Unless Recalled Earlier
Date Due

BRODART, INC.   Cat. No. 23 233   Printed in U.S.A.

Library Services in Theory and Context

Second Edition

Pergamon Titles of Related Interest

CARROLL   Recent Advances in School Librarianship

CHANDLER   International and National Library and
Information Services

COOK   School Librarianship

FRY/HEMON   Government Publications: Key Papers

Related Journals*

Government Publications Review

Information Processing and Management

Information Systems

Library Acquisitions, Practice and Theory

* Free specimen copies available upon request

Library Services in Theory and Context

Second Edition

Michael K. Buckland

PERGAMON PRESS

OXFORD · NEW YORK · BEIJING · FRANKFURT
SÃO PAULO · SYDNEY · TOKYO · TORONTO

U.K.	Pergamon Press plc., Headington Hill Hall, Oxford OX3 0BW, England
U.S.A.	Pergamon Press, Inc., Maxwell House, Fairview Park, Elmsford, New York 10523, U.S.A.
PEOPLE'S REPUBLIC OF CHINA	Pergamon Press, Room 4037, Quianmen Hotel, Beijing, People's Republic of China
FEDERAL REPUBLIC OF GERMANY	Pergamon Press GmbH, Hammerweg 6, D-6242 Kronberg, Federal Republic of Germany
BRAZIL	Pergamon Editora Ltda, Rua Eça de Queiros, 346, CEP 04011, Paraiso, São Paulo, Brazil
AUSTRALIA	Pergamon Press Australia Pty Ltd., P. O. Box 544, Potts Point, N.S.W. 2011, Australia
JAPAN	Pergamon Press, 5th Floor, Matsuoka Central Building, 1-7-1 Nishishinjuku, Shinjuku-Ku, Tokyo 160, Japan
CANADA	Pergamon Press Canada Ltd., Suite No. 271, 253 College Street, Toronto, Ontario, Canada M5T 1R5

First edition 1983

Second edition 1988

Library of Congress Cataloging-in-Publication Data

Buckland, Michael Keeble.
Library services in theory and context/
Michael K. Buckland.—2nd ed.
p.   cm.
Includes bibliographical references and index.
1. Library science.   I. Title.
Z665.B916 1988   88-17864
025.5—dc19

British Library Cataloguing-in-Publication Data

Buckland, Michael K. (Michael Keeble)
Library services in theory and context.
2nd ed.
1. Librarianship
I. Title
020

ISBN 0-08-035755-5 (Hardcover)
ISBN 0-08-035754-7 (Flexicover)

Printed in Great Britain by A. Wheaton & Co. Ltd., Exeter

Contents

Part II: Analysis

Part III: Connections and Extensions

Part IV: Some Problems Reconsidered

List of Figures

Preface to the Second Edition

This book attempts to provide a theoretical framework for considering libraries, yet its aims and origins are pragmatic. The motivation for writing it lay in a series of frustrations. Most immediately there had been a problem of explaining how and why (and to what extent) librarianship is closely related to other apparently similar activities such as archive administration, records management, and museum documentation. Intuitively, one felt that some degree of commonality was there, but identifying and explaining it was another matter. It is not enough to define some common terminology and concepts; it is also necessary to examine thoroughly the adequacy of the common terminology. Hence, this book is a statement of the nature of library services in moderately unorthodox terms.

Another frustration which encouraged the writing of this book derives from the "bittiness" of librarianship: people with radically different backgrounds are busy with quite diverse activities. All of this is under the umbrella of librarianship (or "library-and-information-studies") and, again, one felt that these varied activities are in some way related to each other, but the connections often seemed tenuous at best.

A deeper frustration had to do with the management of library services, which depends a good deal on experience and feel. It may be that "managing by the seat of the pants" is to some extent unavoidable. However, the conviction persists that, if our understanding of the provision and use of library services could be made more *explicit*, then it might be possible to place more emphasis on reason and less on "feel"—or, at least, augment the "feel" with more knowledge.

In addition, there is the background irritation that a number of paradoxes and dilemmas remain. If, as is sometimes claimed, libraries tend not to be adaptive, then how do they manage to survive changing circumstances so stably, even, sometimes, in the apparent absence of effective management? Why does the extensive literature of librarianship have so little to say about optimal library size, which one might have expected to be a central, basic issue? Why does the evaluation of retrieval systems remain elusive? Is a single measure of library "goodness" possible? If so, what is it? If not, why not? It is not claimed that these issues have been resolved in the pages that follow, though each is discussed. We have drawn attention to them because they provided much of the motivation.

Sabbatical leave spent at the University of Klagenfurt, Austria, from January to May 1980, provided an opportunity to address these concerns. On reflection they all seemed to be manifestations of a single problem: an inadequate conceptual framework for considering retrieval-based information services in general, and library services in particular. What seemed most needed was better theory in the broad sense of the term, meaning an explanation of the nature of something. (Theories in the restricted sense of the formal and physical sciences, composed of fundamental laws rigorously testable by empirical evidence may or may not follow.)

The first tasks in the development of theory are to identify the phenomena of interest, to characterize their nature, and to examine the relationships between them. An approach based on five different sorts of processes and on the relationships between them and their environment seemed promising. The next step was to test this approach by applying it in detail to an example of a retrieval-based information service to see how effective it would be, using two criteria: (i) would it be adequate, in the sense of being complete enough to include any and every aspect? and (ii) would it contribute to an improved understanding? Examining library services seemed, for several reasons, the best candidate for developing and testing what was originally conceived as a framework of wider applicability. This book resulted.

This second edition addresses some deficiencies of the first edition with the addition of chapters on the role of collections (chapter 7), on the different aspects of the loosely used concept of "access" (chapter 15), on technology in relation to library services (chapter 17), and on long-term change (chapter 18). A few changes have been made in other chapters, some typographical errors have been corrected, and it is acknowledged (in chapters 6 and 9) that the original emphasis on the role of library services in reducing ignorance understated their role in changing opinions.

As before a large debt is acknowledged to many people, especially within the University of California.

Part 1

Introduction

1

Plan

Intention

The intention of this book is to advance a conceptual framework for considering library services. It is not asserted that what follows constitutes a complete framework, but rather an attempt to take a step toward the development of a framework. The motivation is both intellectual and pragmatic. At an intellectual level, there is curiosity about the nature of things and about how—and why—they work. At a pragmatic level, there is the incentive that a clearer theoretical understanding might bring greater effectiveness in practice.

Theory brings insights, but there is no guarantee that theory will be helpful in practice. Bad theory may bring false and misleading insights, good theory brings helpful insights. However, theory, once developed, can, in general, be tested—and inadequate theory rejected. A necessary condition for progress, then, is to propose theory so that it can be tested.

Organization

In seeking to propose a theoretical framework for library services, the text has been organized as a logical progression in the following stages:

Part I: Introduction

The intention and general arrangement of the book are outlined in chapter 1, and some basic problems in librarianship are identified in chapter 2:

- How do the different facets of librarianship relate to one another?
- Why do library services differ from each other from one context to another?
- Why aren't libraries used more?
- How should catalogs and retrieval systems be evaluated?
- How big should a library be?
- How do libraries survive?
- What is "goodness" with respect to library services?

It is asserted that it is lack of theory which causes these questions to be—and to remain—problems.

The scope and probable nature of appropriate theory are defined in chapters 3, 4, and 5.

Part II: Analysis

Five key aspects of the provision and use of library services are analyzed:

- Inquiries (chapter 6)
- Retrieval (chapters 7 and 8)
- The process of becoming informed (chapter 9)
- The demand for library services (chapter 10)
- The allocation of resources to and within library services (chapters 11 and 12)

Part III: Connections and Extensions

After the separate examination of five key aspects of library service in Part II, Part III seeks to view library service *as a whole* from various perspectives. To what extent could they be regarded as constituting a "system" (chapter 13)? The problem of achieving internal consistency in such a complex situation (chapter 14), the diverse dimensions of "access" to knowledge (chapter 15), measurement (chapter 16), the role of technology (chapter 17), long-term change (chapter 18), and the generalizability of this conceptual framework to other information services (chapter 19) are considered.

Part IV: Some Problems Reconsidered

Some of the basic conceptual problems of library services which were noted in Part I are reconsidered in terms of the ideas discussed in Parts II and III: the relationships between the parts; why libraries differ; criteria for the evaluation of retrieval systems; optimal library size; the internal coherence and consistency of library services; and the nature of library goodness.

Although an evenly balanced overview is desirable, some topics have been given more attention than others. This unevenness derives from two considerations:

1. The development of theory with respect to library services is itself uneven. For example, little seems to be known about how users come to formulate the inquiries which they bring to libraries.
2. Some topics need a longer and more careful exposition than others in order to describe them adequately. For example, the discussion of

censorship issues in chapter 11 (*Allocation*) is much briefer than the treatment of nonmonetary aspects of price in chapter 10 (*Demand*).

A book that presumes to deal with theory might well have been expected to have been more formal and more rigorous. In fact, this has been deliberately avoided. Not only does the state of theory concerning library services hardly seem ready for such treatment but, even if it were, formal, rigorous treatment would probably have hindered communication with many people who would otherwise have been interested. This book adopts an informal, discursive approach. Let us hope that more formal treatment will be developed by those better qualified to do so.

The title of this book, *Library Services in Theory and Context*, reflects a deliberate emphasis. We are concerned with library services and, therefore, with both the provision and the use of these services. The intent has been to focus on the theoretical aspects and the emphasis is on developing a framework—on how the parts fit together and into the context in which the services are provided. Indeed, a suitable subtitle would have been "Toward a conceptual framework for considering the structure and functioning of library services in relation to their sponsors, their users, and their societal context." Most of the literature about library services has to do with specific details such as indexing, classification, logistics, and social mission. It is clearly important to have such detailed treatments. In contrast, however, the pages that follow represent an attempt to provide a general theoretical framework. Ideally, the more specialized theoretical work will fit within and into this more general treatment. The one should complement the other.

2

Origins and Motivation

The origins of, and motivation for, this book lie in the belief that a wide range of intellectual and practical problems associated with library services are caused or, at least, exacerbated by inadequate understanding of what is involved—in brief, by inadequate theory. In this chapter, some examples of these problems will be briefly reviewed. Later, after the components of a theoretical framework have been examined in Parts II and III, these same problems will be reconsidered in Part IV.

Bits and pieces of librarianship

Many quite different sorts of activities take place under the general umbrella of librarianship. For example:

1. The principles of indexing and information retrieval have been studied in an abstract, formal way. The notation of logic is used to formulate the problems and statistical techniques are employed in experimental studies.[1] Since retrieval is central to library services, examination of the basic nature of retrieval can be regarded as fundamental to library services.

2. Since the essence of a library service is providing books[2] to be read, it is only natural to consider *what* messages are being read and what the probable effects of reading them are. For example, stereotyped images concerning the nature and role of particular groups can easily be found. Well-known examples are books which consistently portray boys in roles of leadership and girls in subservient roles. Similar patterns with respect to age, ethnicity, profession, class, and national origin are not difficult to find. The issue is not so much whether such images reflect past roles or not but, rather, where stereotyping exists, whether it may

[1] As examples, see B. C. Brooks, "The Measures of Information Retrieval Effectiveness Proposed by Swets," *Journal of Documentation* 24, no. 1 (March 1968): 41-54; and M. E. Maron and J. L. Kuhn, "On Relevance, Probability, Indexing and Information Retrieval," *Journal of the Association of Computing Machinery* 7, no. 3 (July 1960): 216-44. (Reprinted in *Introduction to Information Science*, edited by T. Saracevic (New York: Bowker, 1970), pp. 295-311.)

[2] The terms "book" and "document" are used here and elsewhere (unless stated otherwise) as generic terms to include all library materials: monographs, serials, periodicals, newspapers, and other formats.

have an affect in reinforcing attitudes and beliefs which tend to limit individuals' ability to fulfill their potential. In consequence, if one's social values lead one to disapprove of these effects, then the indentification of such patterns and the assessment of their effects become important.[3] Literary criticism and social psychology are suitable ingredients in such studies.

3. From a different perspective, one might argue that actually making books physically available is central to library service. To do this, one needs to study patterns of book use—and of failure to find books. Further, one needs to assess as quantitatively as possible the probable consequences of taking various logistical steps to increase the chances of books being available when sought. After all, what use is a library in which one cannot find the books one wants? Measurement and mathematical modeling are called for.[4]

4. Elaborate cataloging rules are needed if the complex range and variety of library objects, e.g., newspapers, books, slides, magnetic tapes, manuscripts, are to be made accessible in a systematic, coordinated way. Some have title pages, others do not. Some have clearly identifiable authors, others do not. The interrelatedness of these objects can be quite complex. The revised *Anglo-American Cataloging Rules* (AACR2),[5] generally adopted in January 1981, extends to over 600 pages. Since bibliography is not a rigidly structured area, the revision represented a major intellectual undertaking—as did the preparation of earlier codes. Even the consistent application of the codes is, in itself, a non-trivial task. Yet, the catalog is the key to the library. Relevant expertise includes a thorough grounding in bibliography and some logic. By way of illustration, the Paris Principles[6] and Wilson[7] can be cited.

5. In library management, a very heavy emphasis is usually placed on experience. Management is not generally regarded as an activity for which the reading of a textbook provides any very adequate preparation, although there is little doubt that reading can be helpful, especially when

---

[3] See, for example, F. M. Blake, *The Strike in the American Novel* (Metuchen, N.J.: Scarecrow Press, 1972); G. M. Bataille and C. L. P. Silet, eds, *The Pretend Indians: Images of Native Americans in the Movies* (Ames, Iowa: Iowa State University Press, 1981); R. Preiswerk, ed., *The Slant of the Pen: Racism in Children's Books* (Geneva: World Council of Churches, 1980).

[4] For example, see P. Kantor, "Availability Analysis," *Journal of the American Society for Information Science* 27, no. 6 (October 1976): 311-19; and M. K. Buckland, *Book Availability and the Library User* (New York: Pergamon Press, 1975).

[5] *Anglo-American Cataloging Rules Prepared by the American Library Association*, edited by M. Gorman and P. W. Winkler, 2nd ed. (Chicago: American Library Association, 1978).

[6] International Federation of Library Associations, *International Conference on Cataloguing Principles, Paris, 1961* (London: Organizing Committee of the International Conference on Cataloguing Principles, 1963).

[7] P. G. Wilson, *Two Kinds of Power: An Essay on Bibliography Control* (Berkeley, Calif.: University of California Press, 1968).

done in conjunction with experience. This is true, more or less, of all fields of management. Yet, there are aspects of libraries which exacerbate the unstructured and, therefore, unsystematized nature of management:

- management specialists have concentrated on commercial rather than public service situations;
- librarians and professors of librarianship have tended to concentrate on books, bibliography, and retrieval rather than on libraries in general;
- there is no dominating criterion of effectiveness for library services comparable with profit in the commercial sector;
- library services are commonly support activities for some larger organization; and
- librarians often have severely limited managerial discretion.

For these and related reasons, one tends to fall back on discussion, on the analysis of cases, and on attempts to transpose to library contexts what is asserted about management in other contexts.[8] Yet, the management of library services should not be lightly dismissed. Its very unstructured nature, which makes it difficult to analyze, also makes it hard to *do* effectively. If library services are to be provided, they have to be organized and managed. Further, a very large proportion of the managing has to be done with and through people, since library services are highly labor-intensive with salaries normally accounting for more than half of the budget.

6. Books are not the only objects found in libraries, but they do pre-dominate, and older books tend to be accessible *only* through libraries. However, to understand properly an older book, considerable knowledge of historical bookmaking techniques is needed. For research in the period 1480 to 1800, in particular, printed documents are primary sources for most disciplines. Several questions need to be asked about this evidence: Are there variant issues of this book? Which version was the original one and which were later? Were the later versions corrections or corruptions of the text? Was the book printed when and where it says it was? To answer such questions one needs to understand past techniques of paper-making, typography, composition, printing, and binding. (The account of the detection by Carter and Pollard of "first editions" fraudulently fabricated by T. J. Wise provides a fascinating illustration of this.)[9]

7. As labor costs rise and computing costs decline, the prospect of using electronic data processing in the massive recordkeeping inherent in library service becomes increasingly attractive. It is, however, a rather specialized field of application and unlike scientific computation or most

[8]   R. D. Stueart and B. B. Moran, *Library Management*, 3rd ed. (Littleton, Colo.: Libraries Unlimited, 1987).

[9]   T. Carter and G. Pollard. *An Enquiry Into the Nature of Certain Nineteenth Century Pamphlets* (London: Constable, 1934).

business data processing. The emphasis is on sorting, storing, and displaying rather than on computation. The internationally standard format for communicating bibliographical data (MARC II) provides for a wide variety of data elements ("fields") which can vary greatly in length, may contain letters and accents as well as numbers, and, indeed, may or may not be present for any given book. Not only are *individual* records long and complex, there are also often a large number of them. As of 1987, the OCLC On-Line Catalog Library Center data base in Dublin, Ohio, was providing access in 6,000 libraries to 15 million records,[10] and the growth in other data bases available from other sources has been equally remarkable. Such systems call for substantial specialized expertize in planning, analysis, costing, programming, and computer and telecommunications technology.

These seven examples are only some of the varied facets of librarianship. One could continue, but the examples already given should suffice to demonstrate two features of librarianship:

1. These activities are, in fact, quite diverse. They call for different sorts of skills, and they are likely to attract different sorts of people with different sorts of interests and different sorts of backgrounds.
2. The relationships between these facets are not very clear. In each particular example, one can make a plausible case for its importance, but what they have in common is a lot less clear. Their interactions, let alone any interdependencies, are less obvious.

The combined effects of these two findings is that it is all too easy for specialists to understand and to value their own area. Tolerance of other specialists is desirable but it is the *understanding* of other areas—and of how they relate to one's own—which is important for effective achievement. In the face of variety, as depicted in this section, what seems to be needed is a conceptual framework within which the interrelationships can be comprehended.

Some fundamental problems in library service

In the previous section, we explored some of the variety of librarianship and argued the need for a conceptual framework to provide a unifying force. In the present section we identify some basic problems in the provision of library services. Only a small selection of such basic problems is considered. The criteria for inclusion were twofold: a belief that the problem was of importance; and a suspicion that it was insufficient understanding of the *nature* of the problem (inadequate theory, one might

---

[10] *OCLO Pac-News* 29 (September 1987): 4.

say) which caused them to remain problematic. If only one had clearer, deeper insights, then maybe each would cease to be a problem.

Why do libraries differ?

Traditionally, libraries have been divided into four groups: academic, school, public, and special (i.e., specialized and usually in support of industry or public administration). *How* they differ is not a mystery: one can recognize which is which. But explaining *why* they differ has not received very much attention. Another sort of difference can be observed between libraries of the same type in different environments. The traditional library service of a German or Austrian university does not resemble a typical North American university library service. Public library services also vary from country to country: in some places they are valued as a bastion of freedom and democratic survival;[11] yet Lenin, his wife, and subsequent communist leaders have seen libraries as an important tool in engineering the triumph of Marxist-Leninist communism;[12] and, in some countries, even some quite wealthy ones, public libraries remain curiously undeveloped. Are these various differences merely accidental?

Why aren't libraries used more?

In the study of the use of library services, there are ambiguities concerning "wants" and "needs." One can understand a user wanting (i.e., desiring) something that he or she needs (i.e., which would solve some problem). However, it is less clear why users sometimes do not seem to desire something they need—at least they may not desire it enough to take action. This can be unsettling for librarians who are uniquely situated to know how the library service could be used to satisfy that need. Hence, users are occasionally believed by librarians to be ignorant or idle in the face of opportunity. Mooers' Law (or, rather, dictum) states that: "An information retrieval system will tend *not* to be used whenever it is more painful and troublesome for a customer to have information than for him not to have it!"[13] This is somehow unwelcome to those who have worked so hard to make information retrievable. How are desires and

---

[11] M. Owens and M. Braverman, *The Public Library and Advocacy; Information for Survival.* (Commissioned papers project, Teachers College, 5.) (Washington, D.C.: U.S. Office of Education, Division of Library Programs, 1974.) Note also the slogan on the current (1983) U.S. 4-cent postage stamp: "A public that reads. A root of democracy."

[12] B. Raymond, *Krupskaia and Soviet Russian Librarianship, 1917-1939* (Metuchen, N.J.: Scarecrow Press, 1979); S. Simsova, *Lenin, Krupskaia and Libraries* (London: Clive Bingley, 1968).

[13] C. N. Mooers, "Mooers' Law or Why Some Retrieval Systems are Used and Others Are Not," *American Documentation* 11 (1960): 204.

needs to be distinguished and, more usefully, how are degrees of desiring and needing to be predicted and assessed?

How should catalogs be evaluated?

One uses books in libraries, but first one must find them. For this, retrieval systems are used whether catalogs, indexes, or subject arrangement on the shelves. The question naturally arises as to how effectively the retrieval systems are working and whether some other system might work better. What, then, is the proper measure of retrieval performance? The simple answer is that books are cataloged and, therefore, retrieved by their attributes. Usually this reduces to what they are "about" and whom they are by. But this has its limitations. One might not know (or care) who the author was and the "subject" (what it is about) also has its deficiencies in practice. An aspect of pharmacy, for example, might best be studied in a book that is not primarily "about" pharmacy. Even a book "about" that aspect of pharmacy might contain only material already known and, therefore, of no new benefit to the inquirer. Instead, it has been argued, the *utility* of the retrieved book to the reader rather than what it is "about" should be the criterion for evaluating a retrieval system. However, this raises additional problems. Not only does it become important to define, measure, and predict utility but a more fundamental problem arises. We are basing the evaluation of the retrieval system on factors (notably the utility to the users) which are extraneous to it and independent of the retrieval system—a seemingly impossible (and unfair) feat. So how should retrieval systems be evaluated?

How big should a library be?

One might reasonably have expected that the question of optimal library size would be a central issue in the extensive literature of librarianship, but it is not. Quite the reverse. There is some literature with a rather thin theoretical base on minimal sizes for some sorts of libraries,[14] and there is a widespread (though not unanimous) consensus that "bigger is better." There has been very little direct discussion of optimal library size. Why so little?

[14] V. W. Clapp and R. T. Jordan, "Quantitative Criteria for Adequacy of Academic Library Collections," *College and Research Libraries* 26, no. 5 (1965): 371-80; R. M. McInnis, "The Formula Approach to Library Size: An Empirical Study of Its Efficiency in Evaluating Research Libraries," *College and Research Libraries* 33, no. 3 (1972): 190-8. Other writings on library size include: K. D. Metcalf, "Is It Possible to Pick the Ideal Size for Large Research Libraries?" in *International Congress of Libraries and Documentation Centres, Brussels, 1955* (The Hague: Nijhoff, 1955), vol. 2A, pp. 205-10; M. D. Cooper, "The Economics of Library Size: A Preliminary Enquiry," *Library Trends* 28, no. 1 (Summer 1979): 63-78; D. Gore, ed., *Farewell to Alexandria: Solutions to Space, Growth, and Performance Problems of Libraries* (Westport, Conn.: Greenwood Press, 1976).

How do libraries survive?

Another intriguing paradox concerning library services has to do with their adaptability and survival. Two basic assumptions in systems theory are that survival depends on adaptation and that adaptation depends on feedback, on information about what is happening so that the organization can know when and how to adapt. However, library staff are often not in a situation to know whether users have found what they are seeking, let alone what they needed. In other words, libraries are often unable to obtain the quantity and quality of feedback that appears to be necessary for adaptation. Hence, one would expect crises and inability to survive.[15]

Nevertheless, libraries do survive remarkably. Not only that, but they are popularly viewed as tranquil, crisis-free places suitable for the employment of quiet, retiring persons. How is it that library services survive while being apparently weak in the mechanisms supposedly necessary for survival?

What constitutes "library goodness"?

How does one know whether one library is better than another, or that a given library is currently improving or degenerating? Can there be a single, usable measure of library goodness? If so, what is it? If not, why not?

This short selection of problems covers some interesting and important issues: Why do libraries differ? Why are they not always used when they might beneficially be used? How should one evaluate the central process of retrieval? How big should a library be? What is goodness as applied to a library service? These questions can hardly be said to be about insignificant details in the provision of library services. Yet, in each case, it could be asserted that the issues are not well understood. In other words, our comprehension of these matters is insufficiently developed to provide enough insight either to provide a coherent theoretical basis for practical action or to demonstrate that the answers are unknowable.

---

[15]   *Cf.* "… organizations could not survive if they were not responsive to the demands from their environment," J. Pfeffer, and G. R. Salancik, *The External Control of Organizations* (New York: Harper & Row, 1978), p. 43.

3

Scope

In the previous chapter, we considered the apparent need for a better theoretical understanding of library services. In the present chapter, we examine what it is we are to theorize about. The purpose is to clarify what it is we are seeking to develop a conceptual framework for. Then, having asserted the need and defined the scope, we will, in the next chapter, discuss what sort of theory might be appropriate.

Library services and information science

It is ironic that the term "information science" should, of all terms, have been used in an uninformative and unscientific way. Unfortunately, it has been carelessly used and even, on occasion, treated as a near synonym for librarianship.[1] It seems desirable, therefore, to review some aspects of information science.

All-embracing information science

After World War II, at least three intoxicating new developments emphasized information. Shannon and Weaver's "information theory" offered a whole new prospect for the scientific study of information.[2] Norbert Wiener's new science of cybernetics proclaimed a new, integrating approach to the study of human beings, machines, nature, and organizations based on the study of information and control. The powerful potential of electronic computers was just coming to be realized. There was the exciting prospect here for a whole new field of study based on

---

[1] A. M. Schrader, "In Search of a Name: Information Science and its Conceptual Antecedents," *Library and Information Science Research* 6, no. 3 (July-September 1984): 227-71. See also the literature review and definition in J. G. Meijer, *Librarianship: A Definition* (Occasional Papers, 155) (Urbana, Ill.: University of Illinois, Graduate School of Library and Information Science, September 1982).

[2] Information theory as developed by Shannon and Weaver is a mathematical analysis of efficiency in the signaling of data. The meaning of the data and the benefit derived from receiving the signal are not considered. For details, see for example, C. Shannon and W. Weaver, *The Mathematical Theory of Communication* (Urbana, Ill.: University of Illinois Press, 1949); L. Brillouin, *Science and Information Theory*, 2nd ed. (New York: Academic Press, 1962).

information as its unifying concept. It might rival, or at least take its place alongside, biological sciences based on life and physical sciences based on energy. Vannevar Bush, then at the National Science Foundation, wrote an influential essay entitled "As We May Think" in which he speculated about an artificial information system which would resemble and extend the power of the human brain.[3]

The fact that "information" is an elusive concept and difficult to define—let alone measure—was not (and is not) cause to despair. After all, "life" and "energy" are not simple concepts either. "Information," it seems, is in good company. The prospect was, and is, exciting. It is also clear that the scope of information science must necessarily be *very* extensive: logic, mathematics, linguistics, philosophy, literature, rhetoric, neurology, electronic engineering, cybernetics, librarianship, studies to do with decision making, mass communications ... all these and others have to do with information. The domain of information science is clearly very large. Two things follow from this. First, many different sorts of people who perceive themselves as having very little in common share in the study of information. Their present interests, techniques, and terminology may overlap little if at all. Each could define his or her area of interest as being "information science" (or, more honestly, *within* information science) without having much in common with the others except for the claim to being active within the field of information science. Second, it is not at all clear who would be capable of providing any integration of this dispersed field nor where such integrators would be found.

This "all-embracing" definition of information science is awe-inspiring. There would appear to be no sensible justification for limiting it in any way. Maybe "all-embracing information science" should be placed on a convenient pedestal to serve as a challenging inspiration to us all and to serve as a corrective for any inhabitant of a part of the field who came to assume that his or her part of the field was, in fact, the whole field rather than merely a part of a larger whole.

Computer science, librarianship, and information science

Computer science and librarianship are the two fields within the domain of information science which have most often used the name of the whole for the name of a part. Both have a valid claim, of course, but not to the whole.

Computer science is unquestionably much involved in the study of information-related matters: the coding of data into machine-readable form; and the transmission, manipulation, storage, and presentation of

3 V. Bush, "As We May Think," *Atlantic Monthly* 176 (July 1945): 101-8.

these data. The manipulation can include information retrieval and the use of inference for artificial intelligence. Yet, the limitation is that these matters are rooted in the computer and the computer is not coextensive with all sorts of information and information handling. Other information-related matters such as human cognition, speech, and indexing systems which are not computer-based can hardly be regarded as computer science.

With librarianship, the case is not stronger, even though one may concede that librarianship has implications and applicability outside what are ordinarily regarded as libraries. It is, in this connection, instructive to observe what is actually taught in schools of librarianship under the heading of "information science" or by professors in these schools who identify themselves as "information scientists." By this empirical definition, information science (librarianship-style) is also something noticeably less than the all-embracing information science. In practice, information science (librarianship-style) is primarily the application (and applicability) of computers to libraries and (mainly bibliographical) data retrieval outside of libraries. To a limited extent, other matters are also included, notably the formal (i.e., theoretical) analysis of information retrieval processes. Actually, the case could be strengthened by including other topics that are also dealt with in schools of librarianship though it has not been traditional to categorize them as "information science." A good example is the study of human information-gathering behavior— traditionally referred to as "user studies" but sometimes viewed in a broader sense as "social studies of information." Also, there is the rather thorough treatment of semantic and practical problems of information storage and retrieval with or without a computer. The causes of this partial use of the term "information science" would seem to be derived from the view in the English-speaking world that the term "science" ought to be restricted to those studies which partake of the characteristics of the "hard" (i.e., physical) sciences, or else not used. The social studies of information are clearly "soft" and within the general area of the social sciences and so tend not to be regarded as part of information science in the same way as the application of computers or of logic area. This squeamishness about the use of the word "science" is not, however, entirely consistent so long as the generic term for the principal degree in librarianship is referred to in North America as being "library science."

The interests of schools of librarianship have in fact been heavily concentrated on libraries. This has been even truer in practice than in rhetoric. Serious interest is now being expressed by some of these schools in a broader definition of their interests to include information-handling activities outside of libraries. How many schools will be able to achieve such a reorientation, how effective they will be with respect to areas outside of libraries, and whether they move outside of retrieval-based information services are key issues. Yet, even if all these things were to be done widely and effectively, one can hardly imagine the scope of such schools expanding to become even nearly coextensive with all-embracing information science.

Both computer science and librarianship have valid claims that they deal with information science. This is not to say that either deals with the whole of information science; if they did, they would no longer be departments of computer science or of librarianship; they would be departments of information science and, presumably, substantially similar to each other. Nor do we suggest that other disciplines, such as business administration and linguistics, for example, do not also share in the broad reaches of all-embracing information science. It might even be beneficial for our understanding of information if even more groups of people were to lay claim to the use of the term "information science." At least that would probably stimulate interest and debate. There remain, however, two dangers in the use of the name of the whole to represent a part: (1) it tends to cause misunderstanding as to what the term covers; and (2) it is liable to lead to preemptive use of the title by those who only deal with a part, thereby impeding others with a valid interest in other parts.

Information science and library science as "sciences"

The traditional view among those who have sought to develop an information science is reflected by Mikhailov and others who argue that any subject which claims to be a science (as the terms "information science" and "library science" appear to) must satisfy the following criteria:[4]

- The subject area and the phenomena to be studied must be specified.
- The basic descriptive concepts must be clarified.
- The fundamental quantitative laws peculiar to the subject must be developed.
- A theory able to relate a multiplicity of phenomena must be developed.

Mikhailov and others think that only the first two of these can be claimed to have been achieved in information science. Therefore, they argue, anyone who wishes to assert that information science is a "science" has the onus of producing the fundamental quantitative laws and the theory. The same would hold true with library science.

---

[4] B. C. Brookes, "Information Science (Excluding IR)," *British Librarianship and Information Science, 1966-1970,* edited by H. A. Whatley (London: Library Association, 1972), pp. 137-49, esp. p. 137. Brookes is summarizing A. I. Mikhailov, A. I. Chernyi, and R. S. Gilyaresvskii, "Informatics: Its Scope and Methods," in *On Theoretical Problems of Informatics* (FID 435). (Moscow: All Union Institute for Scientific and Technical Information, 1969), pp. 7-24.

The issue here is not the accuracy of these statements but their applicability. The specifications quoted above are for a formal, physical science. The subject areas which fit are physics, chemistry, biology, and the like—disciplines which are concerned with physical entities. Not all areas are like that. Theology, for example, which used to be known as "the Queen of the Sciences," has plenty of theory but not much quantification. These specifications would appear to be appropriate if, and only if, information science is deemed to be primarily concerned with physical matter. It may be inherently misguided to expect information science to partake of the same sorts of attributes as the physical sciences even though we might, with whatever motivation, wish it to. A more modern revisionist view is that the study of information services is not only not a "hard" science but a part of the social sciences, and that such social sciences are best regarded as a part of the study of history.[5]

In this book, we are concerned with a theoretical framework for *library services* rather than information science as a science. Reflection on the phenomena of library services suggests that, if any affinities exist, they are likely to be with the social and behavioral sciences since the use of library services is an act of conscious social behavior. Further, since books are read and knowledge acquired, one might expect concepts and theories pertaining to education, linguistics, psychology, and human behavior to be relevant or similar to theory pertaining to library services. Further, management and technology are involved so concepts relevant to them may also be applicable. Whatever sort of theory may emerge, one might also reasonably expect it to have some affinities with philosophy since both library services and philosophy have to do with knowledge.

On the scope of librarianship[6]

The term "librarianship" is ambiguous. It can refer to a set of techniques or it can refer to the occupational field of those who are known as librarians. Neither definition is strictly identical to "library services."

The imagery of librarianship

Rhetoric is used to persuade and imagery is a major part of rhetoric. Images, repeatedly used, however, lead to stereotypes and are liable to

---

[5] P. G. Wilson, "Limits to the Growth of Knowledge: The Case of the Social and Behavioral Sciences," *Journal of Documentation* 50, no. 1 (January 1980): 4-21, esp. pp. 15-17.

[6] This section draws on M. K. Buckland, "Looking Ahead—And Around," *Information Reports and Bibliographies* 7, nos. 4-5 (1978): 15-18; and M. K. Buckland, "Library Education—Meeting the Needs of the Future," *Catholic Library World* 50, no. 10 (May 1979): 424-26.

influence the speaker as well as the audience. Movie star, computer scientist, peasant, librarian ... these labels evoke stereotyped images.[7] Individuals, impelled by social pressures, are liable to adopt, more or less unconsciously, the image and role projected onto them.

The rhetoric pertaining to librarianship is remarkably dominated by the term "library," an institution. In everyday speech, one goes to a "*library* school" to study for a "*library* degree" (usually formally known as a Master of *Library* Science degree), approved, one hopes, by the national *library* association. One reads articles in journals that typically have the word "*library*" in their titles. This heavy emphasis on an institution is less marked in other professions and professional schools. Journalists don't get a "*newspaper* degree" nor do would-be farmers enroll in "*farm* school." We do not refer to teachers as holding a "*school* degree" and attending a "*school* school" sounds bizarre. Librarianship, it seems, is somewhat out of line. One wonders what effect, if any, this imagery may have had.

The rhetoric would suggest that the institution, the library, should dominate the definition of the field of interest of librarianship and of schools of librarianship. Let us explore two alternative ways in which this might be done.

Librarianship and schools of librarianship

A simple approach would be to state that the field of a school of librarianship is coterminous with the institutions known as libraries and the preparation of people to work in them. Since libraries are complex, varied institutions and are fundamentally concerned with the fabric of human knowledge and with intangible values, and since they are labor-intensive with different types of staff, this need not be a simple or a narrow focus.

Schools of librarianship were set up to train personnel for libraries and early schools were often part of a library. The historical explanation of the title "library school" is straightforward. The practice is no longer simple. Schools of librarianship are no longer in libraries but in universities, albeit sometimes somewhat isolated within them. Furthermore, they only train professional librarians. Other sorts of library personnel also need training: library assistants and library technicians especially.

Schools of librarianship are, in fact, well equipped to train people other than professional librarians in that they have a range of specialists, instructors, laboratories, links with other libraries, and good collections of instructional materials. In most cases, the schools have, or could

---

[7] For librarians see, for example, M. Slater, "The Image of the Library Information Worker," in *The Information Worker: Identity, Image, and Potential,* edited by M. R. Raffin and R. Passmore (London: Aslib, 1977), pp. 9-19.

probably acquire, the capacity to handle more students. But, generally, they confine themselves to the Master of Library Science degree and, sometimes, advanced programs, leaving less advanced training to the libraries and to other sorts of schools.

Schools of librarianship, then, do not simply prepare people to work in libraries—only the professional librarians. In doing this, a valuable opportunity has been missed. The syndrome seems still to be to flee the bad old days of undergraduate professional majors in librarianship. It is not, of course, only a matter of the preparation of personnel other than professional librarians to be employed in libraries but also of sharing what is interesting and useful in librarianship with people who are *not* intending to be employed in libraries but who may benefit intellectually and practically from what could be shared. There are a very few schools of librarianship that share in a serious way such topics as the effective use of libraries, children's literature, principles of information retrieval, history of the book, and so on, but this is unusual.

In the other direction, there has been a steady growth of "advanced certificate" and doctoral programs. A notable characteristic of both is that (with rare exceptions) they are based on the Master of Library Science degree as a prerequisite. This point is particularly relevant to the doctoral programs. The doctoral programs tend to be based directly on whether the proposed area of research is within the school's area of interest and on whether the prospective student has sufficient preparation to undertake the specific area of doctoral research. Doctoral study ordinarily requires completion of the Master of Library Science degree and, often, professional practice as a librarian. The inference would seem to be that the schools want to inhibit some of the prospective doctoral students who could study aspects of librarianship and to restrict doctoral work to those who have been formally associated with libraries by acquisition of the professional training and by professional practice in libraries. A Master of Library Science degree, though useful for many purposes, cannot be claimed as the one and only sensible definition of suitable academic preparation for advanced study in each of the sorts of specialized research which schools of librarianship could reasonably be expected to want to foster, e.g., early printing, publishing history, content analysis of books, or foundations of information retrieval.

The preoccupation with the Master of Library Science degree has historical origins. For most of the history of most of the present schools of librarianship, this degree program (however named) and the school were virtually identical in that this was the school's only program. Traditionally, U.S. schools of librarianship require students to have a bachelor's degree in some other subject before undertaking professional education. A reason for this is that librarians deal constantly with knowledge of all sorts and, therefore, a significant level of general education should be required of them. However, the traditional concentration on the first professional degree for librarians who will be working in libraries can interfere with a clear view of the full range and opportunities of librarianship and information science.

This attempt to distinguish between the dominating Master of Library Science degree program and the full potential contribution of schools of librarianship leads to an alternative approach to defining the scope of the field of librarianship. From a naive, academic point of view, it would seem more sensible to take not an institution-derived view, but a conceptual one. In other words, one might seek to identify the concepts, skills, and mysteries which are characteristic of librarianship and to emphasize that body of knowledge as the foundation to be built upon. The addition of "and Information Science" to the names of many of the schools hints at this more basic view. Yet, in practice, the evidence remains thin. The name of the degree has been less frequently changed; the graduates remain headed for libraries. The "information science" tends, on closer inspection, to be mainly data-processing as applied to libraries.

If we are to get beyond the circular definition of librarianship as that which pertains to the provision of library services, then what sort of description would emerge? It seems unnecessary to impose the constraint that this "science" be *unique* to librarianship. Let us consider what is *characteristic*. (We consider later the consequences of any of it also being pertinent to activities which are not associated with libraries.)

Indexing, in its broadest sense, seems a good starting point. Library cataloging and classification schemes are but formal, rather structured, examples of the more general activity. The essence is description and labeling with the expectation that some person or persons as yet unknown will be able, at some future time, to find material that will probably be welcomed by them in the pursuit of some objective that they may have. The phrase, "information storage and retrieval" is appropriate. One might argue that document storage and retrieval is even more descriptive— and so it is in the sense that the units stored are overwhelmingly, if decreasingly, books and other sorts of documents. Yet, the books are there as a source of information and it is what is written in them that is of interest. So information storage and retrieval is an apt phrase, even though it has an aura of formality and machinery that seems out of character in a context that also includes reader's advisers, storytelling, and community information and referral. If we were to develop a more formal description of mission, then "fostering access to public knowledge" would seem likely to be close to the mark, so long as it is recognized that this mission is characteristic of, rather than unique to, library service. If an activity does not have to do with understanding, facilitating, or improving access to recorded knowledge in one way or another, then it probably ought not to be regarded as a part of librarianship.

While we may take indexing as a central feature of librarianship, there are, of course, many other activities necessarily associated with the provision of library services as was noted in chapter 2. Some of these—notably, management skills, communication skills, and a familiarity with relevant technology—are important in such a wide range of non-library contexts as to need little comment. There is, however, in addition to indexing, another area of expertise, which, like indexing, is unusual and is characteristic of librarianship, but is not unique to it. This has to do with what might be described, in words derived from Robert Fairthorne, as "documentary discourse."[8] By this, we mean an understanding of the relationships between author and document, between one document and another, and between document and reader. One can generalize this beyond documents to "recorded knowledge" to include data also. One could hardly implement, for example, a relational data base without this sort of knowledge.

It is probably unnecessary and unwise to attempt to define librarianship too closely. After all, defining things tends to be done by excluding things, and one may come to regret the exclusion.

Libraries only?

So long as librarianship is defined in terms of library services, it can be expected to be perceived only in those terms. However, as soon as we examine the *nature* of what is done, it becomes clear that the "science" of librarianship (or at least some of it) is not entirely unique to libraries, but also occurs in various forms in a variety of contexts: archives, Management Information Systems, records management, data base management, to name a few.

We can respond to this breadth of context in more than one way. Perhaps we should adopt a broad definition of the "science," but then restrict ourselves within it to the extent to which it occurs in or is significantly relevant to library services. But does it make sense to study the reading of library books but not the reading of other books? Is it reasonable to grapple with the arrangement and cataloging of library collections but to ignore problems in the arrangement and indexing of archives and data bases? A narrow view may inhibit broader insights. Yet a broader view may be rather wasteful if our practical aims are exclusively concerned with library services. Library services are almost ideal things to study for those who like challenges. They are long-established, varied, numerous, fraught with non-trivial problems at all kinds of levels, draw on all sorts

---

[8] R. A. Fairthorne, *Towards Information Retrieval* (London: Butterworths, 1961), pp. 95-96; R. A. Fairthorne, "Content Analysis, Specification, and Control," *Annual Review of Information Science and Technology* 4 (1969): 79.

of disciplines, are rooted in intangible social values, and are important enough to society to warrant the attention of good minds. Yet, if we have any significant insights concerning libraries and if the underlying "science" characteristic of library services also occurs elsewhere, then it would seem only responsible for those who inquire—and especially academicians— to offer and test their insights in these other, related, non-library contexts as well. It can hardly be argued, at a time when society appears to be drowning in data and documents, that non-library contexts do not also have problems worthy of the attention of good minds. Perhaps the apparent concentration of interests on library services has been reinforced, at least in part, by the imagery embedded in the phrase "*library* school."

A broader view

If one were to take a broader view than is implied by concentrating on library services, then one might represent it by figure 3.1, in which the theoretical insights from what might be loosely described as "theoretical information science" challenge and are challenged by pragmatic knowledge and empirical evidence relating to a set of retrieval-based information service activities, including library services.

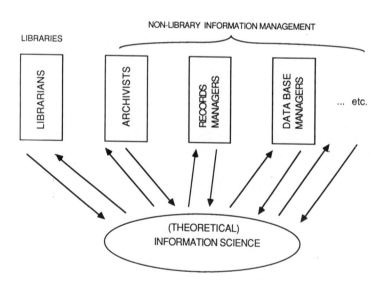

Fig. 3.1   Libraries and related areas

Broadening the field of vision to include activities performed outside of libraries does not come easily, nor is it clear where the boundaries should be. Yet it is difficult to avoid the conclusion that there would be a loss to all parties if attention to phenomena which occur in libraries but are also characteristic of other information retrieval situations were considered only insofar as they are manifest in libraries.[9]

One way of relating library services to other retrieval-based information services and both of these to the broader reaches of information science is to think in terms of representations of knowledge. These representations can be considered in both an abstract sense ("texts") and a physical sense as manifestations of these representations ("text bearing media") such as a printed book, coding in a computer memory, and, in a more fleeting form, words that are spoken. The Gettysburg Address has been printed many times. The different printed versions—physical manifestations of the text— are not identical. However, the words that they bear are, or should be, the same as the words spoken by Abraham Lincoln on November 19, 1863.[10]

If we take the broad and amorphous realm of "all-embracing information science"—or the fields of information study—as being concerned with representations of knowledge in one way or another, we can usefully distinguish a more specific area of concern: the identification, description, manipulation, storage, retrieval, and use of representations of knowledge or information. The processes of arrangement, description, and retrieval, in particular, imply the creation and use of representations of the representations of knowledge. The card catalog in a library is a familiar example of the representation of representations of knowledge.

Information storage and retrieval, then, can be seen as an identifiable subfield within the broader area of information science. We include in this subfield the techniques of storage and strategies for retrieval, indexing, classification, content analysis, and description, and similar sorts of activities.

Yet information storage and retrieval, while not without some technical interest, is sterile when considered in isolation. In order to see information storage and retrieval properly in context, we need also to concern ourselves with information science in the broader sense of concern with representations of knowledge, with knowledge itself, and, indeed, with people insofar as their needs are related through knowledge and representations of knowledge to information storage and retrieval. While the semantics of this whole field leave much to be desired, we can plausibly use the phrase "library and information science" to denote this area of interest, anchored in information storage and retrieval but also concerned with people, their needs, knowledge, and records.

The actual and potential contexts for studying and using "library and

[9]   For further discussion, see Buckland, "Looking Ahead—And Around," pp.15-18; and Buckland, "Library Education," pp. 424-6.
[10]   For further discussion of texts and knowledge in relation to information retrieval, see P. G. Wilson, *Two Kinds of Power: An Essay on Bibliographical Control* (Berkeley: University of California Press, 1968), chapter 1: "The Bibliographical Universe."

information science" are very extensive: libraries obviously, but also on-line retrieval services, archives, records management, and documentation in numerous specialized areas, e.g., museums, litigation, engineering, computer program libraries, planning, and bureaucracies. Nor is the field restricted to document retrieval systems. Data retrieval, information and referral services, and "knowledge availability systems" can all be reasonably included. From this perspective, library services are an area of application for a body of expertise that is best seen as applicable to a range of applications that includes but is not confined to library services.

There are further problems in definition. The techniques and knowledge associated with librarianship appear to be more or less applicable to a range of activities outside of library service as well. In other words, the techniques and knowledge associated with a range of cognate activities appears to coincide or at least overlap to an important degree. This has significant practical implications for those who need, possess, and/or study such techniques and knowledge; but that is not our present concern. The practical implication for this book is to require us to reiterate that we are concerned with "library services" rather than "librarianship." The title, *Library Services in Theory and Context*, was carefully chosen. It could well be argued that, if the techniques and knowledge characteristic of library services have some applicability in other contexts, then perhaps theory pertaining to library services has some applicability in other contexts also. Alternatively, it seems highly probable that the most useful approach would be to think in terms of a general body of theory which is, more or less, common to and applicable in each of these various contexts.

The origin of this book was an attempt to provide such a general conceptual framework not for library services but for a set of cognate activities of which library service was one example. However, generalities have to be tested in specific contexts. So the proper next step seemed to be not the development and presentation of a general conceptual framework for considering retrieval-based information services but, rather, to explore in some detail how well the general framework fitted one particular sort of retrieval-based information service. We chose to consider library services and this book is the result. If the approach is satisfactory for library services, then it is a plausible hypothesis that it will also prove satisfactory for other cognate fields.

Technology and theory

The technology of library services is rich and seductive. Books are interesting as physical objects as well as for the writings they contain. Papermaking, printing, type design, book design, binding—a range of technologies are involved which can be appreciated at several levels. A well-made book can have pleasing aesthetic and tactile qualities in addition to its intellectual interest. Printing and the book have influenced civilization profoundly: Would the Reformation have occurred without printing? Would the Counter-Reformation have been effective without it? How soon would the Copernican view of the cosmos have been reversed if early modern astronomers had not printed astronomical tables?[11] People relate emotionally to books and hesitate to discard them—unless it be to burn them in an attempt to attack abhorrent ideas printed in them.

Computers, too, have their fascination. They have an amazing power to perform computations. The sheer speed at which they work and their wide range of applications astonish. They can be programmed to fly airplanes, to play chess, to sort and shift through masses of data, and much else besides. Yet the consensus is that we have only just begun to develop their capabilities and to explore their potential.

Mathematics is another technology sometimes applied to libraries: queuing theory, linear programming, information theory, and so on. These, too, like books and computers, are strong magic.

The intrinsic interest and practical power of the technologies associated with library services are to be welcomed. Yet their very interest has perhaps been a distraction. To develop theory, it is necessary to look beyond the technology in the sense that an understanding of the potential role in society of access to recorded knowledge is not likely to depend only on a knowledge of the technology of printing. Principles of subject indexing preceded the invention and use of computers.

Technological developments make it more *feasible* to do things that were, in theory, feasible all along. Good theory should permit the more effective *use* of technology. Problems in the application of technology, on the other hand, stimulate thought which fosters the development of theory.[12] We shall consider some aspects of the role of technology further in chapters 7 and 17, but this is not a book about library technology. It

[11] E. L. Eisenstein, *The Printing Press as an Agent of Change: Communications and Cultural Transformations in Early Modern Europe* (Cambridge, England: Cambridge University Press, 1979), 2 vols.

[12] The relationship betwen theory and technology is commonly oversimplified: "The term 'basic research in engineering' causes a great deal of confusion, since engineering is ordinarily thought of as applied by definition. Nevertheless, there are a number of basic scientific disciplines which have become traditionally associated with engineering in universities even though they are pursued largely for their own sake, and are just as fundamental as the disciplines associated with the natural sciences. The basic sciences associated with engineering are primarily those concerned with the behavior of manmade systems—information theory, the theory of structures, the theory of feedback and control systems, computer and systems theory—but they are nonetheless fundamental. Also there are subjects such as fluid mechanics, solid mechanics, and thermodynamics—what might be called macroscopic or classical physics—which have been largely taken over as basic engineering sciences. All these engineering sciences are distinct from engineering as the art of applying the mathematical and physical sciences to the meeting of human needs." H. Brooks, *The Government of Science* (Cambridge, Mass.: MIT Press, 1968), p.187, footnote.

is an attempt to consider library services at a more basic level—at the level of theory.

Summary

The preceding sections concerning the scope of this book can be briefly summarized as follows:

1. The use of the term "information science" has been inconsistent. Any complete view of information ("all-embracing information science") must necessarily be very wide-ranging and presumably include, among other things, the provision and use of library services.
2. The term "librarianship" is ambiguous; it can refer to a group of people known as librarians or it can refer to the techniques associated with libraries. Neither definition is satisfactory for our purposes— the former because it refers to people and the latter because the techniques associated with libraries appear to have some relevance and applicability outside of library services as well as inside them. We are concerned with the provision and use of library services. Possible applications of the techniques of librarianship outside of library services are outside the scope of our present study.
3. We are concerned with theory rather than technology. The technologies associated with library services are rich, varied, and distractingly full of interest. We must, however, look beyond them to a more basic level of understanding because that is our goal and because that should enable us to use the technology more effectively.

We have not attempted a formal definition of library services and their users. Nor do we explore the fringes to ascertain when a library service ceases to be a library service. To do so does not appear necessary. The basic outlines of common sorts of libraries are widely known and our examples and discussions will related to the principal conventional sorts of libraries: university libraries and public libraries, with occasional references to school libraries and the "special" (i.e., specialized) libraries found usually in industrial firms. Discussion will be based on library services as they exist in the United Kingdom and in the United States of America. Open access by readers to the stacks, arrangement of the books by subject, and borrowing will be assumed. Even though patterns of library service do vary from one country to another, the international similarity of librarianship is such that the examples and discussion should be intelligible to those whose experience is quite different from U.K. and U.S. patterns.

Having described the scope of our interest, we explore, in the next chapter, a particular perspective on library services which we expect to be helpful. Library services, their users, and the interactions between them will be considered as a system.

4

Library Services and their Users as a System

Library services as systems

As noted in the previous chapter, the scope of this book is the provision of library services, the users of them, *and the nature of the relationship and interactions between them*. Considering library services in the absence of consideration of the people who use them would seem to have little meaning and less benefit.

From this perspective, it is meaningful to consider library services (and their users) as a system of interacting parts.[1] In fact, we can go further and make some general statements about the nature of this system in the terminology of systems theory.

It is an "open" system. In other words, the activities that take place in the provision and use of library services are not isolated from the rest of the world. Indeed, what takes place in the provision and use of library services appears to be highly susceptible to interference by and interaction with things external to the system as defined:

- dock strikes delay the acquisition of materials;
- floods and earthquakes may affect the building;
- users may decide at any time to switch to some other source of information: another library perhaps, a book shop, or a friend;
- a message for somebody inside the library may interrupt activities;
- changes in the outside world may affect the resources and goal of the library service.

We need not labor the point. The assertion is merely that we can define the library service, the users, and the interactions between them as a "system" of sorts. There is no suggestion that this can be viewed as self-contained.

---

[1]   Other examples of attempts to view library services as systems include J. Orr, *Libraries as Communications Systems* (Westport, Conn.: Greenwood Press, 1977); and D. Smith, *Systems Thinking in Library and Information Management* (New York: Bingley, 1980). See also M. P. Marchant, *Participative Management in Academic Libraries* (Westport, Conn.: Greenwood Press, 1976), esp. chapter 2 "The Library as an Open System."

It is a "large" system. The basic concept of a library is quite simple: some books are placed on the shelves and one or more users may use one or more of the books. Closer inspection, however, reveals that there are many possible interactions. Any one of a large number of people may use the library. When doing so, that one person may interact with one or more documents, with one or more of many indexes, with library staff, with other users. The books are interrelated with each other and with the catalogs and indexes through common authorship, through being about the same sorts of things, through referring to each other directly and indirectly. The consequences in the library may also vary widely: purchasing one book may preclude buying another, longer opening hours may mean less reference service, a noisy user may distract another.

Libraries are generally small in organizational terms. Libraries generally take up limited space and employ few people.[2] Great libraries with an annual budget over $10 million are very rare. However, libraries are invariably "large" or, rather, complex in the terminology of systems theory wherein largeness refers not to the budget, the cubic footage, or other physical features but to the complexity of the interactions.

An important property of systems is their ability to respond to changes, to adapt themselves to their environments, and to maintain sufficient stability to survive. The characteristics of library services in this regard seem contradictory. Library services are generally regarded as being weak on the features needed for adaptation and stability—feedback on what is happening in library use is generally weak, incomplete, or lacking; the goals of library services are usually vague; library services are often criticized for being rather unresponsive; and librarians have little or no control over the environment.[3] On the other hand, library services do exhibit some of the characteristics of systems that are adaptable: library services may have serious problems but rarely dramatic crises; and the popular stereotypic image of libraries is as safe, suitable places for timid

---

[2] A survey of libraries in Indiana in 1973 illustrates the overwhelming numerical predominance of small libraries. The median annual expenditure on books and educational materials (and range) was for public libraries, $4,400 ($202-$591,550); for school libraries, $1,994 ($150-$14,000); for college and university libraries, $38,383 ($1,500-$1,070,501); and special libraries, $6,712 ($315-$120,496). The median annual expenditure for salaries (and range) was: public, $11,489 ($360-$1,960,302); school, $9,300 ($136-$44,000); college and university, $62,000 ($5,000-$1,379,156); and special libraries, $18,500 ($3,841-$581,897). It seems reasonable to suppose that small libraries were more likely to have been omitted from the survey than large ones. Hence, these figures probably overstate the actual sizes. See B. E. Markuson, *The Indiana Cooperative Library Services Authority: A Plan for the Future* (Indianapolis: Indiana State Library, 1974), appendix A. A reasonably complete survey of any region can be expected to yield a similar, highly skewed distribution.

[3] Of course librarians seek to influence their environment. *Cf.* J. R. Euster, *The Academic Library Director: Management Activities and Effectiveness* (New York: Greenwood Press, 1987).

persons to work rather than adventurous, action-oriented "change-agents."[4] Even more significantly, library services do, in fact, *survive*. In other words, there is a paradox: library services do not appear to have the usual characteristics of adaptability, but they do share the crucial feature of adaptive systems—survival. We shall return to this paradox in the final chapter.

Controls and responses

We have deliberately chosen to view library services, their users, and the interactions between them as a system. This approach is chosen not only because it is believed to be helpful for the development of theory, but also because any theory developed with an emphasis on the interactions would seem more likely to be of some usefulness in practical application—in making the provision and/or the use of library services more effective in some sense. How *do* the parts relate to each other? How *might* they relate? What actions or relationships might be more (or less) effective (or economical) with respect to specific goals or outcomes?

Notions of "control" are central to the study of systems. Control, however, is perhaps too strong a term. What is of interest is what *responses* are made. How do parts of the system react to stimuli? How do the responses and interactions of parts combine to form the response of the system as a whole? It is the process of response to stimuli which constitutes the means of change and adaptation, either by internal alteration or by altering the environment. Responses to opportunities and to threats are the essence of achieving goals.

What sorts of controls or responses are at work in the provision and use of library services? Five distinct sorts of responses appear to characterize retrieval-based information services, including library services.

1. *Inquiry* can be viewed as the response to curiosity or to distressing ignorance. It is, ordinarily, an inquiry which causes information retrieval systems to be used.

---

[4] One may not agree and one may deplore such views. Nevertheless, that is the prevailing opinion and it has not been contradicted by studies of the personality traits of librarians who emerge as lacking the traits which are most closely associated with forceful leadership. See P. R. Douglass, "The Personality of the Librarian," Ph.D. dissertation (University of Chicago, Graduate Library School, 1957); P. D. Morrison, "The Career of the Academic Librarian: A Study of the Social Origins, Educational Attainments, Vocational Experience, and Personality Characteristics of a Group of American Academic Librarians," D. L. S. dissertation (University of California, Berkeley, School of Librarianship, 1961). A. McMahon, *The Personality of the Librarian* (Occasional Papers in Librarianship, Adelaide: Libraries Board of South Australia, 5, 1967). J. Agada, "Assertion and the Librarian Personality," *Encyclopedia of Library and Information Science*, vol. 42 (New York: Marcel Dekker, 1987), pp. 144-214.

2. *Retrieval* can be viewed as a response to inquiries. Inquiries are posed to the retrieval system which responds with a set of retrieved signals. One looks in a card catalog or searches at a terminal expecting a useful response in the form of cards or messages bearing data appropriate to the inquiry.

3. *Becoming informed* is the term we use to denote the process whereby people's personal knowledge changes in response to the messages they receive. (One could have used the term "information" to denote this process, but it would be ambiguous since the term "information" is more commonly used to denote the data, signals, or messages, i.e., the stuff as well as the process.)

4. *The demand* for library service is a response to perceived need and the perception of opportunity to do something to meet that need. The scale and nature of the demand will vary in response to a variety of stimulating or inhibiting factors.

5. *The allocation* of resources to and within library services responds to preferences and perceptions by those who have resources to allocate. The actual allocation determines in detail the provision of library services.

At this stage, we merely note and briefly define these five types of "control" or, as we prefer, response. We shall examine each in detail in Part II, chapters 6 to 12 and the interactions between them in Part III, chapter 13.

Some related systems

We have judged it useful to define our system as including library service, the users, and the interactions between them. Anything else is defined as being part of the environment (i.e., outside the system as defined). Defining the boundaries of a system is a rather arbitrary process, especially when dealing with "open" systems. One could redefine the boundaries of the system so that importantly related aspects of the environment come to be considered part of a larger system.

We have already noted that what we have defined is an "open" system capable of affecting and being affected by its environment. It is also important to remember that parts of the system may simultaneously be parts of other systems also. Library users are parts of other systems (universities, disciplines, families, occupational groups), and their information-gathering behavior can be expected to range over numerous other systems in addition to the library service, e.g., colleagues, newspapers, bookshops, other libraries, meetings. A given library service will be only one part of any given user's range of information.[5]

[5]   A. Campbell and C. A. Metzner, *Public Use of the Library and Other Sources of Information* (Ann Arbor, Mich.: University of Michigan, Institute for Social Research,

(cont'd. on p. 31)

Libraries not only have their own internal systems and procedures, but also participate in at least three other, wider sorts of systems: the larger political framework (e.g., university, city, school, firm); the universe of publishing and bibliographical control (e.g., book trade, indexes, citations); and systems of libraries and librarianship (e.g., the professional customs of librarians, and other libraries). Libraries depend significantly on other libraries for interlibrary loans and, more recently, on the collective use of computerized bibliographical utilities. The attitudes and initiatives of the profession of librarians and of schools educating librarians can also stimulate or inhibit the development of library services. Both libraries and their users are intimately involved in the complex and continuously changing web of human knowledge.

So far we have asserted a need for theory, we have described the scope of our present interests, and we have suggested that it would be beneficial to view library services and their users as systems. In the next chapter, we consider what sort of theory would be appropriate when considering library services.

1950), esp. pp. 11-14; C.-C. Chen et al., *Citizen Information Seeking Patterns: A New England Study. Executive Summary Report* (Boston, Mass.: Simmons College, School of Library Science, 1979), (ERIC report ED 186 031) pp. 6-7.

5

What Sort of Theory?

As the next step, we pause to consider what sort of theory would be appropriate when considering library services. After all, if one were to have a mistaken expectation as to the sort of theory, one might fail to recognize it. Ideally, one should seek to reduce the number of preconceived notions about the sorts of theory we might find or develop. Two considerations should encourage us to take a broad view:

1. Ideally, one should be open-minded and objective in analysis. However, each human being has particular values, experiences, and frames of reference and there seems to be no reason to believe that open-mindedness and objectivity are fully attainable. We may be more narrowly oriented that we realize.
2. Knowledge concerning library services is commonly referred to as library *science* and symptoms can be found of a desire for it to be scientific. Yet, at the same time, there is little evidence that it is or can be "scientific" in the ordinary usage of the term which implies characteristics of the physical sciences as opposed to those of the social sciences or of the humanities. As Aristotle observed, "It is a mark of the educated man and a proof of his culture that in every subject he looks for only so much precision as its nature permits."[1]

There have been recurring complaints that knowledge concerning library services "lacks theory." A favorite quotation with those who wish to complain is a statement written by Pierce Butler and published in 1933:

> Unlike his colleagues in other fields of social activity the librarian is strangely uninterested in the theoretical aspects of his profession. He seems to possess a unique immunity to that curiosity which elsewhere drives modern man to attempt, somehow, an orientation of his particular labors with the main stream of human life. The librarian apparently stands alone in the simplicity of his pragmatism: a

---

[1] Aristotle, *The Ethics of Aristotle; The Nichomachean Ethics Translated* (Harmondsworth: Penguin, 1955), Book 1, chapter 3, pp. 27-8. For a discussion of "knowledge outside the matured mathematical-experimental sciences," see J. R. Ravetz, *Scientific Knowledge and Its Social Problems* (New York: Oxford University Press, 1971), pp. 371-7. Also M. Bunge, *Scientific Research: The Search For System* (Berlin: Springer Verlag, 1967).

rationalization of each immediate technical process by itself seems to satisfy his intellectual interest.[2]

When this passage is quoted, there is rarely any discussion of whether or not there might have been any progress in the development of theoretical understanding of librarianship *since* 1933—nor is there, typically, any discussion of the sorts of theory which could be expected with respect to library services. At the very least, it would seem reasonable to explore plausible definitions of "theory" in this context. We might find that the sorts of theory desired are inherently impossible; or we might find that, of the sort which are feasible, there is more evidence than has been generally realized.

Theory defined

Webster's Third New International Dictionary of the English Language Unabridged offers a series of definitions for the varying usages of the word theory.[3] Of these, one appears to be particularly meaningful in the context of library services:

> 3.a.(1) The body of generalizations and principles developed in association with practice in a field of activity (as medicine, music) and forming its content as an intellectual discipline.

A closely related definition would seem somewhat applicable, although more directly to the study of library services than to practice:

> 3.1.(2) The coherent set of hypothetical, conceptual, and pragmatic principles forming the general frame of reference for a field of inquiry (as for deducing principles, formulating hypotheses, undertaking action).

Other definitions provided (e.g., "a judgment," "an unproved assumption," "a systematic analysis") can clearly be used in relation to library services, but the first definition quoted above (3.a.(1)) would seem to fit best in the phrase "theory of library service" and it is the one we shall use for present purposes. It may be noted that one other definition, which we do not adopt here, will be considered later when discussing philosophy, i.e., "2.a. A belief, policy, or procedure proposed or followed as basis for action: a principle or plan of action."

In the next section, we will briefly enumerate examples of notions in

---

[2] P. Butler. *An Introduction to Library Science* (Chicago, Ill.: University of Chicago Press, 1933), pp. xi-xii. See also J. M. Christ, *Toward a Philosophy of Educational Librarianship* (Littleton, Colo.: Libraries Unlimited, 1972), chapter 1 and J. G. Meijer, *Librarianship: A Definition* (Urbana, Ill.: University of Illinois, Graduate School of Library and Information Science, 1982).

[3] *Webster's Third New International Dictionary of the English Language Unabridged* (Springfield, Mass.: Merriam, 1971).

librarianship that would appear to meet the criterion of fitting the above definitions. After that, we consider some aspects of the theory of library service and consider how they relate to theories of other fields. The *Oxford Dictionary* offers two definitions in this sense:[4]

> 4. A scheme or system of ideas or statements held as an explanation or account of a group of facts or phenomena; a hypothesis that has been confirmed or established by observation or experiment, and is propounded or accepted as accounting for the known facts: a statement of what are held to be general laws, principles, or causes of something known or observed.
> 4.b. That department of an art or technical subject which consists in the knowledge or statement of the facts on which it depends, or of its principles or methods as distinguished from the *practice* of it.

It is emphasized that we are concerned with theory in the broad sense of an understanding or explanation of the nature of things, not in the restricted sense, used in formal and physical sciences, of fundamental laws rigorously testable by empirical evidence.

Examples of theory

In this section, we consider briefly some arbitrarily selected examples of notions which would appear to fit either or both of the Webster definitions of "theory" cited above. We will, for convenience, follow our previous breakdown of Inquiry, Retrieval, Becoming Informed, Demand, and Allocation.

With respect to *inquiry*, we find that the higher the level of formal education the higher the propensity to inquire after specific documents and the lower the propensity to make "subject inquiries" in a library.[5]

The area of *retrieval*—including indexing, classification, and the evaluation of retrieval performance—depends heavily on notions of "aboutness," "relevance," "recall," "precision," and "utility" and the relationships between them. Indexing itself depends on logic and linguistics (semantics, syntax, and pragmatics), and for imposing control on indexing (vocabulary control, classification scheme construction, and the syndetic structure of catalogs) set theory, hierarchical structures, and facet analysis. For the actual construction of indexes, technology is needed, especially but not only when computers are used. This depends on the understanding of what alternative technological devices can do and on management tools such as cost analysis and cost effectiveness.[6]

The process of *becoming informed* is characterized by notions of what is likely to be understood by the people to be served, what ancillary services

---

[4] *Oxford English Dictionary*, vol. 11 (Oxford, England: Clarendon Press, 1961), p. 278.

[5] R. Hafter, "Types of Search by Type of Library," *Information Processing and Management* 15, no. 5 (1979): 261-4.

[6] A convenient general textbook is F. W. Lancaster, *Information Retrieval Systems: Characteristics, Testing, and Evaluation*, 2nd ed. (New York: Wiley, 1979).

might facilitate this, and what the limitations of the service are with respect to fostering beneficial knowledge and/or diminishing harmful ignorance. Much of this is largely implicit as in the development of "appropriate" collections of documents and ancillary aids such as dictionaries. Other aspects have been made more explicit in writings on library service in relation to "social epistemology" and "public knowledge."[7]

The *demand* for library services has a substantial literature based mainly on surveys of use (which is not the same as the demand) and focusing mainly on how things are at a given point in time rather than on the dynamics of demand (which would be more useful).[8] These more tractable aspects yield consistently reported findings which can and sometimes do form the basis for planning. The more quantitative analysis of the logistics of document delivery derive in part from theoretical notions derived from operations research.[9]

The politics of *allocation* of resources and priorities to and within library resources is reflected in conclusions and exhortations in the literature on library management. More formally, concepts drawn more or less directly from welfare economics are used to explain and justify the noncommercial nature of libraries.[10] Here, we are concerned with theory used for analysis and comprehension. The choice of social values implicit in advocating the adoption of specific allocations of resources will be discussed subsequently in relation to the philosophy of librarianship. Concepts used to describe political and managerial activities in relation to library services are largely derived from the literatures of management and the study of organizations.[11]

---

[7] See, for example, P. G. Wilson, *Public Knowledge, Private Ignorance: Toward a Library and Information Policy* (Westport, Conn.: Greenwood Press, 1977).

[8] M. G. Ford, "Research in User Behavior in University Libraries," *Journal of Documentation* 29, no. 1 (March 1973): 85-106. [Reprinted in *Reader in Operations Research for Libraries*, edited by P. Brophy et al. (Englewood, Colo.: Information Handling Services, 1976), pp. 293-306]; J. M. Brittain, *Information and Its Users: A Review With Special Reference to the Social Sciences* (Bath, England: Bath University Press, 1970).

[9] See, for example, P. M. Morse, *Library Effectiveness: A Systems Approach* (Cambridge, Mass.: MIT Press, 1968); C.-C. Chen, *Applications of Operations Research Models to Libraries* (Cambridge, Mass.: MIT Press, 1976); M. K. Buckland, "Ten years of Progress in Quantitative Research on Libraries," *Socio-Economic Planning Sciences* 12, no. 6 (1978): 333-9. Also chapter 16, below.

[10] For example, see F. M. Blake and E. L. Perlmutter, "Libraries in the Market Place," *Library Journal* 99, no. 2 (January 15, 1974): 108-11; W. Schwuchow, "Fundamental Aspects of the Financing of Information Centers," *Information Storage and Retrieval* 9 (1973): 569-75. See also footnote 6 of chapter 10.

[11] See, for example, R. D. Stueart and B. B. Moran, *Library Management*, 3rd ed. (Littleton, Colo.: Libraries Unlimited, 1987).

Structure as theory

Some of what will be described has to do with the description of "structure," i.e., how things relate to each other. For example, mathematical theories of bibliographical obsolescence are descriptions of document usage in relation to time. In an important philosophical sense, the description of structure *is* theory, in that structure is, by definition, the relationship between things; and theory can only be expressed in terms of the relationships between things. Material on structural relationships in library service constitutes an important part of "the body of generalizations and principles developed in association with practice."

It should be noted that an empirically found structure can be examined theoretically without any theory as to *why* it occurs. This happened with Zipf. His empirically found "Zipf's law" of patterns in the distribution of various social behaviors has found widespread acceptance. His elaborate explanation of *why* this pattern is found—his "principle of least effort"—has not found acceptance.[12]

Good theory, useful theory, provisional theory

So far, we have not considered the notion of "goodness" of theory. The view implicitly adopted throughout can be summarized as follows: Theories are, by definition, mental constructs. They may be *expressed* in written and graphical form. They may well inspire and guide practical achievements of a concrete form. Yet a theory remains a mental construct. A "good" theory is one which *matches* well our perception of the objects that the theory is about. The closer the match the better the theory. It is to be remembered that the matching is with our *perception* of the objects. This explains why a theory can seem perfectly adequate in relation to what is known, but then has to be rejected as "bad" when more has been learned. This change from "good" to "bad" can happen when either of two things happens: (1) another mental construct—another theory—is developed which "fits" even better the perceptions of the objects regarded as relevant; or (2) additional objects are discovered such that the perceptions of these new objects are incompatible with the original theory. Even if the additional objects have been inaccurately perceived, the theory will cease to be regarded as a "good" theory and efforts can be expected to develop a better theory. Of course, it could happen that the

---

[12] Zipf's principle of least effort means that a person will strive to minimize the probable average rate of his work-expenditure over time. See G. K. Zipf, *Human Behavior and the Principle of Least Effort* (New York: Hafner, 1965, reprint of 1949 edition). See also M. K. Buckland and A. Hindle, "Library Zipf," *Journal of Documentation* 25, no. 2 (March 1969): 58-60; and R. A. Fairthorne, "Empirical Hyperbolic Distributions (Bradford-Zipf-Mandelbrot) for Bibliometric Description and Prediction," *Journal of Documentation* 25, no. 4 (December 1969): 319-43.

additional objects had been wrongly perceived and that, with a later revised view of these objects, the original theory might be reaffirmed as being good after all. Goodness of theory, then, is not a moral attribute but a matter of closeness of match between the mental construct and the perception of entities to which the theory pertains.

A theory can be useful insofar as it serves to assist and guide the development of further understanding (whether formalized as "theory" or not) and/or of practical activities. Yet, theory should always be regarded as provisional. This is necessary because it is always possible that mental effort might result in a new or revised theory which would match the perceptions of relevant objects even better and because perceptions of relevant objects are likely to change. New objects may be discovered. The perceived relevance of old or new objects may change. Each of these cases means that the theory must now match something different and that the closeness of match—the goodness of theory—must be reassessed.

The consequence of all this is that every theory should be regarded as strictly provisional—and as a challenge not only to our mental powers to develop better theories which might match our perceptions much better, but also to the accuracy and extent of our powers of perception of relevant objects. The so-called "scientific method" is precisely this: a systematic two-pronged assault on theory intended to supersede good provisional theories with better provisional theories. On the one hand, the formulation of a hypothesis is, in effect, the drafting of potentially better theory. On the other hand, scientific experiments are systematic attempts to perceive relevant objects which the theory cannot fit or match. In this way, scientific knowledge is corrected and the theoretical frameworks (the "paradigms" of science as described and popularized by Kuhn)[13] are overthrown. In fields of study which do not deal with observable objects, the challenge must come by persuasion, for example, by the demonstration of conceptual inconsistencies, as in philosophy. Nevertheless, the approach and process are basically the same.

It follows from all this that, insofar as theory can assist understanding and guide practice, the most useful consequence of this book would be for it to be promptly superseded by new, better theory and by fuller perceptions of relevant aspects of library services and of their users. Even the most favorable view of this book, then, could only be that it is a tentative, provisional statement to be rendered obsolete as soon as possible.

[13] T. C. Kuhn, *The Structure of Scientific Revolutions* (Chicago, Ill.: University of Chicago Press, 1964).

Unique to and characteristic of

In discussion of theory in relation to library services, the assumption appears to have been, either explicitly or implicitly, that the theory ought to be unique to librarianship (e.g., Houser and Schrader).[14] This constraint would seem to be both unnecessary and contrary to the available evidence. Library services must surely be unique in the sense that the phrase denotes a particular set of activities in a particular set of contexts. The *combination* of notions pertaining to this particular set of activities in these particular contexts may well be unique as a *combination* of notions. However, even if we assume that the *combination* of notions is unique, it does not necessarily follow that *any single* notion is unique to library service, only that no other activity will be characterized by the identical *combination*. Individual aspects of what happens in libraries in general can be found to have characteristics which also characterize one or more activities outside of libraries. It is to be expected, therefore, that analysis of the theory which is pertinent to a non-library context will be more or less pertinent also in the library context and vice-versa. A sensible approach would seem to be to welcome the practical consequence of these common characteristics and not to regret a sense of diminished uniqueness. In this regard, uniqueness may be flattering to the sense of self-esteem of a librarian, but would also appear to be counterproductive for practical purposes of getting on with the development of the theory and the practice of library service.

The relationship between notions in library service and comparable notions outside of library services is not necessarily straightforward.

1. *The notion may be distinctive to library service only in its specific application.* For example, in analytical cost studies of library services wherein the attempt is made to ascertain how much of the cost of a service can properly be attributed to one objective (e.g., support of research) rather than another (e.g., support of teaching), concepts and techniques are used which are proper for this aspect of librarianship but also happen to be entirely standard and characteristic for cost analysis in other contexts than libraries: cost centers, overhead, and accounting principles concerning the attribution of cost. However, the detailed problem of attributing the cost of books and journals to and between cost centers would appear to be a problem unique to libraries and the accounting principles adapted for it would seem to be unique to librarianship for that reason.

2. *Notions developed outside librarianship may be incomplete.* Particular manifestations of theory concerning library services may be different

---

[14] L. Houser and A. M. Schrader, *The Search for a Scientific Profession: Library Science Education in the U.S. and Canada* (Metuchen, N.J.: Scarecrow Press, 1978).

from other fields in which theory may have been unevenly developed. The incompleteness may be significant when it comes to the use of that area of theory in librarianship. One might speculate that this is the case with theories of linguistic ambiguity, where it has been suggested that "referential" approaches are fine for the philosophers who developed them and that "structural" approaches are fine for linguists interested in sentences, but that new and different approaches with respect to vagueness in the definition of entities and with respect to the pragmatics of actual and artificial languages are needed both for a fuller development of linguistic theory and, more to the point, for the effective use of linguistic theories in information retrieval.[15]

3. *A notion may originate as unique to library services and spread to other fields.* Bibliometrics, in the sense of the quantitative analysis of bibliographic citations, was developed largely in the context of librarianship. Bradford was concerned with the completeness of bibliographies;[16] Garfield developed citation indexing as a complement to subject indexing;[17] and others have examined the growth and obsolescence of literatures. Subsequently, the quantitative analysis of bibliographical citations has become a major tool used in studies of the sociology of knowledge. The underlying notions are common to both sorts of uses.

4. *Apparently common notions may be misleading.* In the economic analysis of commercial enterprises, the price mechanism is dominant. The existence of monetary prices payable by the user forces a continuous reevaluation by users of the services or goods being offered. The dependence on these payments by users as the supplier's source of income forces the supplier to be responsive to market pressures. It has even been argued that library services ought to introduce monetary charges in order to make library services more responsive.[18] While it is probably correct that introducing charges would engender a sharper responsiveness to market pressure, the assumption that theory characteristic of the economics of commercial situations should also be regarded as characteristic of

---

[15] K. Sparck Jones and M. Kay, *Linguistics and Information Science.* FID publ. no. 492. (New York: Academic Press, 1973).

[16] S. C. Bradford, "Sources of Information on Specific Subjects," *Engineering* 137, no. 3550 (January 1934): 85-6. (Reprinted in Brophy et al., eds, *Operations Research for Libraries*, pp. 170-4 and in *Collection Management* 1, nos. 3-4 (Fall-Winter 1976-77): 95-103). S. C. Bradford, *Documentation* (London: Crosby Lockwood, 1948).

[17] A citation index inverts bibliographical references and so permits one to move backwards from a cited article to the article that cites it. The assumption is that, if a reference has been made from one article to another, the content of the articles is likely to be similar in some significant way. See E. Garfield, *Citation Indexing—Its Theory and Application in Science, Technology, and Humanities* (New York: Wiley, 1979). See also chapter 7.

[18] R. L. Ackoff, et al., *The SCATT Report: Designing a National Scientific and Technological Communication System* (Philadelphia: University of Pennsylvania Press, 1976), p. 41. *Cf.* M. Getz, *Public Libraries: An Economic View* (Baltimore: Johns Hopkins University Press, 1980), pp. 162-3.

libraries' services is vulnerable to criticism on two grounds: (1) introducing monetary charges, while possibly beneficial in some regards, would also interfere seriously with the purposes for which libraries exist (either by distorting usage relative to the funders' intentions or by diverting resources into administering the accounting) and (2) the arguments for the introduction of monetary charges in order to effect responsiveness fail to take into account nonmonetary aspects of price and the existence of presently available (and, perhaps, underutilized) mechanisms for responsiveness. (Further discussion can be seen in chapter 10.)

Whether or not one concludes that monetary charges for library services would be a good idea, there are grounds for asserting that notions drawn from the economics of commerce should not be regarded as *directly* transferable to the library context. This does not, however, preclude the possibility that a more general theory could not be developed to include both.

What is shared theory?

What, one might ask, is signified by the assertion that theory characteristic of an aspect of librarianship is also characteristic of some other field? There would appear to be two answers to this—one mild, one stronger.

A mild response would be that theory pertaining to, say, retrieval processes in libraries, *resembles* the theory pertaining to retrieval processes in, say, engineering documentation or machine translation. This is not a strong assertion though it may well be helpful, since one can systematically set out to look for parallels and analogs. A theory or a practice in the one context might well be transferable (with some adaptation) to another. Even though resemblance may seem to be a mild degree of sharing, recognition of it could be quite powerful in its practical consequences. One can systematically examine the features of one and explore their applicability to the other.

A stronger response would be that there is a commonality of theory. For example, one might assert that the theory of library retrieval processes *is also* the theory of machine translation. Yet, this is untenable since it implies complete identity and the one would have to be a synonym of the other. Theory deals with mental constructs of a set of perceived objects and, if the two sets of perceived objects are not identical, the theory should not be regarded as identical. "Machine translation" is not coterminous with "retrieval processes in libraries." Complete commonality, then, is not possible. Nevertheless, this does leave scope for partial coincidence or commonality. For example, one might assert that retrieval processes in libraries are basically linguistic processes. One might further explicate this by asserting that, since retrieval processes are linguistic or quasilinguistic processes, some (or all) of the theory of information retrieval processes can also be considered part of the theory of linguistics. Alternatively, one might assert that, at some level of abstraction, a common theory is applicable to both. To make such assertions, a critical assumption is necessary: that the matter to be theorized about does not have to be viewed as pertaining only to *one* broader area. In other words, library automation does not have to be viewed as *either* an area of librarianship *or* an area of computer studies. Instead, *any* area can be viewed as being a part of two or more larger fields simultaneously. If, therefore, we were to assert that the allocation of resources to and within library services is a political process, then the implication that this process can be viewed as a part of the field of politics does not prevent us from continuing to view the process as also being a part of library service. By the same token, library automation can be regarded simultaneously as a part of the field of computing and also a part of the field of library service. Similarly, asserting that retrieval processes in libraries *are* basically linguistic processes would imply that the study of retrieval processes in libraries can be viewed as part of the field of linguistics without requiring that we cease to view them as part of library science. Of course, there may not be agreement as to whether a particular topic should be regarded as constituting the partial coinciding of two particular fields.

In this book, frequent reference is made to aspects of library services as also being "characteristic" of other fields or as being "related to" other fields. At the very least, this implies resemblance. If the relationships asserted in this book cannot be accepted even at the level of resemblances, then little has been achieved. Acceptance of a degree of resemblance in most of the relationships posited would seem to be a necessary and sufficient requirement for the conceptual relationships proposed to constitute a meaningful theoretical framework. However, even though it may not be strictly necessary for acceptance of the principal arguments, we do also assert the stronger relationship of partial coincidence in several important areas.

Several consequences would seem to follow any accepted claim to partial coincidence: It may well be important to relax some of the ingrained attitudes derived from territoriality of academic disciplines which develop in spite of the original meaning of the name "university." If, for example, the allocation of resources to and within library services is viewed not merely as "resembling" political processes but also as being an area "common" to both the fields of political science and library service, then some practical consequences follow. It is implied that good theory should be viewed as part of the literature of both political science and librarianship. An effective analyst of this topic could, in principle, approach it from a disciplinary background in librarianship or in political science. Once developed, a truly persuasive theory can be expected to be regarded as good by the rest of both fields.

However, some difficulties can be expected over and beyond the human jealousies which academic and disciplinary territoriality can engender. If the commonality has not previously been widely recognized or if the two fields have already developed separate technical vocabularies and/or different (provisional) theories, then the development of mutually acceptable theory is likely to be difficult. No discipline or field is ever fully developed and it could happen that prevailing theory in one or both may be insufficiently developed with regard to special features in the area of commonality. Indeed, if that were not the case, this book (or something like it) would probably have been written years ago. It is not only, therefore, that commonality may not have been recognized. The area of coincidence could conceivably be a relatively undeveloped area.

If the assertion of partial coincidence in theory is accepted, then more and better tools may be at hand than have been recognized and critical analysis in a more collaborative mode is indicated.

General comments on theory in library services

Certain general conclusions concerning the "theory of library services" would seem to follow from this discussion.

While the overall combination of theory may be unique to librarianship, there appears to be no reason to expect that particular theoretical notions are unique to library services. As a practical matter, it would seem advantageous to share notions characteristic of libraries with other fields in which they are also characteristic. The rationale is that progress in theoretical understanding is more likely to occur if more and different sorts of people are working at it. Further, theories are better tested from two perspectives than from one. The desire for theory unique to library service may stem from a human desire for the status which comes from being distinctively different. The continued expectation of unique theory may have been prolonged by the isolation of librarians understandably preoccupied with library services.

Much of library service has to do with human activities: it is labor-intensive in nature; it is concerned with service to people; and evaluation needs to deal with relatively undefinable aspects of human behavior. There is, therefore, difficulty in achieving definitions. The field is inherently and, one supposes, inescapably a "soft" field in terms of definability.[19]

---

[19] The term "soft" is used following the custom of distinguishing between "hard" and "soft" disciplines. In this sense, hardness/softness refers to the extent to which the concepts can be unambiguously defined. "Hard" sciences include mathematics, physics, and chemistry; whereas sociology, psychology, and education are generally regarded as "soft" sciences. Hardness (in this sense) should not be confused with hardness in the sense of difficulty. Arguably, intellectual progress is more difficult in "soft" disciplines than in "hard" ones. See chapter 8.

A good deal of "the body of generalizations and principles developed in association with practice" is *implicitly* understood by those providing library services. That is to say, much of what is known has not been formally explicated and presented as "theory." There would appear to be a great deal of work to be done in eliciting, explicating, and revising what is implicitly known or not yet consciously thought out. It would appear to be a difficult field for would-be theorists. Exploring characteristics which are shared with other fields may very well be a fruitful—though difficult—strategy.

The sorts of theory which we have used as examples above are not very fashionable in terms of the social respectability of hard sciences especially since World War II. Definition is difficult. Quantification is even more so.[20] It would seem to be necessary to accept the conclusion that library science is not a hard science. Investigators who yearn for the respectability of a hard science will have to restrict themselves to some relatively quantifiable part of it, or, if that is unacceptable, abandon the study of library science for some other field which is. To do that, it would seem necessary to move altogether outside of retrieval-based information services for people to use.

A final paradox

Much of this chapter has been concerned with arguing that each of the various parts of the theory of library service is probably not unique to library service or, at most, is unique in detail of application only. Further, it has been argued that this very lack of uniqueness would seem beneficial from a practical point of view because it permits librarians to collaborate with others in shared theoretical problems. At the same time, there would appear to be no reason not to regard the *totality* or *combination* of the theoretical aspects of library service as being unique to librarianship. On reflection, this could seem to be an ideal outcome: Librarians can take pride in having something unique and take advantage of the fact that they share so much with others.

[20] For a survey of progress in quantification in library services, see chapter 16 below which is based on M. K. Buckland, "Ten Years of Progress in Quantitative Research in Libraries," *Socio-Economic Planning Sciences* 12, no. 6 (1978): 333-9.

[21] C. Oldman, "Scientism and Academic Librarianship," in *Information in Society: A Collection of Papers,* edited by M. Barnes et al., (Leeds: School of Librarianship, Leeds Polytechnic, 1981), pp. 15-29.

Part II

Analysis

6

Inquiries

Definition

We have been viewing library service as an information service. Indeed, we have been viewing it as an example of a broader class of information services that involve retrieval. In this chapter, we are concerned with the *motivation* for using library services. However, in doing so, we encounter problems since it is not clear that all use of library services fits the usual notions of using an information service. College libraries are extensively used as study halls, as places where one may use seats and tables to work with materials that are not library materials. Parents can and do take small children to public libraries in order that their children can borrow books. One motivation, possibly a dominant one, may be that the *reading* of the books would foster the child's reading skills. Some library services, notably those provided by special interest groups and by governments as part of their cultural foreign policy (e.g., U.S. Information Agency, British Council) are expected not only to inform but also to influence attitudes.[1] In a quite different direction, the recreational reading of escapist literature is hardly informational in the customary usage of the word. How, then, are we to deal with these quite diverse activities if we are to view library services as information services?

First we suggest that most library services are designed as and intended to be information services in the customary sense. We suggest further that information—the process of being informed—should be interpreted in a very broad sense. Ordinarily in writings about information, a narrow, utilitarian perspective is adopted: one uses an information service because one needs "facts" in order to *do* something—to make a decision concerning what to do, say, write, or believe. Verifying a reference, checking on an address, looking up a physical constant, discovering

---

[1] O. Stephens, *Facts to a Candid World: America's Overseas Information Policy* (Stanford: Stanford University Press, 1955); *International Book and Library Activities: The History of a U.S. Foreign Policy*, edited by P. P. Price (Metuchen, N.J.: Scarecrow Press, 1982); D. C. Hausrath, "United States International Communication Agency," in *Encyclopedia of Library and Information Science* 32 (New York: Marcel Dekker, 1981): 70-112; R. C. Swank, "International Values in American Librarianship," in *The Cornell Library Conference, ... 1962*, edited by G. H. Healey (Ithaca, N.Y.: Cornell University Library, 1964), pp. 115-29.

someone else's line of argument, ascertaining the actual wording of a text, finding instructions on how to build a wall are examples of the use of a library service in the traditional instrumental sense of an information service. These sorts of activities fit very well our approach of viewing library services as information services. One can speak in general terms of the individual's desire for knowledge. That would be a positive way of describing what we are concerned with, though we prefer, at risk of sounding negative, to invert the discussion and to discuss library and other information services in terms of "the reduction of distressing ignorance" on the grounds that exposition is made clearer.

However, the definition needs to be broad enough to allow for "informing" to include the altering of opinions and there remains the question of recreational reading. Some recreational use may be of the practical nature of the examples just given, but not all recreational use is. One might stretch the definition of desired knowledge—or distressing ignorance—to include "idle curiosity." One would consider an impulse to read *Catch 22* as a desire to reduce one's distressing ignorance of what that novel is about. At least one might for the first reading of it, but it is less clear that rereading the book for a second or third time could be so regarded.

It would seem to be a better approach to follow Pratt in arguing that the traditional practice of restricting "information" to practical, utilitarian purposes is simply too narrow.[2] Instead, one could take a broader, more fundamental view of "informing" to include the receipt of signals for a variety of purposes—functional, aesthetic, sensual.

We can illustrate the difference between the utilitarian view and the broader view by considering the use of a music recording in a library. On the utilitarian view, a musicologist who listened to the recording in order to ascertain how the player had interpreted or adapted the composer's score would be said to have been informed, but someone who had simply listened to the music for enjoyment and relaxation would not be regarded as having been informed—only entertained. On the broader view of information, one would argue that signals were received by both individuals and that these (audible) signals "informed" their brains in some way. The experience of one may have been mainly aesthetic in nature and the experience of the other may have been primarily utilitarian. Nevertheless, on this broad view, both were examples of being informed.

This broader definition of information has two advantages. (1) It is based on information as a physiological *process* rather than on the vagaries of *motivation* for the process or on possible *consequences* of the process. It is a simpler, more general definition and is highly compatible

    [2] A. D. Pratt, *The Information of the Image* (Norwood, N. J.: Ablex, 1982). See also J. H. Shera, *The Foundations of Education for Librarianship* (New York: Becker and Hayes, 1972), esp. pp. 115-25.

with biological and system concepts. (2) It enables one to treat a broad spectrum of library and information services as part of a varied but continuous whole without having to demarcate by using unsatisfactory distinctions between terms such as educational, recreational, utilitarian, instrumental, and the like in order to define information.[3] Further, it enables one to recognize that an act of information can have various effects (inspirational, recreational, utilitarian, educational) singly or in combination, expected or unexpected.

Although, in this book, we concentrate discussion on the utilitarian, instrumental use of information services, we nevertheless adopt Pratt's broader view of information. With this definition, there is no difficulty in including recreational reading within the view of library services as information services, libraries as a means of influencing opinions, and parents' use of books to foster reading skills in their children.

As for more eccentric uses, as, for example, those who use libraries for shelter, one can observe that means can become ends and be glad that human beings are versatile enough to find uses for institutions over and beyond those for which they were intended.

Concentrating, then, on library services as information services, we start our analysis by considering inquiries—their origin and characteristics.[4] Subsequently, we shall consider how library services respond to inquiries.

For our framework, we need only assume that inquiries originate. It is not essential to understand how and why they arise. However, it does seem plausible to view inquiries as being in response to distressing ignorance. We are all enormously ignorant in the sense that there is a very great deal that we do not know. Some things we are unacquainted with. Some things we do not understand. One has only to peruse an encyclopedia or to contemplate a library to realize how little of human knowledge one possesses. Yet, any encyclopedia is but a very select abstract of the totality of human knowledge and, beyond that, there are the things that are not yet part of human knowledge.

In a very important sense, this colossal individual ignorance does not matter. People can (and do) live pleasant, happy lives unaware of the characteristics of the moons which circle Jupiter, ignorant of the early history of the Danube basin, and unable to tell anyone the chemical formula for common salt.

Ignorance becomes important to the extent to which it becomes distressing or harmful. We use the term "distressing" to denote occasions when an individual is not only conscious of ignorance but also feels a

---

[3] D. Waples et al., *What Reading Does to People* (Chicago, Ill.: University of Chicago Press, 1940), p. 13.

[4] For a convenient summary of recent studies, see B. Dervin and M. Nilan, "Information Needs and Users," *Annual Review of Information Science and Technology* 21 (1986): 3-33.

desire to acquire knowledge in order to reduce the ignorance and, thereby, the distress. Such ignorance would seem to reflect an incongruence in the individual's knowledge. It may be a gap in personal knowledge. For example, one may want to fly from San Francisco to New York, but not know the departure times of the flights. In this case, not knowing the times of the flights makes it difficult to make detailed arrangements for the journey—which is distressing. There are two possible solutions: one can inquire, in which case the knowledge acquired fills the gap and removes the ignorance; or one can decide not to travel after all, in which case the ignorance remains, but, since the intention of going has been removed, the ignorance ceases to be distressing and is, therefore, no longer of concern.

There are also less clearly motivated examples of distressing ignorance. One might, for example, like to know something of the history and culture of Austria. It is not that one's life or physical well-being would be spoiled for lack of such knowledge but, rather, that there is a curiosity, a desire to know. Failure to acquire such knowledge may not have any obviously deleterious effects on one's life and, in contrast to ignorance concerning the flights to New York, there may be no urgency. Nevertheless, in one's personal system of values, a positive value has been assigned to the acquisition of such knowledge and so the lack of it is in some way distressing. The degree of distress may be only very mild, depending on the value attributed to the knowledge. Similarly, one may feel impelled to verify a footnote or to track down a reference.

We have assumed, implicitly, that ignorance is a matter of gaps in our knowledge. This is not necessarily the case. We may have acquired conflicting knowledge, as when we hear two apparently irreconcilable accounts of the same event. This constitutes ignorance in the sense that we do not know what to believe. Perhaps we do not care. If we do care, the incongruence or dissonance becomes another case of distressing ignorance.[5] Inquiries, then, we define as attempts to acquire knowledge in order to reduce distressing ignorance.[6]

Other writers, notably Wilson,[7] have used the phrase, "harmful ignorance." We prefer to use the phrase "distressing ignorance" for inquiries

---

[5] *Cf.*, the notion of "cognitive dissonance" as developed by L. Festinger, in *A Theory of Cognitive Dissonance* (Stanford, Calif.: Stanford University Press, 1957).

[6] For the similar notion of "anomalous states of knowledge," see N. J. Belkin, R. N. Oddy and H. M. Brooks, "ASK for Information Retrieval: Part I. Background and Theory," *Journal of Documentation* 38, no. 2 (June 1982). 261-71. See also B. K. Swigger, "Questions in Library and Information Science," *Library and Information Science Research* 7, no. 4 (October-December 1985): 369-83; S. D. Neill, "The Dilemma of the Subjective in Information Organization and Retrieval," *Journal of Documentation* 43, no. 3 (September 1987): 193-211.

[7] P. G. Wilson, *Public Knowledge, Private Ignorance: Toward a Library and Information Policy* (Westport, Conn.: Greenwood Press, 1977).

which originate from an individual on the grounds that inquiries would not originate unless the individual felt some degree of distress, even if only in the form of curiosity. One might argue that anything distressing is by definition harmful, but that requires a particular definition of harmful and also interferes with the use of the term harmful for situations in which the individual is unaware of, and, therefore, undistressed by genuinely harmful ignorance. For example, if the public water supply were infected with dangerous germs, the people using that water supply would be in dangerously "harmful" ignorance. Yet, so long as they remain unaware of the danger, they would not be "distressed." The supplier of the water, however, if conscious of the problem, would know that the consumers were in harmful ignorance and ought to inform them of the danger so that they could boil the water or take other precautionary measures. *Harmful* ignorance seems a particularly useful term to use in relation to those who plan information services or diagnose information needs *for others.*[8] We use the term "knowledge" to denote what people believe to be true. There is no guarantee that this knowledge may not subsequently be regarded as untrue or that there would necessarily be agreement as to what is or is not harmful.

Response to inquiries

Given that an inquiry has arisen, i.e., that one seeks knowledge to reduce distressing ignorance, there are several possible courses of action. The distress might be eliminated rather than the ignorance. One might decide not to travel to New York or lose interest in the history and culture of Austria. One might seek to replace the ignorance by mental effort alone. Perhaps by searching one's memory the desired knowledge might reappear. Perhaps, by mental effort, one might conclude that two apparently conflicting accounts of the same matter can be reconciled. One might seek to extend one's inquiry to others. One might ask a friend, telephone an office, look in a book, or interrogate a data base. There are numerous possibilities. The connection with library services arises when inquiries reach the library. The principal question then becomes: What happens as a result of this inquiry?

A related matter of considerable interest has to do with inquiries that might have reached the library but did not. It would seem entirely likely that some inquiries reach libraries which might have been better directed elsewhere, and that some inquiries directed elsewhere might have been better directed to libraries. However, to examine this issue, it is necessary

---

[8] For example, "To be culturally literate is to possess the basic information needed to thrive in the modern world. ... Cultural literacy constitutes the only sure avenue for disadvantaged children ...," D. Hirsch, *Cultural Literacy: What Every American Needs to Know* (Boston: Houghton Mifflin, 1987), p. xiii.

to understand not only the nature of different sorts of inquiries and how different sorts of library services can help but also how other non-library sources of information might help. For this we need to probe the basis of library service and the actual and potential roles of library services in society.

At any time, the person with the inquiry may decide that the degree of distress does not warrant the probable effort of further attempts to acquire the knowledge which is expected to reduce the distressing ignorance. This matter will be discussed more fully in chapter 10. At this point, we will simply stress that not all sources of information involve the same probable effort. Telephoning a knowledgeable friend requires far less effort than traveling to and using a large library, for example. It can be a rational strategy to try a less informative source before a more informative one if the probable effort involved in using the former is significantly less than in using the latter.[9] It is also entirely rational to abandon an inquiry when the probable effort in pursuing it exceeds the probable benefit of acquiring the knowledge sought.

Types and taxonomies of inquiries

Inquiries posed in libraries have been classified in a variety of ways.[10] Particularly common is a three-part typology:

- bibliographical, i.e., inquiries about documents;
- factual or subject inquiries; and
- directional inquiries, e.g., Where is the catalog?

Another common practice is to analyze inquiries by the time taken to answer them. Hieber proposed a five-part classification scheme based on

    [9] V. Rosenberg, "Factors Affecting the Preferences of Industrial Personnel for Information Gathering Methods," *Information Storage and Retrieval* 3 (1967): 119-27; T. J. Allen and P. G. Gerstberger, *Criteria for Selection of an Information Source* (Cambridge, Mass.: MIT Sloan School of Management, 1967); I. W. Harris, "The Influence of Accessibility on Academic Library Use" (Ph.D. thesis, Rutgers University, New Brunswick, N.J.: 1966; University microfilms order no. 67-5262).

    [10] For proposals and reviews, see S. Rothstein, "The Measurement and Evaluation of Reference Service," *Library Trends* 12, no. 3 (January 1964): 456-72; C. E. Hieber, *An Analysis of Questions and Answers in Libraries* (Studies in the man-system interface in libraries. Report no. 1) (Bethlehem, Pa.: Lehigh University, Center for the Information Sciences, 1966); G. Jahoda, *The Process of Answering Reference Questions. A test of a descriptive model* (Tallahassee, Fla.: Florida State University, School of Library Science, 1977). Markey refines the earlier analysis by Taylor who proposed four levels of question formulation: the actual ("visceral") but unexpressed need for information; the conscious, within-brain description of the need (the "conscious" need); the formal statement of the need (the "formalized" need); and the question as presented to the information system (the "compromised" need). K. Markey, "Levels of Question Formulation in Negotiation of Information Need During the Online Presearch Interview: A Proposed Model," *Information Processing and Management* 17, no. 5 (1981): 212-25; and B. C. Vickery and A. Vickery, *Information Science in Theory and Practice* (London: Butterworths, 1987) chapter 7: Intermediaries and Interfaces.

on the precision required in the answer.[11] Jahoda discussed a variety of ways in which reference questions can be classified:

- heading the patron toward the answer versus providing the answer;
- types of answer;
- size of answer—single versus multiple facts, documents;
- recall versus discovery;
- types of tools used; and
- types of training required of the person answering.[12]

However, choosing between alternative taxonomies depends on having a criterion for deciding which is better. In the absence of a criterion, any one would be as good as another. The bibliographical/fact-subject/directional breakdown is useful for determining the sort of staff needed, since little professional expertise is needed for directional questions. Analysis by time taken is useful in determining the amount of staffing needed.

Our present interest is in the structure and functioning of library services. Hence, we are interested in the origin of inquiries, the factors that determine their nature, and their characteristics insofar as these affect the provision and use of library services.

Known item search and subject search[13]

Of particular importance is the traditional distinction between searching for a "known item" (i.e., an already identified document) on the one hand and, on the other hand, a "subject" search (i.e., a search for knowledge regardless of, or in ignorance of, any particular documentary source).[14]

This distinction is very significant for the design of library services because a known item search needs different sorts of provision than does a subject search. Author and title indexes are needed for the former; subject indexes and open access to books arranged by subject are needed for the latter. There is no doubt that the distinction between these two sorts of search is of practical usefulness in the detailed design of library services. Nevertheless, closer scrutiny suggests that, however useful, the distinction is a superficial rather than a fundamental one.

The search for knowledge can be illustrated as follows: If we seek to know the population of Klagenfurt in 1900, the cosine of 36°, Nelson's last words, or the chemical composition of citric acid, then we are seeking

---

[11] Hieber, *Questions and Answers in Libraries.*

[12] Jahoda, *Answering Reference Questions.*

[13] This section is based on M. K. Buckland, "Types of Search and the Allocation of Library Resources," *Journal of the American Society for Information Science* 30, no. 3 (May 1979): 143-7.

14. *Cf.,* F. W. Lancaster, *The Measurement and Evaluation of Library Services* (Washington, D.C.: Information Resources Press, 1977), chapters 2 and 14.

highly specific information. More generally, we may seek familiarity with some area of knowledge. Some writers have distinguished between a "factual" inquiry and a "subject" inquiry. While this may be helpful for some purposes, we prefer to regard both as searches for information, albeit differing in the degree to which inquiry can be precisely defined. Yet, these searches do not, in themselves, call for any particular source. There may be any number of documents that contain the desired information. For some inquiries there might only be one source—or even none if the answer is not known or not recorded.

The searcher for a document, on the other hand, might wish to examine, for example, *The Life and Adventures of George Augustus Sala, written by himself* (1895), or *Human Behavior and the Principle of Least Effort* by G. K. Zipf (1949). Reading either document might prove more or less amusing, stimulating, or informative on one or more of a variety of topics whether or not the reader had been seeking specific information. These are examples of highly specific searches for precisely identified information and for unambiguously described documents respectively. It should be recognized that either search could be less specific. One might want to familiarize oneself with Klagenfurt as a possible vacation resort: the precise size of the population might not be of particular interest, and the situation in 1900 even less so. At the same time, one might wish to acquire one or more Agatha Christie stories to read on vacation or one or more items from a reading list of books on the history of Austria. In either case, a limited number of titles have been defined but not any *single* document. Searches, then, may be more or less "information specific," or they may be more or less "document specific."

It is customary to treat information ("subject") searches and document ("known item") searches as entirely separate, different, and independent. However, we suggest that consideration of actual inquiries leads to the conclusion that any given search can and should normally be viewed as *simultaneously both* information specific and document specific in various degrees. We further suggest that any combination of high and low degrees of specificity appears possible. We can examine this further by considering the four combinations which result from combining high and low information specificity with high and low document specificity. This represents a substantial departure from the orthodox dichotomy of "known item" searches and "subject" searches.

The combination of high document specificity and high information specificity is characterized by precisely defined information sought in a clearly identified document: How does Pastor's *History of the Popes* cite the biography of Eugenius IV written by Abert? Does G. K. Zipf cite the related and contemporaneous work of S. C. Bradford in his *Human Behavior and the Principle of Least Effort* (1949)? A less obvious example in this category would be: What is the collation of the 1630 Sheffield edition of the Sermons of Josiah Bloggs? In this case, the inquirer probably has no desire to be informed by the textual "content" of the document. Nevertheless, the searcher does seek to be informed by the physical document on a precisely defined matter.

High document specificity and low information specificity is characterized by clearly identified documents but rather vaguely defined objectives so far as subject matter is concerned. A conscientious future historian of information science might wish to read S. C. Bradford's *Romance of Roses* (1946), not because of any specific interests in gardening but because doing so might provide insight into the author who is better known for having enunciated the bibliometric "law of scattering" now named after him.

Low document specificity but high information specificity represents searches for specific information for which there may be several sources. Either several identified documents could provide the information or it is not known which documents, if any, contain it. What *was* the population of Klagenfurt in 1900? A good example of this category would be a search for priority: Did anybody explicitly combine Bradford's law of scattering with bibliographical obsolescence in order to examine optimal library size prior to 1968?

Low document specificity and low information specificity includes searches that are vague in scope and vague as to source. It would include "What's new in my field?" if the field is not too specifically defined, or "What is new in librarianship this year?"; "Do you have any adventure stories?"; "I am bored with reading this, what else is there in this library that might interest me?"

For the sake of exposition, just two levels of specificity of each type have been examined. Intuitively, specificity should be regarded as a continuous variable and one which is not easy to measure. What we might demonstrate is that, although library users may either ask for a particular document or pose a subject inquiry, in practice the underlying inquiry can involve both a document and a subject search. We shall consider this issue further after a brief discussion of browsing.

Browsing

Studies of book provision in libraries have tended to concentrate on the library's ability to serve users seeking specific documents.[15] A good reason for this is that the logistics of satisfying searches for documents are more tractable than are other sorts of searches. Studying formal

---

[15] For example, see M. K. Buckland, *Book Availability and the Library User* (New York: Pergamon Press, 1975); P. Kantor, "Availability Analysis," *Journal of the American Society for Information Science* 27, no. 6 (October 1976): 311-19.

subject searches is feasible but difficult. Most difficult to study is the rather casual behavior known as browsing.

In the context of our discussion of information specificity and document specificity, it becomes possible to offer a definition of browsing as informal searching which is low on document specificity but might at any level be of information specificity. The adjective "informal" is important. Without it, browsing, an essentially unsystematic activity, would be coterminous with all subject searching. We use the term "informal" in order to exclude searches characterized by the systematic use of formal tools for subject access. Our definition includes both vague searches for anything that might be of interest and accidental, "serendipitous" situations in which highly specific information was found in an unsystematic way.

It is important to remember that, just as our ignorance is massive, many aspects of it may be at least mildly distressing in a nonurgent way. It follows that we can expect many inquiries to be latent at any given time. Therefore, perusal of a heterogeneous set of documents is statistically likely to yield something relating to at least one of these more or less latent inquiries—and the more curious the mind, the greater the probability of gratification, of serendipitous discovery.[16]

Documents as surrogate definitions of desired knowledge

After the brief digression on browsing we now resume our exploration of the nature of inquiries and especially the ways in which inquiries manifest themselves as searches for documents and/or knowledge in libraries.

Let us imagine a world without books or any other retrieval-based information services. What would we do when distressing ignorance arises? We could ask other people and ask them to find out if they don't know the answer themselves. Probably, however, we should adopt the following indirect approach:

1. seek to identify somebody who might have the requisite knowledge;
2. try to find that person; and
3. ask that person for the information desired.

At stage 2 one would be seeking a person, not because that person is wanted as an individual but as a source of the knowledge desired. If it were discovered that the person did not have the requisite knowledge, then one's interest in that person would end. In other words, the interest in that person is solely as a repository of desired knowledge. The person *represents* the desired knowledge. This is an indirect approach in that, at

---

[16] For data on accidental discovery of information see S. S. Guest, "The Use of Bibliographic Tools by Humanities Faculty at the State University of New York at Albany," *The Reference Librarian* 18 (Summer 1987): 157-72, esp. p. 169.

stage 2, we should be asking directly for the person as an indirect means to becoming informed. It is worth considering the circumstances under which we are likely to prefer this indirect approach to the more direct approach of just asking the first person encountered. These circumstances would seem to occur:

- if we were shy about publicizing our particular distressing ignorance;
- if we suspected that the people most conveniently at hand were unlikely to know the answer to our question or to even understand the question; and/or
- if it were particularly difficult to describe the information we were seeking.

In each of these cases, the indirect approach would be preferable in the sense that less discomfort and/or less effort would be involved. Similarly, it is commonly easier to ask for a book than to define the knowledge desired to reduce the distressing ignorance, especially since the information may well be contained in a book on a more general topic.[17] For example:

- "Where are books about Austria?" may suffice for an inquiry concerning the treatment of Croatian and Slovenian minorities in Austria.
- "Where is the *Encyclopedia Britannica*?" may suffice for an elementary inquiry concerning the Coptic church.
- "May I use the San Francisco telephone directory?" is certainly simpler than asking for a particular individual's telephone number.

Often, if the document requested does not contain the desired information, it may well have pointers to where else the information might be found.

We infer from these examples that, when a specific document is sought, what is happening is that the name of the document is being used as a surrogate definition of the knowledge actually sought. It may or may not be the case that the document specified is the *only* source of the information desired—or even that it contains it at all. Most likely, to the person doing the search, specifying a particular document appears to be the easiest way of acquiring the knowledge desired. However, specifying a particular document may prove to be a less than perfect solution. The document may not, in fact, include the information expected to be in it. This is not to say that specific books may not be sought for themselves as books. This would be true for bibliophiles, book-collectors, historians of the book, and library acquisitions and interlibrary loan departments. However, these are specialized and atypical examples of requests for specific books.

---

[17] *Cf.* " ... the query for the location of a specific title may thus be an indicator that the real query has not been asked." Jahoda, *Answering Reference Questions*, p. 87.

In all this we reiterate our distinction between an inquiry and a search. An inquiry is an attempt to acquire knowledge in order to reduce distressing ignorance. A search is a set of actions taken in the process of resolving an inquiry.

We conclude that all inquiries are subject inquiries in that they are attempts to acquire knowledge. It often seems easier to express the inquiry in terms of specific documents which are believed to contain or lead to the knowledge sought. In other words, the specifying of a particular document as being the object of the search is likely to be, in effect, an indirect definition of what is actually being sought. This tendency to specify not the objective of the inquiry but rather the presumed address of the answer to the inquiry would apppear to be characteristic of retrieval-based information systems.

Urgency and importance

We have noted that, during the course of an inquiry, the search may be more or less specifically defined in terms of the information desired; and more or less defined in terms of specific documents. Two more characteristics are needed to complete the categorization of searches in order to relate the design of library services to them:

1. The perceived importance of the inquiry, reflecting the degree of distress felt, will determine how much effort the individual is willing to exert and the point at which he or she is willing to abandon the search. In effect, the *importance*, in conjunction with the perception of probable effort, determines whether (or how far) a search derived from an inquiry will be pursued.
2. The *urgency* attributed to the inquiry will determine *when* it is pursued. The urgency of a given inquiry can be expected to vary over time.

The distinction between urgency and importance is necessary to explain why less important but more urgent inquiries are attended to before more important but less urgent inquiries.

Summary

In this chapter, we have considered the motivation for using library services. We have argued for a broad definition of "information," one based on the process rather than on the motivations for using the process.[18]

---

[18] For a colorful account of why people read, including motives that "are downright vicious," see P. Butler, *An Introduction to Library Science* (Chicago, Ill.: University of Chicago Press, 1933), pp. 58-76.

In doing so, we would assert that traditional discussions of information have restricted themselves altogether too narrowly to the consideration of situations in which information had, or was expected to have, an instrumental role leading to utilitarian consequences. Instead, we would argue, an act of information—reading, listening, observing—for aesthetic pleasure is just as much an act of information as asking for and being told a telephone number in order to transact business. Information is not simply the reduction of uncertainty.

Of course, it does not follow that those who *pay* for the provision of library services will be indifferent as to the sort of use made of it, or to the sorts of services provided. This will be discussed in later chapters.

7

Collections

Introduction

Having considered the sorts of inquiries that may be posed in a library, we shall now consider retrieval—the process whereby data or documents are found in the attempt to deal with the inquiries that have been posed. There are two related processes: arranging for selected materials to be collected for use, which we address in this chapter; and the retrieval of material from collections, which we shall explore in the next chapter.

In the mind's eye, libraries and their collections are almost synonymous. One tends to visualize libraries *as* collections, with rows upon rows of shelves of books. Much of what you see in a library is its collection. The number of volumes remains the most prevalent indicator of how good a library is. Assembling and maintaining collections accounts for much of libraries' budgets, labor costs, and space needs.

Writings on library collections have, understandably, concentrated on procedural aspects of selecting material.[1] The *purpose* of the library collections is generally discussed briefly, if at all, with a vague phrase about how, for example, a university's library collections "support the academic programs." The library is often referred to as a center for the community, as the heart of a university, or as the laboratory of the humanities, but studies of library use have concentrated heavily on surface phenomena, such as frequency of visit or loan statistics. There has been far less examination of *how* the use of library materials relates to learning, to research, and to the broader context of library service. What are people *doing* with library materials when they use them? How is the *role* of a collection related to other aspects of library service? How does the cultural context in which the library is set affect the collection?

[1] For an introduction see G. E. Evans, *Developing Library and Information Center Collections*, 2nd ed. (Littleton, Colo.: Libraries Unlimited, 1987); A. Curley and D. Broderick, *Building Library Collections*, 6th ed. (Metuchen, N.J.: Scarecrow Press, 1985); W. A. Katz, *The Selection of Materials for Libraries* (New York: Rinehart & Winston, 1980); *Collection Development: A Treatise*, edited by R. D. Stueart and G. B. Miller (Greenwich, Conn.: Jai Press, 1980); R. K. Gardner, *Library Collections: Their Origin, Selection, and Development* (New York: McGraw-Hill, 1981); M. Moskowitz, "Collection development and the college library: a state-of-the-art review," *Collection Building* 6, no. 4 (Summer 1984): 5-10; R. D. Johnson, "The College Library Collection," *Advances in Librarianship* 14 (1986): 143-74.

In this chapter we shall consider the astonishing richness of materials as sources of information; the important distinction between library materials and the activity of collection development; the role of collections as part of the retrieval process; ways in which library materials are used; the tendency for any given library's collection to contain materials that are "preprocessed" for ease of use; the diminishing returns associated with increasing investment in collection size; the significance for collection-development activities of the technical medium (paper, microform, data base) of materials; and the tendency for libraries' collections to conform to the cultural values of its social context.

Richness and diversity

The range of objects that libraries and library-like institutions such as archives and museums collect is remarkable. Most obviously, large research libraries have truly massive collections of books and journals. The 118 members of the Association of Research Libraries, for example, reported more than 321 million volumes and 233 million microform units as of 1986.[2]

Images are also assembled: photographs and slides, movies and videos, paintings and prints, also often in millions.[3] Sounds are collected: speeches, songs, music, and language lessons are accumulated in libraries, language labs, museums, and schools. Easily overlooked are the often very extensive collections of objects, both natural objects and artifacts. A large city is likely to have an art gallery and a local history museum. A large university is likely to have a herbarium, a rock collection, an historical or anthropological museum, skeletons, fossils, and much more besides.

We are concerned here with *library* collections, which although ordinarily thought of in terms of books and serials, actually contain a very broad range of materials: manuscripts, archives, photographs, recordings, movies, and much else. Not only will a particular collection include different sorts of objects, but some objects combine textual, visual, audio, and artifactual aspects. Further, the same object can be of interest for quite diverse reasons. Photographic collections illustrate this complexity rather well. One can wonder at the technical skill involved, especially in the nineteenth century. Imagine Roger Fenton working with wet plates in a dark room on wheels in the middle of the Crimean War in 1855, or Matthew Brady in the US Civil War—or Carleton Watkins,

[2] Association of Research Libraries, *ARL Statistics, 1985-86* (Washington, D.C.: ARL, 1987).
[3] A survey of the nine campuses of the University of California located an unexpectedly high total of 17.5 million photographs. *University of California Directory of Photographic Collections*, compiled by S. Conkelton (Riverside: University of California, Museum of Photography, 1985), p. vi.

wandering around California with pack mules and a tent to serve as a darkroom. A 1911 account of how to make an albumen negative on a glass plate starts with "The whites of five fresh eggs are mixed ...."[4] The modern, automatic, single-lens reflex camera is a marvel of chemical, optical, mechanical, and electronic engineering; and of design and manufacture.

There is also the artistic skill involved: the sense of composition, of arrangement, the point of view, the inspired choice of moment. These are reflected in the early portraits by Julia Margaret Cameron, in Ansel Adams' ability to find a picture in a view, and Karsh's famous portrait of Sir Winston Churchill, when he snatched Churchill's cigar away and caught a momentary and characteristic flash of anger.

Photographs also excel in capturing history in views of times, places, and events. How little we would know of ballet without the camera, or of the growth of towns, or of the appearance of people unlikely to have their portraits made by painters. Similarly, there is the major role played by photography in many areas of study, such as astronomy, particle physics, aerodynamics, and natural history.

In quite a different dimension there is the human interest in what is depicted. There is the emotional impact of portrayals of the human condition, as in the Depression era photographs of Dorothea Lange. There are also the sociological and psychological questions raised by, for example, the nineteenth-century interest in photographing dead children.[5]

Books, manuscripts, movies, and other objects can similarly be of interest from each of these different perspectives. The range is remarkable.

The purpose of library materials

The standard phrase concerning collections of library materials is that they "support" the purposes of the community served and that those served "use" the materials in the collections. The terms "support" and "use" are not very evocative. However correct the words may be, they do not tell us much about *how* the materials support the programs, nor about *how* the materials are used, and even less about *why*. More formally it is said that collections contain "relevant information," a phrase composed of two words which have been used in varied and confusing ways. Nevertheless, if these terms have a meaning that can be understood, then it should be possible to rephrase and discuss them usefully in other terms.

---

[4] *Encyclopaedia Britannica*, 11th ed. (New York: Encyclopaedia Co., 1910-11) Vol. 21, s. v. Photography, p. 487.

[5] A more prosaic explanation is that only in this condition did children remain still long enough to be photographed with early, slow films.

The intrinsic interest of photos, books, fossils, paintings, etc., is enormous. However, this interest needs to be balanced against the purpose of the library. In general the purpose of the library is, or should be, to constitute a resource for answering inquiries that arise, as discussed in the previous chapter. We have been using the term "inquiries" in a very broad sense, ranging from research concerning matters apparently not known to anyone, through learning what is not known to the individual, to perusing texts for vague curiosity and amusement. The intended *outcome* is that library users will become better *informed*, as will be discussed in chapter 10.

Library materials as evidence

One learns from the examination of various sorts of things. In order to learn, texts are read, numbers are tallied, objects and images are inspected or listened to. In a significant sense library materials are used as evidence in learning—as the basis for understanding. One's knowledge and opinions are affected by what one sees, reads, hears, or experiences. Textbooks and encyclopedias provide material for an introduction to a subject; literary texts and commentaries provide sources for the study of language and literature; arrays of statistical data provide input for calculations and inference; statutes and law reports indicate the law; photographs show what people, places, and events looked like; citations and sources are verified; and so on.

In each case it is reasonable to view library materials as *evidence*, though without implying that what was read, viewed, listened to, or otherwise used was necessarily accurate, useful, or even pertinent to the user's purposes. Nor need it be assumed that the user did (or should) believe or agree with what was read. In this view collections are regarded as selections of material of actual or potential usefulness in meeting the sorts of inquiries regarded as appropriate for the people for whom library service is provided. The next sections will review some implications of this view. Unfortunately, in the apparent absence of well-defined and widely accepted terminology, any such discussion is liable to suffer from the need to coin new terms or to use existing terms in ways that are not quite standard. In particular, the terms "evidence," "interpretation," and "summarizing" will be used in ways that are not customary in the literature of librarianship, and that are not entirely satisfactory.

Viewing library materials as selections of potential or putative evidence enables us to examine library use more deeply. What do people do when faced with evidence? They sift, they excerpt, they evaluate, they summarize, and they may well add to the cumulation of evidence.

Sifting: an inquiry for a local telephone number is ordinarily straightforward—the telephone directory usually suffices. Someone inquiring into the role of women in eighteenth-century England could benefit from a very wide range of materials: helpful evidence might be found in literature, diaries, sermons, pictures, in contemporary materials of almost any kind, and in commentaries of many sorts written in the centuries since. Much of the evidence is likely to be indirect, in the implications of texts and images created for quite other purposes.

Excerpting and *summarizing* permit copying and condensing of evidence for the convenience of the inquirer, whether by hand, photocopier, or computer.

Evaluation of and *inference* from the texts, images, and objects in the collections leads to understanding, insights, and new ideas. These, in turn, may lead to new material (more or less related to the earlier material) in new articles or books, which may include commentary on the old, thereby increasing the accumulation for the future.

The library is, in essence, a resource for inquiry. A fundamental feature of library collection development is the continual effort to make resources of library materials more conveniently available in a manner that corresponds to the local use of evidence.

Interpretation and summarizing of evidence

Much of the material assembled in library collections is not raw data but material that has already been processed and refined. This is to be expected. For most inquiries the original data are not what would be most helpful. It would not be sensible to refer every individual with a question about Mark Twain to the Mark Twain archives. That would be unhelpful for the inquirer and bad for the archives. Almost always a book about Mark Twain, which may be based on material in the archives, would be sufficient and more practical for all concerned. The book about Mark Twain could well have drawn on and condensed information from other sources, and explain or interpret the relevant ideas and evidence. These two processes, which we shall refer to as "interpretation" and "summarizing," are central to understanding both the nature and the use of library materials.

Interpretation

We use the term "interpretation" in a broad sense, not just as a matter of translation from one language to another but in the sense of explaining: "to explain the meaning of, to elucidate, unfold, show the purport of; to translate into intelligible or familiar terms."[6]

---

[6] *Chambers' Twentieth Century Dictionary*, rev. ed. (Edinburgh: Chambers, 1959), s.v. Interpret, p. 555.

Some books in a library contain original data, but many, if not most, of nonfiction material involves explanation or interpretation of more detailed material.

In the case of foreign literatures, both interpretation and summarizing can be seen. The original writing is not always the first choice. Suppose, for example, that there was an interest in Swahili literature. In North America, an English translation is likely to be the preferred choice, or a book about Swahili writings, perhaps containing abridged texts or translated excerpts, or even an encyclopedia article. Yet each of these options, while progressively more convenient, also contain progressively less of the original evidence. Something is always lost in translation or in summarizing.

Summarizing

The notion of summarizing or reducing evidence can be illustrated most conveniently using examples from the sciences. In statistical studies the goal is usually to reduce large amounts of data into progressively smaller summaries: large quantities of numbers can be aggregated into summary tables; tendencies and patterns in the data can be briefly expressed as, for example, an average, a curve representing the relationship between two variables, and so on. Useful though this simplification and diminution in physical size can be, some of the evidence is necessarily lost in the process of reduction. The essence of statistical technique is the desire to maximize the reduction while minimizing the loss of evidence. Similarly, in chemistry an important goal is taking some material or a process, analyzing it, and working out how to describe it by a succinct formal statement, such as a chemical formula.

In biology one can illustrate this process of reduction, this trade-off between convenience and loss of evidence. Suppose that one were interested in woodpeckers. Some aspects of woodpeckers, such as woodpecker behavior, can be learned only from live woodpeckers, preferably woodpeckers in the wild. For other, fewer purposes, a dead woodpecker would suffice. Studying live woodpeckers, however, is less convenient than studying dead ones, which can be housed and handled more easily. Similarly, more can be learned from a film of a woodpecker than from a still photograph, but the latter is easier to make and to examine. A set of measurements of woodpeckers is even easier to deal with, but much less can be learned from measurements than from photos or films or actual woodpeckers.

Reproductions, even photographs, of works of art and museum items cannot reflect all the evidence of the originals. However, they may well suffice for many purposes and have two striking advantages: they can be made much more widely available and can be used without wear and tear of the originals.

We have used the term "summarizing" with some hesitation. There is no question that the summarizing, condensing, and interpreting of evidence pervades recorded knowledge. In the case of statistical studies, "summarizing" is an apt description of the process of making evidence more convenient and, indeed, more understandable. In literary and historical studies, however, where words rather than numbers are the principal basis for description, the commentaries intended to render the original more understandable can easily be larger than the original. (Consider for example the relative sizes of some originals such as the Bible or the works of Shakespeare with the corpus of writings *about* the Bible or Shakespeare.) Further, commentaries are more likely to *complement* the original (and each other) than to serve as a substitute. In the humanities, interpretation and summarizing is likely to be an expansion![7]

Education, scholarship, and debate—and, therefore, library collections— are permeated with these processes of interpreting and summarizing. Articles and books summarize, cite, refute, and build upon earlier work. This is especially noticeable in the scholarly literature where the growth of material has created the need for abstracting and indexing services, for guides and reviews. Encyclopedias, handbooks, and textbooks, all examples of summarizing and interpretation, perform a very useful role.

Implications for library service

So far we have emphasized two key features of library materials that are important for library service: (i) the *potential* range of informative material is truly enormous in extent and variety and (ii) much of what is held in collections summarizes or explains other evidence. This is both understandable and desirable: not all evidence is equally intelligible or convenient; not all inquiries are equally complex; not all inquirers are equally motivated or bring equal personal knowledge or cognitive skills. It is therefore important that a library collection include material at various levels of explanation: there would be little point in an English primary-school library having *Aesop's Fables* in the original Greek instead of in English—or *Heidi* in German.

Nor is this only a matter of language, since materials at the forefront of most fields of scholarship are difficult or unintelligible to most non-specialists because the concepts and specialized terminology are not

[7] For an extended critique of library planning from the perspective of research in the humanities see B. Fabian, *Buch, Bibliothek und geisteswissenschaftliche Forschung: Zur Probleme der Literaturproduktion in der Bundesrepublik Deutschland* (Gottingen: Vandenhoeck & Ruprecht, 1983). For an English language summary see *Minerva* 23 (August 1985): 433-40. A similar discussion by Fabian is "Libraries and the Humanistic Scholarship," *Journal of Librarianship* 18, no. 2 (April 1986): 79.

understood. Hence summaries and introductory works such as textbooks are useful.

It follows that collection development—the combination of selection, duplication, and retention policies—needs to be based not only on what a book is about, but also on its suitability as evidence from which people can learn. Given constraints of funding and space, the challenge is how to select from the colossal universe of all possible materials in order to achieve collections that will, it is supposed, constitute the most useful resource for whatever the groups to be served, the pattern of inquiries, and the goals of the library service may be. Hence the material selected and retained for any given collection needs to meet two requirements:

1. The language and difficulty of the texts should match the competencies of the users. In the example of foreign literatures, for example, this would tend to imply original foreign texts for some, but translations for others.
2. The evidence needs to be sufficiently detailed for the sorts of inquiries for which the service is provided.

These two requirements are potentially in conflict: the first argues for simple explanations; the second against simplification.[8] (The intelligibility and adequacy of collections will be considered further in discussing "access" in chapter 15.)

Material versus collection

In ordinary discussion it is easy to use the terms "library materials" and "collections" more or less interchangeably. But the distinction is fundamental to any serious understanding of the present and future role of collections. We use the term "library materials" to denote text-bearing, image-bearing, or other objects of the sort that libraries collect that could be informative for the people that the library seeks to serve. (The phrase is potentially misleading since they do not have to be *library* materials to be informative: a privately owned copy of a book is not intrinsically less informative than a copy owned by a library.)

The assembling of collections is a matter of practical convenience, a matter of logistics and convenience. A book does not have to be in any particular collection to be useful. Ideally one would have one's own copies of what one needed and hence neither need nor want to use a

---

[8] This aspect of collection development has received remarkably little explicit attention in the professional literature. Katz (*op. cit.*) does stress consideration of the library's "audience" and analysis of the community to be served is often urged, but generally the need for library materials to be both intelligible for the users and complex enough for the expected use seems to be implicit or ignored. As will be discussed in chapter 10, library users tend to adapt to what is provided.

library. In practice, however, the cost and bulk of books preclude this possibility, with the exception of a limited quantity of the materials which one might expect to use a great deal. The point is important, however. Like compiling a bibliography or a catalog, *the building of a collection is—and is no more than—a practical device intended to facilitate access to materials.*

Collection as the first stage of retrieval

Assembling collections of library materials serves two different purposes:

1. Preserving a copy of potentially useful material that might otherwise be lost to present and future users is an *archival* role.
2. Arranging for copies of selected materials to be collected and housed locally for the greater convenience of local users is a *logistic* role.

It is a very significant characteristic of the use of books that it *is* very helpful to have copies stored locally, a point we shall examine further in considering the implications for collection development activity of changes in the technical medium of library materials. The overwhelming preponderance of libraries' collections, even of research libraries, serve the second, logistic purpose in the sense that most of the materials acquired also exist elsewhere in other copies in other libraries. Imagine how much different, smaller, and more economical libraries would be if only the archival role mattered, and just one or two copies were acquired nationwide or worldwide.

The assembling of a library collection, therefore, can reasonably be regarded as the first stage of the process of retrieving material for use. One might also argue that collections themselves serve as a form of bibliographic retrieval system analogous to the catalog in that by inspecting the array of books on the shelves one can discover works on particular topics. Ordinarily "retrieval" is thought of only in terms of catalogs, indexes, classification schemes, or other devices that provide pointers to the documents or data that might satisfy the inquiries that arise. (The next chapter will discuss retrieval in this more customary sense.) However, it is important to recognize that, regardless of the terminology used, the archival role of library collections is, in an important sense, a necessary precondition for, or first stage of, retrieval—and the logistic role greatly facilitates convenient retrieval. Material that has not been collected at all is simply not available for retrieval by anyone. Material that has not been added to local collections is not available for convenient retrieval by individuals at that location. It is true that material that has not been collected locally can still be obtained by purchase, by reproduction, or by interlibrary loan, but all of these involve delay and expense, and are best seen as procedures that are corrective of failures in collection development—or else as fallback options for handling truly exceptional and unexpected inquiries for which acquisition would have been impractical or extravagant given constrained resources.

As will be discussed in chapter 10, the use of library materials is characterized by three patterns:

1. The use of materials is unevenly dispersed across titles, some being used more often than others.
2. Use of materials tends to diminish with age.
3. Usage varies with convenience of access.

These three aspects of collection use—scatter, decay, and inertia—reflect and define, in general terms, the profile of demand in any given library context. The challenge for the librarian is to develop a collection of materials appropriate to that situation, given the inevitable constraints on space, labor, and funds. Most of the effort will be concerned with assembling locally the most suitable collections. Some of the effort should be devoted to arrangements for ensuring that everything likely to be needed by anyone will be preserved somewhere, if not locally.

Collection development decisions

The development of local collections in support of the logistic function of collections is essentially a compromise between the physical convenience that can be achieved and the resources allocated to this purpose. The choices of outcomes include the completeness and appropriateness of the range of materials relative to the demand, the standard of availability of the materials in relation to the pattern of demand, and the physical accessibility of the collection. Specific decisions include: whether to create another collection; where to locate it; relationships with other collections, coordination with other collections within the same system, and cooperation with collections outside the system; and the selection, duplication, loan policies, form of storage, and relegation of individual documents. None of these decisions create new materials: they only deploy copies of existing materials.

Preservation and conservation

As we noted at the outset, if material has not been collected at all, it is not available for anyone. Not only must it be collected, it must also be preserved for future use.[9] With the obvious fragility of the photographic

[9] This section has benefited from the advice of Barclay Ogden. For further reading see P. N. Banks, "Preservation of Library Materials," *Encyclopedia of Library Materials*, Vol. 23 (New York: Marcel Dekker, 1978), pp. 180-222; C. C. Morrow, *A Conservation Policy Statement for Research Libraries* (Occasional Papers, 139) (Urbana, Ill.: University of Illinois, Graduate School of Library and Information Science, 1979).

media and the gradual self-destruction of most extant books from acid traces in the paper, it is clear that there are massive problems beyond the effects of ordinary wear and tear through usage. As a practical matter collections can be divided (in principle) into three categories.

- *Consumables*, such as duplicate copies of textbooks or popular novels, which can be discarded or replaced when they have deteriorated or are no longer needed.
- *Reproducibles,* which can be copied. For example, the text of a dissertation can be preserved through being microfilmed, the image of a photograph can be rephotographed, and a sound recording copied. There may be some loss in the process of reproduction, which may or may not be significant.
- *Irreplaceables*, which need to be retained, preserved, and, if need be, restored, typically because they are unsuitable for copying or because the artifacts themselves are too valuable to lose.

We have discussed above the "interpretation" and "summarizing" of library resources. However, the original evidence may need to be preserved. Future inquiries cannot be fully known in advance, and so for some inquiries the wrong sort of reduction may have been done—instead of measures of the length of woodpeckers, measures of the weight or width are requested. For other sorts of inquiries, any reduction or interpretation may be too much. For a study of Arabic calligraphy even a transcription, let alone a translation, would be too much. It will sometimes be necessary to go back to the original, or as close as is feasible. Commonly it is not feasible: archivists cannot keep all records; scientists do not keep all observational data indefinitely; not all evidence of daily life can be preserved.

There is the additional division of priorities between attention to the conservation and restoration of individual items that are reproducible or irreplaceable and the preventative measures such as air filtration, humidity, and temperature controls which reduce the rate of deterioration of the collection as a whole.

Collections and the changing technology of library materials[10]

Any change of technology is a change in the nature (usually a loosening) of the constraints upon what one might wish to do. There is much interest in the rise of electronic and optical digital "machine-readable" forms of storage, currently for bibliographical and numerical data and, imminently, for text, sounds, and images.[11] In this case the changes are substantial and,

[10] For fuller discussion see M. K. Buckland, "Library Materials: Paper, Microform, Database," *College and Research Libraries* 49, no. 2 (March 1988): 117-22.
[11] F. G. Kilgour, *Beyond Bibliography* (London: British Library, 1985).

as a result, there are substantial practical consequences which are outside the scope of this book. Change in technology has an additional interest because thinking tends to be formed by what we consider feasible. A change in technology is a change in constraints, a change of what is feasible. There is, therefore, at least some likelihood that thinking, planning, and actions will continue to be formed by obsolete notions of feasibility, by technological constraints that are no longer present.

Libraries and library users are concerned with ideas and knowledge, but through *recorded* texts and images—in very large quantities. As a result, any change in the technology of the media for recording or storing texts and images could have enormous significance for libraries. The characteristics of data bases are different from those of paper, and do not fit into current library practice very well. Examples of lack of fit include the following:

1. Special equipment is required to use data bases.
2. A library can provide data base service without either the user or the data base necessarily being "in" the library or the use being restricted to the library's opening hours. Library staff may not be at hand to offer assistance.
3. Data bases customarily involve costs based on the amount of use, making expenditures difficult to project or to control.

Exploration of the underlying characteristics of the different media seems a good basis for reconsidering the assumptions concerning collections that have been built up on the basis of library materials on paper.[12]

Characteristics of library materials on paper

Libraries evolved to provide access to resources on paper with characteristics that are so familiar to librarians and library users that they tend to be overlooked.

1. No special equipment is needed to read them.
2. They are strictly localized: the reader must read a printed book, pamphlet, map, or journal where that item is. The reader must go to the book, or the book must be physically transported to the reader. Possibly another copy can be acquired or made, but each copy would still have to be where its reader is. Any given copy is suitable for being read only by a single person at a time and in the one place where that copy is located. Obvious though this may seem, it is a massive constraint on library service since the use of the material is, in practice, highly sensitive to location: a book at hand is used more

---

[12] J. R. Euster, "Changing Views on Library Collections," *Library Issues* 6, no. 5 (May 1986): 1-2.

than a book elsewhere, let alone at a distant library.[13] As a result, expenditure on the selective duplication of library materials in different libraries on the same campus or in the same public library system is generally needed, and there is at least mild contention for unduplicated material of interest to two or more groups at different locations. The size of *locally held* collections is taken to be the measure of the worth of the library.[14]

3. Material on paper, like a telescope, is unsuited for simultaneous viewing by two or more people. Either another copy must be found (or made) or users must take turns.

4. Library materials on paper are treated as a capital, public good: they are acquired and made available without charge. They are bought at a one-time cost as an investment, the cost is not passed on to the reader, and, until the copy becomes worn out, there is no additional cost involved in it being read by one more person (other than circulation and reshelving workload). If demand exceeds supply, three options exist: rationing use by limiting loan privileges; increasing supply by adding another copy; or lowering the standard of service by letting additional would-be readers wait.[15]

5. Paper materials are not easy to correct, revise, or update, except for isolated minor alterations to individual copies. Devices such as errata slips are not very effective. It is more effective to replace the entire document. But, after the copies of an edition have been distributed, who would know where they all are to replace them, or to make the corrections?

Library activities, and especially library budgetary practices, are based on these characteristics.

Characteristics of microforms

The first major programs of microfilming library materials began with newspapers in the 1930s. Use of microforms increased greatly in the 1960s as microfiche were used for the dissemination of technical reports

---

[13] For branch libraries see both D. A. Wells, "Individual Departmental Libraries vs. Consolidated Science Libraries," *Physics Today* 14, no. 5 (May 1961): 40-1 and J. H. Shera, "How Much is a Physicist's Inertia Worth?," *Physics Today* 14, no. 8 (August 1961): 42-3. For a recent review see R. A. Seals, "Academic Branch Libraries," *Advances in Librarianship* 14 (1986): 175-209. For interlibrary loan see T. J. Waldhart, "Patterns of Interlibrary Loan in the U.S.: A Review of Research," *Library and Information Science Research* 7, no. 3 (July-September 1985): 209-29; T. J. Waldhart, "Performance Evaluation of Interlibrary Loan in the United States: A Review of Research," *Library and Information Science Research* 7, no. 4 (October-December 1985): 313-31.

[14] For discussion of library "goodness" see chapter 20. Also M. Buckland, "Concepts of Library Goodness," *Canadian Library Journal* 39, no. 2 (April 1982): 63-6.

[15] *Cf.,* M.K. Buckland, *Book Availability and the Library User* (New York: Pergamon Press, 1975).

by government agencies.[16] Microfilms and other microforms represented a significant departure from paper materials, yet they differ on only one of the characteristics noted above—special equipment is needed to read them. This adds a requirement for libraries to maintain a new sort of equipment: microform readers and printers. Microforms are therefore even more localized than paper materials: not only must the would-be reader and the microform be in the same place, there must also be a usable machine on which to read it at that place. Furthermore, copies are less convenient to make and cannot, like paper, be annotated. They are even less suitable for correction or revision. Nevertheless, the low cost of acquiring and, especially, storing microforms makes them a reasonable choice for some kinds of information (such as old newspapers) in spite of their unappealing form and attributes.

Characteristics of data bases

Machine-readable data bases, as typically used in library contexts, have tended to differ from paper not, like microforms, on just one of the characteristics of paper-based materials, but on all five:

1. As with microforms, special equipment is required to read them—equipment that is substantially more complex, more expensive, more useful, and more obsolescent than microform readers. Not only is the equipment used to provide access to information in data bases more elaborate than is that of microforms, but the equipment has two other novel features:

    (a) A microfilm reader displays an image of the text and does little else, except maybe, produce a copy. Computers used in conjunction with data bases allow not only retrieval but also a very great deal of manipulation: (i) bibliographical data can be reorganized, reformatted, and combined with other machine-readable text; (ii) texts can be edited and stored again in revised form; and (iii) numerical data, such as census tables, can be retrieved and subjected to statistical manipulation. A census table on paper or microform would have to be transcribed by hand and/or keyed into machine-readable form.

    (b) The equipment used to gain access to data bases is, in general, usable for other purposes also. A scholar's personal computer can be used for word processing, electronic mail, statistical

---

[16] Convenient introductions can be found in: *ALA World Encyclopedia of Library and Information Sciences* (Chicago: American Library Association, 1980), s. v. Micrographics, pp. 370-3; and *Encyclopedia of Library and Information Science*, Vol. 18 (New York: Marcel Dekker, 1976), s.v. Microform, pp. 76-99 and Microform Publication, pp. 99-114.

analysis, and manipulation of personal data as well as accessing data bases. Moreover, there should be a convenient linking of each of these functions such that data could flow conveniently between them.[17]

2. Usage of a data base is not inherently localized. For example, thousands of people all over the world use the data bases made available through the Lockheed DIALOG service, but few of these people have ever been to Palo Alto where the data bases reside.[18] There is a strong trend for at least faculty and graduate students to have workstations, either terminals or microcomputers, that enable them, in principle, to read data bases from their offices, laboratories, and homes as an alternative to using workstations in libraries. Data bases can be copied and scholars will probably tend to have their own copies of parts or all of some sorts of data bases even though, given telecommunications, data bases can be used and shared from a distance. In this sense, data bases lend themselves to cooperative, shared provision much better than do library materials on paper or microform. Just as it does not matter to a library user where a book borrowed on interlibrary loan has come from, so long as it does come in a timely and reliable manner, so it does not matter to an online searcher where the data on the screen have come from so long as they too come in a timely and reliable manner. (There could well be cost differences that may matter to the librarian, but that is a separate issue.)

3. Further, given suitable equipment, users of data bases can, in effect, make simultaneous use of the same data base, whereas it is not practical to make simultaneous use of the same book. Contention for the same book is a major source of frustration for the library user.[19]

4. The use of data bases has, in general, not been budgeted as a capital, public good. Typically, data bases have been provided on a "pay-as-you-use" fee basis, including telecommunications, computer charges, and other elements. These expenses—real, monetary charges—are passed on to the users, except to the extent that libraries feel able to

[17] For example, M. K. Buckland, "Combining Electronic Mail with Online Retrieval in a Library Context," *Information Technology and Libraries* 6, no. 4 (December 1987): 266-71.

[18] "The logic of print on paper is local availability through multiple outlets of multiple copies of a particular document. Printing entails a multiplicity of local booksellers and libraries. The logic of the new information technology is quite different—it is that of multiple access via telecommunications networks to a single copy of a document remotely held in machine-readable form. Neither logic is implemented in pure form—local book supplies are supplemented by interlending networks ... and local forms of electronic store are becoming available," B. C. Vickery and A. Vickery, *Information Science in Theory and Practice* (London: Butterworths, 1987), pp. 323-4.

[19] *Cf.* M. K. Buckland, *Book Availability and the Library User* (New York: Pergamon Press, 1975).

absorb the charges. These charges had no real precedent in library budgets. This situation is reflected in the common practice of referring to bibliographical data bases as "commercial data bases," even though it is the final stage of retail marketing, not the data, that has been in commercial pay-as-you-use mode.[20]

5. In general, data bases are designed for routine updating with corrections and additions.

These characteristics of library materials on paper, in microform, and as machine-readable data files are summarized in table 7.1.

TABLE 7.1   Comparison of some attributes of
library materials in different media

		Paper	Microform	Data base
1.	Equipment required	No	Yes	Yes
2.	Remotely accessible	No	No	Yes
3.	Simultaneous use	No	No	Yes
4.	Capital, public good	Yes	Yes	No, but could be
5.	Revisable?	No	No	Yes

Some assumptions reconsidered

Since access to information on data bases is a desirable part of the mission of a library, and yet does not "fit" existing practices, it may be useful to retreat toward first principles.

1. The purpose of making printed books, microforms, and data bases available is the same—to provide access to potentially useful information. It would therefore seem sensible to budget for data bases in the same way as is already done with paper and microform materials, if feasible.

2. There is no obvious reason why data bases could not be purchased unless the publisher chose not to sell them as a matter of marketing policy. It seems reasonable to expect that most data bases will become available for purchase or lease. Some, indeed, may become available inexpensively enough for individuals to purchase copies.

3. Similarly, data bases may also be available on a rental or subscription basis. This would be a matter of the library leasing the data base or negotiating access to it for a fixed fee, and allowing users to make what use of it they can.[21]

[20] One approach is for libraries to buy or lease data bases. There is some precedent for this. U.S. public libraries commonly rent collections of bestsellers ("McNaughton collections") that help take care of temporary peaks of demand. Some reference works (e.g. *Magazine Index* and some Dun & Bradstreet directories) are available only on a lease basis.

[21] *Cf.* B. Quint, "Journal Article Coverage in Online Library Catalogs: Next Stage for Online Databases?," *Online* 11, no. 1 (January 1987): 87-90.

4. "Fee-as-you-use" access to data bases would still be needed in two cases: (i) when the publisher refuses to allow any other arrangement; and (ii) when usage or, more exactly, the cost, is so low that purchase or subscription are not worthwhile. (This is comparable to reliance on interlibrary loan of paper and microform materials in lieu of purchase. It does not follow that the fee would necessarily have to be passed on to the user. Indeed, some cases of very low usage might well be handled by coordinated acquisitions of data bases between libraries and reciprocal search access in the historic tradition of cooperative collection development.)

   It is at this point that the distance-independent characteristic of data bases becomes important. Depending upon assumptions about telecommunications and levels of demand, one copy anywhere in a library system or consortium might suffice for all users in a way that would not have the disadvantages that remote storage has for material on paper or on microfilm.

5. The economic trade-off between purchase, lease, and usage-based fees will be largely a matter of technical analysis of the varying costs of computing, telecommunications, administration, and storage. Optimization of this sort would become all the more practical if all systems seemed similar to the user as they would with the general adoption of a "linked systems protocol" for connecting online bibliographical systems.[22]

On this approach it is not difficult to image a hierarchy of levels of access to data bases. Very popular, inexpensive ones might be held at a campus, or even branch library, level; less popular, more expensive ones might be held at a university level; yet other rarely used data bases might be held regionally or nationally by universities or commercial services and used as needed, rather like interlibrary loans.

For paper materials not held in a library's collection, recourse is made to interlibrary loan. While this is not the same as doing a fee-for-use search of a remote data base, the effect is quite similar. A non-trivial cost is incurred by the borrowing library for each interlibrary loan transaction. In part this is inevitable, since no library can afford to buy everything. It is, however, a sensible strategy to avoid purchase, processing, and storage costs of some materials not expected to be much used, and deliberately to

---

[22] NISO Draft standard Z39.50. For discussion see M. K. Buckland and C. A. Lynch, "The Linked Systems Protocol and the Future of Bibliographical Networks and Systems," *Information Technology and Libraries* 6, no. 2 (June 1987): 83-8; and M. K. Buckland and C. A. Lynch, "National and International Implications of the Linked Systems Protocol for Online Bibliographic Systems," *Cataloging and Classification Quarterly* (forthcoming).

plan on recourse to interlibrary loan if demands were to arise.[23] With either paper materials or data bases, as the level of usage increases, other approaches (purchase or lease) deserve consideration.

Individual collections in context

Scope and diminishing returns

A library collection is not expected to be an entirely random compilation, but to have some scope or coverage. Some important features of decisions concerning what to include and what not are: (1) Any definition of scope implies that the universe of items that *could* be included can be divided into more or less definable subsets (e.g., History, Engineering, Works written by Austrians, Books printed in England, etc.); and (2) There are gradations of inclusion within the scope. At one extreme there is minimal inclusion: "Even if we were given it, we would not keep it." At the other extreme is exhaustive collecting: "We want at least one copy of everything written by or about Paracelsus." The terminology used for these gradations is not and, perhaps, cannot be completely standardized. A good example is the terminology developed for the American Library Association:[24]

A. Comprehensive level. A collection in which the library endeavors, so far as is reasonably possible, to include all significant works of recorded knowledge (publications, manuscripts, other forms) for a necessarily defined field. This level of collecting intensity is that which maintains a "special collection;" the aim, if not the achievement, is exhaustiveness.

B. Research level. A collection which includes the major source materials required for dissertations and independent research, including materials containing research reporting, new findings, scientific experimental results, and other information useful to researchers. It also includes all important reference works and a wide selection of specialized monographs, as well as an extensive collection of journals and major indexing and abstracting services in the field.

C. Study level. A collection which supports undergraduate or graduate course work, or sustained independent study; that is, which is adequate to maintain knowledge of a subject required for limited or generalized purposes, of less than research intensity. It includes a wide range of basic monographs, complete collections of the works of important writers, a selection of representative journals, and the reference tools and fundamental bibliographical apparatus pertaining to the subject.

D. Basic level. A highly selective collection which serves to introduce and define the subject and to indicate the varieties of information available elsewhere. It includes major dictionaries and encyclopedias, selected editions of important works, historical surveys, important bibliographies, and a few major periodicals in the field.

E. Minimal level. A subject area in which few selections are made beyond very basic works.

---

[23]   See, for example, G. S. Lawrence and A. R. Oja, *An Economic Criterion for Housing and Disposing of Library Materials, Based on Frequency of Circulation* (Berkeley: University of California Systemwide Administration, Library Studies and Research Division, September 24, 1979), Research Report RR-79-2.

[24]   American Library Association, Collection Development Committee, *Guidelines for Collection Development*, edited by D. Parkins (Chicago: ALA, 1979).

Also, of course, there is the "out-of-scope" level at which nothing is kept.

There is often a major ambiguity in discussing these issues due to the difference between "about" and "relating to." Pharmacy is a good example. The number of publications actually *about* pharmacy is small compared with the number of publications that could be regarded as *relating* to pharmacy but are *about* physiology, biochemistry, ethics, medical services, marketing, etc. These sorts of relationships are not always self-evident. For example, O'Neill found that, although different sorts of engineering are generally associated together politically and organizationally (as in a School of Engineering with a consolidated engineering library), the intellectual relationship for each branch of engineering is heavily oriented to a cognate science rather than other sorts of engineering[25] (e.g., electrical engineering with electronics; mechanical engineering with mechanics; chemical engineering with chemistry, etc.).

We do not propose to examine in any detail the theory and practice of "collection development." That is extensively discussed elsewhere.[26] We merely note the activity and look at how it relates to the wider framework.

The financial consequence of changing from one level of collection to another, especially from level C to level B, or from B to A, can be considerable. So, therefore, is the opportunity cost in that increased expenditure for collection development prevents the use of those resources for other desirable purposes inside or outside the library. There needs to be, therefore, a significant perceived benefit in the accumulation of the collection if there is to be any degree of rationality.

A benefit, however, implies a value. Hence, discussion of the scope ought to be related to the choice of values. The collection of books for their own sake—bibliophilia—could be such a value, but it is more likely to be the increase in knowledge of one sort or another within a particular group of people that the library is expected to serve. At least, we will assume that this is the case and defer consideration of some other sorts of values until chapter 10.

Now, if the growth of knowledge is to be the determining value and if resources are limited, the only rational procedure is to relate the scope of the retrieval system to those items likely to facilitate the growth of knowledge in the most cost-beneficial way, insofar as one can. For example, if a copy of a book were never to be used, it is difficult to see how it could have facilitated the growth of knowledge; and, since it took resources to

---

[25] E. T. O'Neill, "Journal Usage Patterns and Their Implications in the Planning of Library Systems" (Ph.D. thesis, West Lafayette, Ind.: Purdue University, School of Industrial Engineering, 1970. University of microfilms o/no. 70-18, 704).

[26] See footnote 1, p. 60.

acquire, to process, and to store it, its acquisition was not merely not beneficial, but counterproductive, since those resources might have been used in some other way to foster those values. Every cost is also a lost opportunity. In every library, there are some books that are apparently used little if at all.[27] In large libraries this can represent a very substantial investment. One might conclude, then, that a major pruning of libraries' collections would be cost-beneficial. However, there are three major theoretical reasons why this would be difficult to do:

1. It is not known which titles will be used. Prediction of probable future use is a major element in book selection but the reliability of the predictions appears to be low, especially among titles not in high levels of use.

2. In open access libraries, most of the use is not recorded in any way. So that, if the books were used, it is unlikely that the librarian would know about it. The use of items retrieved from storage and items borrowed is recorded (or, at least, can be) but use of books on open shelves is generally unrecorded. There is some evidence that recorded use and unrecorded use correlate even on a title-by-title basis.[28] However, this is not very well established and, even if it were, it is still a matter of probabilities.

3. Even if one were to know that particular books already in a library would not be used in the future, the cost of discarding them, with present manual records, might well outweigh the probable savings. When uncertainty remains concerning future use, the costs and benefits of weeding become even less favorable.[29]

Therefore, we reach the rather unsatisfying conclusion that a combination of inability to predict the future, lack of management information, and present technology conspire to make collection development an imprecise art. One cannot be sure that one will have all (and only) the documents that will be needed.

Cultural constraints

So far we have assumed that collection development is a trade-off between limited resources and the selection of what would be most informative,

[27] M. K. Buckland, *Book Availability and the Library User* (New York: Pergamon Press, 1975); R. W. Trueswell, "User Circulation Satisfaction vs. Size of Holdings at Three Academic Libraries," *College and Research Libraries* (May 30, 1969), pp. 204-13; A. Kent, *Use of Library Materials: The University of Pittsburgh Study* (New York: Marcel Dekker, 1979).

[28] A. Hindle and M. K. Buckland, "In-Library Book Usage in Relation to Circulation," *Collection Management* 2, no. 4 (Winter 1978): 265-77.

[29] J. A. Urquhart and N. Urquhart, *Relegation and Stock Control in Libraries* (Stockfield, Eng.: Oriel Press, 1976).

but it is not that simple, as will be discussed in greater detail in chapters 11 and 12 on the allocation of resources to and within the library services. The library exists in a political and cultural environment. In this environment the funders, the users, and the librarians have social values that form part of the context of the library's mission. Library collections are constrained to be compatible with those social values. It is for this reason that a library's collection will *not* always contain the most informative material even where it can be afforded—or, if it is afforded, usage is likely to be partially restricted. For example, a child with an inquiry concerning sex is not likely to find the most informative material because the most informative material is likely to be contrary to local cultural norms of decency.[30] Similarly funders, librarians, and (most) users would probably prefer their library *not* to include material that facilitates or encourages topics deemed socially undesirable, such as poisoning public water supplies, dangerous drugs, pederasty, or how to make bombs. There is some tendency to regard such decisions as censorship and outside librarianship, or somehow separate from selection and collection development. Until one can find a library service that has no context, these cultural constraints are best viewed as an inherent part of selection and collection development.

A diminution of localness

For the user, meanwhile, access to remote data bases is very different from interlibrary loan with its lengthy delays. The distance-independence of data bases—in contrast to the localness of paper—is important even for what is stored locally, and it is much more important for what is *not* stored locally. In effect, since the use of data bases is not localized, the difference between what is locally held and what is not is of diminished importance. Stated more directly, local holdings lose their overwhelming significance, which is a radical departure from traditional assumptions about libraries' collections. (It is also a radical departure for assumptions about library catalogs which are, by definition, restricted to locally held collections. As locally held collections come to constitute less and less of what is conveniently accessible, the catalog also becomes progressively less complete as a guide to what materials are available.)[31]

For library services *not* to include access to data bases, local or remote, would be rather like a fifteenth-century library refusing to acquire the

---

[30] "Research indicates that librarians give strong support to the concepts of intellectual freedom and open access to information but do not necessarily implement these concepts in their libraries." M. Pope, *Sex and the Undecided Librarian: A Study of Librarians' Opinions on Sexually Oriented Literature* (Metuchen, N.J.: Scarecrow Press, 1974), p. 184.

[31] M. K. Buckland, "Bibliography, Library Records, and the Redefinition of the Library Catalog," in *Library Resources and Technical Services* (forthcoming).

newfangled printed books in addition to manuscripts because they did not "fit" traditional views of library provision. Data bases do not fit library collection development practices, but that is not the real problem. Data bases are part of the evolving world of communication and of scholarship. The real problem is that collection development practices do not yet fit that world.[32]

Summary

Inquiries need resources for their resolution. The range of materials available is enormous. The technology used affects what can be done. In a significant sense library materials can be viewed as evidence that needs to be suited both to the inquiries and to the library users served by each library. Suitability is not only a matter of subject content, but also of the complexity of inquiries, the intelligibility of the materials, the expertise of the users, and the social values of the library's context. In any discussion of these matters it is important to distinguish clearly between library materials (physical resources) and collection development (the logistics of deploying copies of materials). Collection development practice could reasonably be expected to change with changes in the nature of materials[33] and in emphasis on the different roles that collections play: preservation; indication of what exists;[34] and location of materials conveniently near to users.[35] Libraries make resources available in a series of stages: material expected to be useful is preserved; copies of selected materials are collected locally to assure convenient access; and various techniques of retrieval are used to find particular pieces of material as and when needed. The next chapter will examine retrieval in this last sense.

[32] Cf., P. Briscoe et al., "Ashurbanipal's Enduring Archetype: Thoughts on the Library's Role in the Future," *College and Research Libraries* 47, no. 2 (March 1986): 121-6.

[33] The argument that collection development practice, i.e., library logistics, may need to vary with changes in the nature of the material to be deployed is consistent with Licklider's statement that "any concept of a library *that begins with* books on shelves is sure to encounter trouble" (emphasis added). J. C. R. Licklider, *Libraries of the Future* (Cambridge: MIT Press, 1965), p. 5.

[34] For the relationship between shelf arrangement and library use see R. J. Hyman, *Shelf Access in Libraries* (Chicago: American Library Association, 1982).

[35] "Near to" users is importantly different from "where the users are." See R. T. Jordan, *Tomorrow's Library: Direct Access and Delivery* (New York: Bowker, 1970).

8

Retrieval

Having considered the assembling of copies of materials into collections, we shall now consider retrieval—the process whereby data or documents are found in the attempt to deal with inquiries that have been posed.

Definition: the retrieval process

We view the retrieval process as having three stages:

1. Susceptible person with an inquiry
2. Expressions of inquiry in the language of the retrieval system
3. Set of retrieved signals

It is important to distinguish between these three stages because the transformations between them are significant.

By a "susceptible person with an inquiry," we refer to the fact that library services are for *people* to use. The "susceptibility" indicates that the person with the inquiry is vulnerable to becoming informed. For the purposes of analysis we take the unorthodox step of separating the retrieval process (this and the previous chapter) from the process of becoming informed (next chapter). Therefore, in our analysis, the susceptibility is in a strict sense not *directly* relevant to the retrieval process, narrowly viewed. Nevertheless, it is clearly important to the system as a whole and is, therefore, well worth noting.

The first transformation that takes place—between stages 1 and 2—is the formulation or expression of the inquiry in the language of the retrieval system. It would be an exaggeration to say that this transformation is well understood. Some features, however, can be outlined.

A person is likely to advance only those inquiries which he or she thinks the system may be able to cope with. This is no more than rational behavior on the part of the user. The expectations with respect to the system may not be accurate. Indeed, they might be wildly *un*realistic. Nevertheless, we can expect the user's decision to advance the inquiry to be conditioned by:

- the importance and urgency of the request,
- the perceived effort involved in using the system, and
- the perceived ability of the system to yield a worthwhile response.

This is recognized by librarians who feel the need to publicize the scope of the resources available in their libraries, and in the provision of instruction in library use. They may be correct in asserting that users are often unaware of the power and scope of the retrieval tools available. However, it is also possible for librarians who are intimately familiar with the bibliographical power of their libraries' apparatus to underrate the efforts involved from the users' perspective and to overrate the relevance, range, and accuracy of the retrieval systems. We have discussed this briefly in chapter 6 and will do so again in chapter 13.

The manner in which the inquiry is presented will be influenced by the linguistic, cultural, and technical orientation and personal knowledge of the user; and the user's expectations as to what form of inquiry will be acceptable and/or intelligible to the retrieval process. (This appears to be the case whether the inquiry is made to a librarian or to the retrieval system.)

It is not to be expected that the user will have sufficient understanding of the retrieval system to know exactly what form of expression will produce the response most appropriate to the inquiry. Indeed, only the designer of the retrieval system or someone intimately familiar with it could be expected to approach such knowledge.

Since every individual has a particular conceptual framework and vocabulary, since the retrieval system has its own technical vocabulary, and since the user cannot be expected to have an intimate knowledge of the retrieval system, a greater or lesser degreee of distortion is to be expected in the transformation of the inquiry into the language of the retrieval system.

Librarians recognize that some degree of distortion is to be expected. The short-term solution is for the librarian to initiate a dialog or negotiation with the user. This is commonly referred to as the "reference interview."[1] Inevitably, as in any human interaction, there is more

[1] G. Jahoda and J. S. Braunagel, *The Librarian and Reference Queries: A Systematic Approach* (New York: Academic Press, 1980); E. Z. Jennerich, "Before the Answer: Evaluating the Reference Process," *RQ* 19 (Summer 1980): 360-6; G. Jahoda and P. E. Olson, "Analyzing the Reference Process, " *RQ* 12 (Winter 1972): 148-56; M. T. Lynch, "Reference Interviews in Public Libraries," *Library Quarterly* 48 (April 1978): 119-42; G. B. King, "Open and Closed Questions: The Reference Interview," *RQ* 12 (Winter 1972): 157-60; M. E. Murfin and L. R. Wynar, *Reference Service: An Annotated Bibliographical Guide* (Littleton, Colo.: Libraries Unlimited, 1977), esp. chapter 9. Barnes found very superficial levels of interaction in practice: M. Barnes, "Staff/User Interaction in Public Libraries: A Non-Participation Observation Study," in *Information in Society* , edited by M. Barnes et al. (Leeds: School of Librarianship, Leeds Polytechnic, 1981): 61-81. Question negotiation can have adverse effects: F. W. Lancaster, "MEDLARS: Report on the Evaluation of Operating Efficiency," *American Documentation* 20, no. 2 (April 1969): 119-42.

involved than a simple exchange of verbal statements. (See, for example, Shosid's psychological analysis of the reference encounter.[2])

At some stage the inquiry is expressed in the language of the retrieval system, since there is no other way of using it. In a sense a retrieval system can be regarded as responding to any inquiry addressed to it. But, if alien terms are used (e.g., subject terms not represented in a subject catalog), there is no positive response. The retrieval system will only be responsive to terms it recognizes.

The second transformation is the process between stages 2 and 3 of our definition—the yielding of a set of retrieved signals in response to an inquiry in the language of the retrieval system. We use the word "set" advisedly since the retrieval system may yield nothing—an empty set.

Once the inquiry has been posed in the language of the retrieval system, the outcome is automatic. The search is predetermined. Headings in the catalog lead directly or indirectly to catalog records. In this sense, retrieval systems are automatic devices, machines, in which any given input will yield one and only one output, which is predictable given a sufficient understanding of how the system works. The only exception to this is that there may be mechanical failures: a connection may be lost in a computerized system, or a card misfiled or overlooked in a card catalog. Barring temporary mechanical failures, retrieval systems are like automata in that the same inquiry repeated will yield the same predictable response. This may seem contrary to experience in that two different people with the same initial inquiry (or the same person with the same inquiry at two different times) can and often do end up with different results. There are two explanations for this, both compatible with the view of retrieval systems as automata:

1. Retrieval systems are usually in a state of continuous, gradual revision: data are added or withdrawn; new index points inserted; syndetic relationships changed. A library catalog may seem to be a particularly *un*dynamic object, but the appearance is misleading. It follows that, when the same inquiry is presented at different points in time to what is ostensibly the same retrieval system, the system has, in fact, changed somewhat. It is, therefore, in an altered state— updated, most likely—and, therefore, while still an automaton, it has become a slightly different automaton. The slight difference may well be significant for some inquiries.

---

[2] N. Shosid, "Problematic Interaction: The Reference Encounter," in *Varieties of Work Experience* , edited by P. L. Stewart and M. G. Cantor (New York: Schenkman, 1974), pp. 224-37. See also R. M. Harris and B. G. Michell, "The Social Context of Reference Work: Assessing the Effects of Gender and Communication Skill on Observers' Judgements of Competence," *Library and Information Science* 8, no. 1 (January-March 1986): 85-101.

2. There is scope in sophisticated retrieval systems like most on-line bibliographical search systems and complex card catalogs for changes in the expression of the inquiry. For example, one might conclude that the rendering of the inquiry in the language of the retrieval system has not been done well and that a modification of the phrasing would improve it. Another possibility is that the initial formulation of the query may yield too little (or too much) by way of retrieved signals—and so the formulation of the search may be expanded (or restricted) accordingly.

On-line bibliographical retrieval systems are usually postcoordinate systems wherein complex searches are formulated from their constituent concepts at the time of searching instead of depending on selecting complex descriptions composed when the document was cataloged (as in the case of precoordinated systems such as traditional library subject catalogs). It is, therefore, comparatively easy to expand (or restrict) searches. One can add (or relax) restrictions (e.g., "written in English," "published since 1975," and "pertaining to rabbits"). In precoordinated systems, such as library card catalogs, one can simply decide to exclude some of the richness offered (e.g., by not following "see also references" or by considering only works by a particular author). Alternatively, one can expand the expression of the search by formulating it more broadly in the language of the retrieval systems.

In both cases, the change in the set of retrieved signals from one posing of the inquiry to another represents not an unreliability on the part of a stable retrieval system but a change in the state of the retrieval system or in the formulation of the inquiry.

Data retrieval and document retrieval

The signals retrieved are data in one form or another. The distinction is sometimes made between data retrieval and document retrieval. A "data retrieval system" is one in which specific data are retrieved—the specific information requested in the inquiry.

The term "document retrieval" is ambiguous. It can refer simply to systems in which a document is retrieved. Ordinarily, however, it is used to refer to a retrieval system in which the data retrieved are the description and address of one or more documents; and it is these documents that will contain the data desired. For example, suppose one wanted a list of strong and irregular German verbs. A data retrieval system that enabled one to retrieve such a list directly would have to permit one to use a search command such that the list of strong and irregular verbs would appear. In a document retrieval system this would not happen. Instead, one would specify the need for a book on German grammar, specifying either a particular known work or any German grammar. Assuming that the system does contain details concerning German grammars, the response might be, for example,

Luscher, R. & Schapers, R.
Deutsch 2000: A Grammar of Contemporary German.
München: Hueber, 1976.

This response does not, in itself, inform us about strong and irregular verbs. However, it is a reasonable assumption that, if we were to examine the book, it would contain a list of strong and irregular German verbs and their principal parts. In finding them, however, we may well use another information retrieval system, the index. Looking in the index under either "irregular" or "strong" indicates that, in this case, a list can be found starting on page 274.

There is, it would seem, a basic distinction between a data retrieval system designed to provide *directly* what one thinks one wants and a document retrieval—or, better, a "reference retrieval"—system that merely points one toward the desired data in one or more steps. However, difficulties arise. Suppose, for example, instead of wanting a list of strong and irregular German verbs, we had wanted to know the title of a German grammar by Luscher and Schapers—or, indeed, of any German grammar. The inquiry could have been formulated in the same way and posed to the same bibliographic retrieval system in the same way. The exact same response might well have been received as that given above. The difference is that the desired datum has been retrieved, without further searching being needed. In this example, the exact same system used in the same manner constitutes both a data retrieval system and a reference retrieval system. The only difference is in the intention of the user. This being so, we need to reexamine the distinction more closely. If it is not to be abandoned, then the following options remain:

1. We can classify such a retrieval system as being a data retrieval system or a document retrieval system on the basis of the intention of the person using it; or
2. We can define retrieval systems according to whether they are capable of functioning as a reference retrieval *as well as* a data retrieval system. This capability would appear to extend to any system in which the data stored are capable implicitly or explicitly of indicating further sources of data. From this perspective, we can consider data retrieval systems as a limited, primitive category within the larger class of retrieval systems.

Although the example used was bibliographical, other sorts are possible. The example, in museum documentation, the reference is likely to be to an actual artifact rather than to a book. More generally in data retrieval systems, the inclusion of some kind of reference to further documentation is likely to be provided whether explicitly or implicitly, even if only to indicate the source, authority, or definition of the data retrieved.

Multiple retrieval systems

The ability of a retrieval system to retrieve signals (which, according to the intentions of the user, can be regarded either as the data desired or pointers toward the data desired) can be illustrated by considering some of the many examples of retrieval mechanisms in a library.

One user might treat the subject arrangement of the documents on the shelves (arranged according to the Dewey Decimal Classification, perhaps) as a retrieval mechanism and go directly to the shelves associated with the Dewey number(s) expected to contain the signals (books) desired. (That is, indeed, an example of document retrieval in a literal sense.)

A second user might approach the library catalog and examine subject headings and note the bibliographical data recorded on the cards there. That may be all that the user wanted if verifying a bibliographical citation and willing to rely on card catalog data instead of inspecting the documents themselves.

A third user might do exactly the same as the second user but the data recorded on the cards do not constitute the goal, only the directions to the document on the shelves.

A fourth user might go to the librarian and express the inquiry verbally. The librarian, acting as a retrieval system, would endeavor to convert the inquiry into the terms of the library system and deliver the data required, whether this is a whole document or merely a mention of specific data from within a book. When a document is found, further retrieval mechanisms— index, table of contents—may be used to identify more specifically what is wanted. Dictionaries, encyclopedias, and bibliographies—all examples of retrieval mechanisms—may well be used independently or in conjunction with other means of searching. It is clear that many examples of retrieval systems occur in libraries and that they can be used independently or sequentially.

Retrieval languages I: Notation

Describing things is a linguistic problem. Even concepts in formal logic have to be defined linguistically at some stage.

One readily recognized distinction in descriptive labels is between "natural" language and "artificial" languages. For example, in a bookshop texts on economics are likely to be shelved by a sign bearing the label "ECONOMICS." The very same books in a public library might bear the sign "330," the symbol denoting Economics in the artificial notation of the Dewey Decimal Classification.

From the point of view of achieving an acceptable *address*, the labeling doesn't matter very much so long as it is intelligible and accurate. Also, from the point of view of achieving acceptable *definition*, the choice of notation, language, or meta-language doesn't matter very much as long as the description is sufficiently precise and intelligible for the purposes intended.

It is common for a major distinction to be made between "classification schemes" based on artificial notations (such as Dewey) and natural language indexes. Both will be reviewed.[3]

Natural language systems

In natural language indexing systems, words or terms from the language of choice are used as descriptors. The simplicity is highly attractive. However, as increasing numbers of terms are used, various problems emerge.

Since terms in natural languages overlap in meaning and in appearance, some kind of control is usually imposed. Examples of these include homographs: two or more words spelled the same way but different in meaning. For example, the word CHARACTER means different things to a playwright, a typewriter mechanic, a theologian, and an architect. Similarly, information about a TANK that would interest a general would not necessarily help a plumber. In these cases, the terms need to be expanded or differentiated in some way, or else inappropriate signals are likely to be retrieved.

Different words for the same concept or entity (synonyms) cause other problems. A retrieval system with information under AGRICULTURE might yield nothing in a search under FARMING. Straightforward one-to-one relationships can be handled by imposing further control. Typically, one term becomes the "preferred" term and the other term is used only for redirection. "For FARMING see AGRICULTURE." In practice, more difficult to handle are near-synonyms where the overlap is incomplete, e.g., AGRICULTURE and LAND USE. A list of subject headings,

[3]   The present discussion isolates a few aspects. For a fuller treatment, see L. M. Chan, *Cataloging and Classification: An Introduction* (New York: McGraw-Hill, 1981); R. Hagler and P. Simmons, *The Bibliographic Record and Information Technology* (Chicago: American Library Association, 1982); J. E. Rowley, *Organizing Knowledge: An Introduction to Information Retrieval* (Aldershot, England: Gower, 1987); and B. S. Wynar, *Introduction to Cataloging and Classification*, 7th ed., edited by A. G. Taylor. (Littleton, Colo.: Libraries Unlimited, 1985). For the more specialized topics of information retrieval theory and testing see G. Salton and M. J. McGill, *Introduction to Modern Information Retrieval* (New York: McGraw-Hill, 1983); *Information Retrieval Experiment,* edited by K. Sparck Jones (London: Butterworths, 1981); *Information Retrieval Research,* edited by R. N. Oddy et al. (London: Butterworths, 1981). For a detailed treatment of indexing and classification systems as "documentary languages" see W. J. Hutchins, *Languages of Indexing and Classification: A Linguistic Study of Structures and Functions* (Stevenage, England: Peter Peregrinus, 1975).

or thesaurus, enumerating terms and relationships between them and other terms is used. The process of control is usually known as vocabulary control or authority control.

Another complexity has to do with hierarchical relationships where material on a topic, such as dairying, can be found not only in books specifically on dairying listed under the heading DAIRYING, but also within more general books on agriculture listed under AGRICULTURE. Alternatively, there might be no general work on agriculture but books dealing with aspects of agriculture such as dairying, horticulture, aquaculture, and so on. Retrieval systems vary in the extent and manner in which they contain references to narrower (more specific) topics and to broader (more general) ones.

So far, only simple definitions have been considered. In practice, the topics of inquiry often require some complexity in description. Consider, for example, "TEACHING METHODS IN AUSTRIAN UNIVERSITIES FROM 1918 TO 1939." Natural language indexing systems can handle such combinations ("coordinations") of concepts in either of two ways. In a manual system, it is convenient to compose ("precoordinate") a single (but complex) entry following agreed conventions concerning the order of the aspects (more technically "facets") of the concept. In a traditional library subject catalog one would expect to find a book on this topic listed under a heading of the following form "AUSTRIA, *Higher education*, 1918-1939. Teaching methods" and probably only under that heading.

If this precoordination were not done, one would need to look at each item listed under AUSTRIA, under HIGHER EDUCATION, under 1918-1939, and under TEACHING METHODS and select only those items which had been entered under *all* those labels. Technically, this is known as "postcoordination" since the expression of the relationship—the coordination—is done at the time of the inquiry, after the time of indexing. It is obviously laborious.

In computer-based systems, where the computer can take on the chore of doing the "coordinating," it is customary not to express the coordination at the time of indexing. Various appropriate index terms would be assigned. In a postcoordinate search, the searcher enumerates the index terms that are expected to be helpful in identifying desired material, and the computer assumes the task of finding the books which have been assigned whatever combination of terms the searcher has specified. In this example, one might try the following terms:

HIGHER EDUCATION or POST SECONDARY EDUCATION
    or UNIVERSITIES
TEACHING METHODS
AUSTRIA

One might also be able to specify the historical period though, in this case, it would probably be quite convenient to browse among the items retrieved by the above terms.

These coordinate relationships can be ambiguous, since the mere occurrence of words may be insufficient to define the topic. A textbook example is the difference between a "venetian blind" and a "blind Venetian." Similarly with the three words "bites," "dog," and "man"—"dog bites man" is not the same syntactical relationship or meaning, nor is it as newsworthy, as "man bites dog."

These relationships can properly be described as syntactical in exactly the same way that syntax denotes grammatical relationships. On the whole, syntactical relationships tend to be ignored in indexing languages, but there are notable exceptions, such as relational indexing.[4]

An often overlooked attribute of natural language indexing systems is that each system is natural to a particular time, place, and cultural environment. Subject headings used in the *British National Bibliography* are different from those assigned for a comparable purpose by the U.S. Library of Congress. Special groups of any kind—professional, social, technical, cultural, regional—will tend to use their own particular vocabularies. A natural language indexing system appropriate to one group is likely to be more or less unnatural and inappropriate to another. This limited applicability is also true to a lesser degree in the case of indexing languages with artificial notation in that they too reflect the conceptual arrangements (even though not the language) of a particular group.

Classification schemes with artificial notation

Since they are intended to perform a similar role, it is not surprising that classification schemes with artificial notation tend to have characteristics similar to those of "natural" language systems.

1. Homographs (words with identical spelling but different meaning) are avoided since the concepts are identified and distinguished prior to the assignment of the labels.
2. Synonyms should also be avoided since, having established a label for a concept, subsequent labels for the same concept need not be created.
3. Hierarchical relationships need to be handled in the same sort of way. The relationships are typically embodied in the notation, e.g.,

⁴ J. Farradane, "Semantic Analysis. Farradane's Relational Indexing System," *Journal of Information Science* 1, no. 5 (January 1980); 267-76; 1, no. 6 (March 1980): 313-24. "International Symposium on Relational Factors in Classification, University of Maryland, 8-11 June 1966. Proceedings," edited by J. M. Perrault, in *Information Storage and Retrieval* 3, no. 4 (December 1967): 147-410.

942   History of England
942.7   History of Northwestern England
942.76   History of Lancashire
942.769   History of Lancaster

4. With complex topic such as "teaching methods in Austrian Universities, 1918-1939," the same solutions are available as with "natural" language, e.g. 378.1709436 in the Dewey Decimal Classification. Since most use of existing classification schemes are designed for human rather than computer use, complex precoordinate labels are used.

Precoordination, however, is not a necessary characteristic of classification schemes with artifical notation any more than it is with natural language indexing schemes. It is true that most existing schemes *are* precoordinate, but in recent decades most thinking about classification has been based on analysis into a number of "facets," which, in combination, define the topic concerned. This faceted approach, which is detectable in revisions to existing schemes such as the Universal Decimal Classification (UDC), lends itself to postcoordinate searching by computer, because the elements which have been "precoordinated" remain identifiable and could, therefore, be used for a postcoordinate search also.

Similarities and dissimilarities

As the foregoing discussion illustrates, natural language indexing systems and classification schemes with artificial notation are substantially similar in structure, controls, and uses. A natural language indexing system with a fully worked-out relationship between topics will require the same degree of analysis and control as a classification scheme for the same range of topics. From this perspective, it seems helpful to regard them both as part of the generic category of indexing systems. The difference in notation is just one of the differences between them and not necessarily the most important.

Other differences are as follows:

1. Since the construction of a classification scheme with an artifical notation implies analysis of the relationships between topics, such schemes ordinarily have a great deal of "syndetic" control, i.e., rules concerning the preferred choice of indexing term and the relationships between terms. The development of syndetic control is not a necessary part of using natural language indexing systems, although it may be desirable. Consequently, the amount of syndetic control varies in practice from essentially none to very detailed control.

Intuitively, it seems needed; in practice, there is some question as to whether the benefits justify the costs.[5]

2. A classification scheme with artificial notation will need a natural language index to it—a "relative index"—if it is to be conveniently used.

3. Classification schemes with artificial notation permit the designer to arrange topics that are similar or related to be collocated. In natural language indexing systems, the juxtaposition of concepts will depend on accidents of spelling in the language concerned.

4. The labels used in classification schemes with artificial notation tend to be shorter, though there can be considerable variations in this. For example, "Bibliography of the Economic History of Hungary" would be "330.9439016" in the Dewey Decimal Classification but "ML,E2" in the Bliss Bibliographic Classification.

The foregoing discussion indicates that indexing systems vary in several ways: in fineness of detail; in degree of vocabulary control; in syndetic structure; and in choice between pre- and postcoordination. The principal conclusions from tests of retrieval systems are that, despite these variations and the ingenuity of their designers, there is little difference between them in effectiveness, even though they tend to retrieve different material even when the same inquiries are posed in identical circumstances.[6]

Retrieval languages II: Attributes

In the previous sections we restricted our attention to subject indexes using natural languages or artificial notation. This provided a convenient introduction to some semantic and syntactical aspects. However, it is important to emphasize that "subject" access is only one example of retrieval. Documents and data can have "contextual" attributes assigned to them for the purpose of retrieval, such as author, publisher, and date of creation. Indeed, in academic libraries, more use is made of author entries in the catalogs than of subject entries. The principal means of arrangement and approach for archival materials is their administrative provenance. As noted in chapter 6, attributes of authorship and provenance can also have connotations of subject content.

A citation, by means of which an author refers in one document to

---

[5] "The results of Cranfield II were rather unexpected because, taking both recall and precision into account, the index languages performing best used uncontrolled single words, that is, they were natural-language systems, such as Uniterms, based on words occurring in document texts." Lancaster, *Information Retrieval Systems* p. 275. *Cf.* E. M. Keen, and J. Digger, *Report of an Information Science Index Languages Test* (Aberystwyth, Wales: College of Librarianship, 1972), Part 1, pp. 166-7.

[6] E. M. Keen, "Laboratory Tests of Manual Systems," in *Information Retrieval Experiment,* edited by K. Sparck Jones (London: Butterworths, 1981), pp. 136-55.

another document, implies a relationship between the two and constitutes *prima facie* evidence that if one document is relevant to an inquiry, so might the other be.[7] Citation indexes can be viewed as a form of subject index even though the attribute that forms the basis for retrieval is cited-ness rather than a description of what the document is about. The argument is that the usual custom in scholarly research is to cite closely related work. Such citation is, therefore, indicative of a close relationship, usually in subject matter. Hence, the citation of one article by another generally implies similar subject matter. Since the description is in the form of a citation, not in the inconstant terminology of subject indexes, a citation index has some advantages when it comes to the use of articles in foreign languages or on subjects without standardized terminology.[8] This is reminiscent of our argument in chapter 6 that a document description can be a surrogate description of a subject inquiry.

This point has been stressed because of our assertion that retrieval is primarily a linguistic process, drawing on:

- *semantics:* the study of the elements of a language from the point of view of meaning;
- *syntax:* the study of the formal interactions that exist between the elements of language; and
- *pragmatics:* the study of the relationships between signs of linguistic expressions and their uses.

Since retrieval systems are based on indexing "languages" which share (more or less) the attributes of ordinary languages, they derive from the culture of their context and their study can be asserted to be a form of linguistic study.[9] We can note that this assertion assumes that linguistics does or can include the study of "artificial" languages. How far this assertion can be pushed is a matter for debate. It is suggested that all retrieval systems could be included on the grounds that all depend on

[7] For a study of the significance of citation see T. L. Hodges, *Forward Citation Indexing: Its Potential for Bibliographical Control* (Ph.D. dissertation. University of California, Berkeley, School of Librarianship, 1972. University Microfilms order no. BGD73-16787). B. Cronin, *The Citation Process: The Role and Significance of Citations in Scientific Communication* (London: Taylor Graham, 1984). T. A. Brooks, "Evidence of Complex Citer Motivations," *Journal of the American Society for Information Science* 37, no. 1 (January 1986): 34-36.

[8] "For example, suppose you want information on the physics of simple fluids. The simple citation 'Fisher, M. E., Math. Phys., 5, 944, 1964' would lead the searcher directly to a list of papers ... a significant percentage of the citing papers are likely to be relevant. ... In other words, the citation is a precise, unambiguous representation of a subject that requires no interpretation and is immune to changes in terminology." E. Garfield, *Citation Indexing—Its Theory and Application in Science, Technology, and Humanities* (New York: Wiley, 1979), p. 3.

[9] C. Beghtol, "Bibliographic Classification Theory and Text Linguistics: Aboutness Analysis, Intertextuality and the Cognitive Act of Classifying Documents," *Journal of Documentation* 42, no. 2 (June 1986): 84-113.

indexing "languages," that all indexing languages depend on the assignment of attributes and on the labeling of these attributes, and that a proper understanding of these systems depends on semantic, syntactical, and pragmatic analysis. This is more easily understood in the case of "word"-based subject indexes than in others, but we speculate that it is also true of all "non-word" indexes using artificial notation, all contextual indexes, all citation indexes, and even systems based on the statistical association of attributes of data or documents.

Objects, concepts, and definability

So far, we have simply assumed that a "descriptor," whether drawn from natural language or concocted in some artificial notation, can suffice to describe concepts. This is not the case. A descriptor can act as a label. It may also serve as an address. It may define the topic, more or less, but it is unlikely in all cases to provide sufficient definition to describe completely the topic in relation to other topics. The extent to which definition is needed will vary with respect to at least two considerations:

1. The number of different entities to be described. In a trivial example of an information retrieval system that retrieves data concerning only two or three items (e.g., the number of chairs, tables, and lamps in a warehouse), the need to define will be trivial. In contrast, a chain of furniture shops or a large furniture museum will need detailed definitions to distinguish one type from another.
2. The definability of the entities concerned. It is clear that not all concepts are equally easily defined. Consider the following sequence of concepts:

- Seat 34C on flight PA 6 from San Francisco airport on January 29, 1980.
- An elephant
- Heat
- Lassitude

The airline seat is easily unambiguously defined. An elephant is quite difficult to describe but can be recognized from pictures. Once one knows what an elephant looks like, there is usually little doubt as to whether a particular object is an elephant or not. Heat can only be indirectly illustrated. It cannot be seen directly, though sometimes it causes or effects can be. It can be sensed, however, if one is close enough and it can be defined and measured in physical terms. Lassitude can be sensed and symptoms of lassitude can be observed. Not at all clear, however, is the relationship between lassitude and related concepts such as ennui, tiredness, weariness, exhaustion, boredom, etc. Unlike the aircraft seat, the elephant, and heat, there would appear to be no precise accepted definition of lassitude. If one were to search in an information retrieval system for material about "lassitude" one would probably have to try a variety of search terms, and the items retrieved as a result of the search would probably vary in the extent to which they were about lassitude.[10]

Areas of study appear to vary in the extent to which the concepts they deal with are definable. Physical sciences tend to have "hard," i.e., relatively definable concepts such as temperature, molecular weight, size, velocity, etc. This is reasonable since the physical sciences deal with physical objects and the physical relationships between them. The "hardness" of these properties permits relatively easy measurement and calculation. One development can build upon another because the earlier achievements are clearly defined. The progress in achievement in the hard sciences is, in consequence, more palpable than in other areas of activity such as education, literature, political science, or social welfare.[11]

The "softer" areas tend to be those which deal with human behavior and social values.[12] Each area of study appears to have a characteristic degree of intellectual hardness/softness. There seems to be variation within areas (e.g., welfare economics seems "softer" than econometrics) and subjects may change in hardness/softness over time. In other words, definability does not appear to be itself a linguistic problem. If it were, then coining new words might solve many difficulties. Rather, there appears to be something more basic that has effects which are difficult to handle linguistically. Bunge comments that "vagueness or blurredness has no positive aspect and is a conceptual rather than a linguistic disease, hence it is rather more difficult to cure."[13]

The extent to which formal, logical notation and quantification are used is an indicator of hardness. It is an imperfect one since the use of such notation and quantification is not necessarily appropriate or well rooted in realistic definitions.

[10] *Cf.* Fugman's Axiom of Definability: "The compilation of information relevant to a topic can be delegated only to the extent to which an inquirer can define the topic in terms of concepts and concept relations," R. Fugman, "The Five-Axiom Theory of Indexing and Information Supply," *Journal of the American Society for Information Science* 36, no. 2 (March 1985): 116-29.

[11] Note also the distinction between "uncertainty", which ordinarily decreases with more information, and "equivocality" or "ambiguity," characterized by multiple and conflicting interpretations and less easily remedied by more information; *cf.* R. L. Daft et al., "Message Equivocality, Media Selection, and Manager Performance: Implications for Information Systems," *MIS Quarterly* 11, no. 3 (September 1987): 355-66.

[12] It is sometimes argued that "soft" disciplines are immature disciplines that have not yet developed to a mature, "hard" state. It seems as likely that "soft" disciplines are, at least to some extent, inherently and incorrigibly "soft" by the nature of their concerns.

[13] M. Bunge, *Scientific Research 1: The Search for System* (Berlin: Springer, 1967), pp. 97-8.

The terminology of hardness and softness is potentially misleading. One of the meanings of the word "hard" signifies a firm consistency and its opposite is "soft." In that sense, the imagery of *intellectual* hardness and softness is appropriate. A different meaning of the word "hard" is "difficult." For that meaning, the proper opposite is "easy" rather than "soft." It is in the second connotation of hardness as an indicator of difficulty that this imagery is misleading with respect to *intellectual* hardness and softness. The pages of formal notation and algebra which characterize writings in physics and chemistry look particularly unintelligible to the lay person. However, in an important sense it is even more difficult to make progress in fields where definitions are "soft" and unreliable, than when they are relatively "hard" and dependable. The foundations built by previous scholars cannot so easily be taken on trust but may need redefinition. New work may need to be built *into* rather than *onto* prior work. However one may view *difficulty*, let us simply accept that the definability of concepts—the intellectual "hardness" and "softness"—varies from one field of discourse to another.

To the extent to which terms are relatively low in definability, information retrieval is likely to be less satisfactory since retrieval, being a linguistic process, depends heavily on definitions.

In view of the importance of definition in communication, one would expect definability to emerge as fundamental in information studies in general and information retrieval in particular. Storer has referred to the distinction between hard and soft sciences as being possibly "the most powerful single variable in explaining disciplinary differences in the cultural realm."[14] So far, however, research appears to have been limited. Studies of the information gathering habits of social scientists indicate a general similarity with the habits of physical scientists. Hindle has suggested that in patterns in use of books and journals, "softer" subject areas are characterized by much more diffuse reading than "harder subjects."[15] In other words, the use of documents is more widely spread over different titles and over materials of a wider range of ages.

"Signaling through time" and indirectness

Robert Fairthorne's delightful description of information retrieval as "marking" and "parking" catches nicely the expectation that what is

---

[14] N. W. Storer, "Relations Among Scientific Disciplines," in *The Social Contexts of Research*, edited by S. Z. Naagi and R. G. Corwin (London: Wiley Interscience, 1972), 229-68, on p. 239.
[15] M. K. Buckland, "Are Obsolescence and Scattering Related?" *Journal of Documentation* 28, no. 3 (September 1972): 242-6; see pp. 244-5.

marked and parked may be retrieved after some lapse of time.[16] If that were not the case, then "discarding" or "dumping" would be more appropriate. The same emphasis on the elapse of time as a feature of information retrieval was made more explicitly by Calvin Mooers in a short paper that is said to contain the first use of the term "information retrieval."[17] Mooers describes information retrieval as "communication through time."

The image of information retrieval as communication through time helps explain the lack of direct link between the originator of the message and the recipient. One can readily imagine messages (data, documents) as having hooks (tags, labels, or descriptors) attached to them and then being placed in some timeless void where they remain until an inquiry in the form of a set of one or more hooks reaches into the same void and pulls back any messages which have one or more hooks coinciding with those of the inquiry.

So far so good. However, as one starts to work around the edges of this definition it becomes a little frayed. In one special case of information retrieval, there is an attempt to minimize the lapse of time. This occurs when every new batch of marked and parked information is automatically searched for material pertaining to specific inquiries. In professional jargon, a standing profile of reader's searches is routinely searched against a file in order to provide S.D.I. (selective dissemination of information). One might regard this as a sort of preemptive information retrieval, although the notion of a standing order would seem closer. Yet even here, some delay, even if minimized, is necessarily present because each of these processes of acquiring, marking, parking, and retrieving must take some time. Even in prompt on-line processing, the indirectness and sequential, discontinuous, two-stage nature of the process necessarily involves some time—even though it might be very little.

A different sort of problem emerges from other examples of communication which take time and which do not easily fit accepted definitions of informal retrieval. A letter sent through the mail will take time to arrive. (Strictly, all communication processes must take *some* time even though they may be trivial.) A notice that is posted on a fence, such as "Trespassers

---

[16] "... all retrieval systems demand marks of some kind. ... An object can be marked by changing it intrinsically in some recognizable way—as by painting it, punching a hole, or introducing it to a skunk. This I call 'inscribing.' Or it can be changed relative to its environment by putting it upside down, on one side, in an inscribed pigeon-hole, and so forth. This is called 'ordering the item.' Better terms for less formal contexts are 'marking' and 'parking'!" R. A. Fairthorne, "The Patterns of Retrieval," *American Documentation* 7, no. 2 (April 1956): 65-70. (Reprinted in R. A. Fairthorne, *Towards Information Retrieval* (London: Butterworths, 1961).)

[17] C. Mooers, "Information Retrieval Viewed as Temporal Signalling," in *International Congress of Mathematicians. Cambridge, Mass., 1950. Proceedings* (Providence, R.I.: American Mathematical Society, 1951), vol. 1, pp. 572-3.

will be prosecuted," or on a refrigerator, "Don't drink all the milk," will continue to inform people for as long as it remains posted. A documentary article in a newspaper may consciously be intended to inform readers in posterity.

The simplest conclusion from all this would seem to be that, although information retrieval can properly be regarded as communication through time, it is not the only form of communication in which time may be significant. Delay, one could conclude, is a necessary attribute of information retrieval but not exclusive to it. In information retrieval, the indirectness or discontinuity of communication permits and, indeed, *ensures* delay over and above the time required for communication itself. Both time and indirectness would seem to be significant in information retrieval and will be considered further in chapter 9.

Time

In some cases, library catalogs compiled more than a century ago are still in active use. The disadvantage of old catalogs is that older cataloging practice differs from contemporary cataloging in two ways. Descriptive cataloging (choice of form of entry for author, title, etc.) has evolved over the years. An extreme example—found in an ancient English library in a book-form catalog printed in 1790 and still in use—is the entry of books by the author, "Smith," under the letter F—because the genitive case of the Latin word for a smith (*faber*) begins with an F. Those whose work requires them to use old catalogs tend to learn how to allow for some of these vagaries. More serious is the shift in terminology for describing things over the years. In all aspects of human activity, new terms are coined and existing words change their meaning. Language evolves. Objects themselves may evolve. Consider, for example, the computer. Its appearance, power, and function have all changed radically in less than half a century. Finding antiquated terminology in library and other sorts of catalogs can be a source of amusement, of irritation, and of failure to retrieve. Inevitably, the use of words reflects the parlance and perspectives of the day. For example, Berman has drawn attention to the use of indexing terms which reflect sexist and racist attitudes which are now less acceptable in the United States than they used to be.[18] From the point of view of information retrieval, the shifting of word usage over time and the evolving of new concepts, objects, and terms (which seem inevitable and behind which retrieval systems seem bound to lag) will mean that the retrieval system itself tends to become less accurate

---

[18] S. Berman, *Prejudices and Antipathies: A Tract on the LC Subject Heads Concerning People* (Metuchen, N.J.: Scarecrow Press, 1971). See also J. K. Marshall, *On Equal Terms: A Thesaurus for Nonsexist Indexing and Cataloging* (New York: Neil-Schuman, 1977).

and less effective over time. The already imperfect description and definition, which are pivotal to effective retrieval, get worse.

Ideally, of course, the books should be recataloged continually according to contemporary cataloging practice, especially with respect to the subject headings used to describe what they are about. This requires, however, relatively expensive intellectual labor and the cost and benefits need to be weighed against the alternative uses of such money as is available. Most library users would be properly upset if their librarians ceased to buy new books of current interest in order to divert resources to the recataloging of old books which may be of limited interest.

Indirectness

By the "indirectness" of information retrieval systems, we refer to the characteristic that the designers and operators do not know who will seek the indirect communication that the information retrieval system provides. Not only does one not know *who* , one álso does not know *why* they will seek to use it or what perspectives and vocabulary they will have when they seek to use it. To some extent, this lack of prior knowledge is shared by other communication systems, notably in mass communication. One is, in general, unable to predict or later ascertain who heard a radio broadcast, read a newspaper, or heard a speech to a crowd—or how much of it they understood—or how beneficial the message was to them. In information retrieval situations, however, there is a further problem and that is that the user—with or without someone else acting as a mediator—needs to define what it is that needs to be retrieved. The vocabulary of the would-be user is necessarily somewhat different from that of the designer of the retrieval system, since no two persons' vocabularies are exactly alike, and may be substantially different especially if the designer (a category within which we include the indexer for present purposes) is distant in time, education, and culture from the would-be user.

This problem of predicting rather than knowing what each future user of the system is likely to ask for and how he or she is likely to ask for it has long been recognized. Indexing and cataloging are, in part, predictive pastimes since the formal description of what data represent and what documents are about has to be modified by estimation of the probability that they will be sought and of the probable ways in which they will be sought.[19] For the most part, this seems to have been assumed more or

[19] "Among the several possible methods of attaining the objects, other things being equal, choose that entry (1) that will probably be first looked under by the class of people who use the library. ..." C. A. Cutter, *Rules for a Dictionary Catalog*, 4th ed. (Washington, D.C.: Government Printing Office, 1904), p. 12. This issue recurs in discussions of "probabilistic indexing": M. E. Maron and J. L. Kuhns, "On Relevance, Probabilistic Indexing and Information Retrieval," *Journal of the Association for Computing Machinery* 7, no. 3 (1960): 216-44; A. Bookstein, "Probability and Fuzzy-Set Applications to Information Retrieval," *Annual Review of Information Science and Technology* 20 (1985): 117-51.

less implicitly. In analysis, it has been described in terms of "thought experiments."[20]

The importance in practice of this indirectness varies according to the circumstances and, we suspect, with the degree of definability. Previously, we have noted three factors as affecting definability:

1. The range of choices available: limited in most management information systems; unlimited in general libraries and archives.
2. The definability of the things that might be retrieved: from specific aircraft seats to vague cultural concepts.
3. The extent to which the individual seeking to use the system can describe what he or she needs to reduce distressing ignorance: from a telephone number to, say, background material on stoicism in modern Western culture.

Time and indirectness would both seem to reduce the closeness of match between the designer and the user in terms of approach to description and definition. Both, therefore, would seem to exacerbate the problems of matching characterized by these three dimensions.

Strictly speaking, it is the fact of indirectness which *permits* the matching of definitions and it is the fact of time which inhibits adaptation of the system to the user. The user can, heuristicly, learn to understand the system better and the system, if computer-based, might be programmed to facilitate this heuristic learning. With either manual or computer-based systems, other humans can, and often do, play a mediating role, as, for example, in doing a literature search on behalf of someone else who is too busy or less familiar with the retrieval systems available. Significantly, ascertaining what the user wants and translating it into a form suitable for the system(s) to be used are both regarded as important processes which not only take time but require special training. We conclude that:

- information retrieval involves communication through time, although not all communication through time is information retrieval;
- information retrieval is necessarily indirect communication;
- both the delay and the indirectness are liable to exacerbate existing difficulties caused by problems of definability.

Relatedness, relevance, responsiveness, and retrieval

Introduction

The design, use, and evaluation of retrieval systems depend heavily on

---

[20] W. S. Cooper, "Indexing Experiments by Gedanken Experimentation," *Journal of the American Society for Information Science* 29, no. 3 (May 1978): 107-19.

various sorts of relatedness. There have been two problems in discussions of this area: (1) the elements and relationships have not always been analyzed in enough detail; and (2) terminology has not always been clear and consistent. In particular, the *utilization of retrieved data* has not always been adequately distinguished from the *retrieval process* and the term "relevance" has been loosely used for more than one sort of relatedness.[21] An attempt will be made to clarify the concepts and terminology involved.[22]

The mechanism by which retrieval systems operate is the association (usually but not necessarily the matching) of arbitrarily chosen but predetermined attributes of the set of data that is to be susceptible to retrieval. The attributes that are used include authorship (as in a library catalog), date of publication (as, sometimes, in bibliographies), age (as in museum documentation), occurrence of words (as in the searching of texts), and so on. The list of possible attributes that could be used seems endless: location, size, chemical process, origin, etc. Nor need attributes be used alone: systems retrieving bibliographical data, for example, commonly operate on two or more attributes in combination, e.g., authorship, date of publication, language, and subject matter. The retrieval system responds to an inquiry by yielding such data as it finds that are highly associated with the attributes specified in the inquiry.

"Aboutness"

Writings about retrieval and especially about the evaluation of information retrieval systems have been dominated by just one of the apparently unlimited range of attributes: subject matter, i.e., what documents are about.

The term "aboutness" can be conveniently defined as referring to a coincidence of concepts, that is to say, if a book is "about" Austria, we infer that the book contains concepts that we associate with the subject "Austria." If it did not do so, we should deny that the book is "about" Austria. This is not entirely an objective matter since concepts have to be perceived and there may be some scope for disagreement in the perceptions by different people as to the concepts they perceive in a book and even in the concepts they associate with the subject "Austria" (Austria-Hungary, Austrian Empire, Republic of Austria, etc.). Hence, there is

---

[21]   For a convenient introduction to the literature concerning relevance, see A. Bookstein, "Relevance," *Journal of the American Society for Information Science* 30, no. 5 (September 1979): 269-73; also T. Saracevic, "The Concept of 'Relevance' in Information Science: A Historical Review," in *Introduction to Information Science*, compiled by T. Saracevic (New York: Bowker, 1971), pp. 111-51.

[22]   For a similar discussion see M. K. Buckland, "Relatedness, Relevance, and Responsiveness in Retrieval Systems," *Information Processing and Management* 18, no. 4 (1983): 237-41.

scope for honest difference of opinion as to what a book is about. Consider, for example, an allegory. A person who fails to perceive the allegorical symbols will have a different opinion concerning what the text is "about" than someone who does perceive them. In an extreme case, most persons who saw a book on Buddhist mythology written in Tibetan would be able to perceive so little of the concepts that they would, if honest, have to say that they did not know what the book was about. This is a matter of conceptual perception as well as a linguistic problem. If the book on Buddhist mythology were translated into a language they could understand, then, if the concepts were unfamiliar, they would probably still understand little of what the book was about. It is unwise to assume that a document has a single subject matter. It would seem more sensible to recognize that a document may, by general consensus, be concerned with a particular topic and yet have quite different meanings for particular individuals on particular occasions.[23]

In addition to the problems of the recognition of the concepts, there is also the problem of the definability of the concepts. Even with accurate perception, if there is not a rigorous, exclusive, unambiguous use of terms, the defining of the concepts perceived in the book may vary from one reader to another. This might simply be a matter of using alternative and equivalent synonyms. However, to the extent that concepts are not susceptible to description in unambiguous terms—they are vague or "soft"—then it is to be expected that statements by different individuals as to what a book is about, i.e., which set of concepts they perceive to be represented, will vary. Different people will state different nonequivalent definitions as to what the book is about.

The scope for honest disagreement concerning what something is about is important. However, in any given point in linguistic and cultural time and space, there is likely to be a great deal of agreement.[24] If there were not, then subject indexes would not work. On the assumption that indexes are expected to indicate what things are about, one can state that the effectiveness of indexes depends on and is determined, in part, by the degree of uniformity in perception of concepts, and common definition and labeling of those concepts.

[23] A library user who was studying Third World dialects of English complained that a book on politics by an African politician had been classified in the politics section when "It is African use of English." The library had acquired the book specifically to support this user's research. See Beghtol, "Bibliographic Classification, Theory and Text Linguistics: Aboutness Analysis, Intertextuality and the Cognitive Act of Classifying Documents," *Journal of Documentation* 42, no. 2 (June 1986): 84-113.

[24] L. E. Leonard, *Inter-Indexer Consistency Studies, 1954-1975* (Occasional Papers, 131) (Urbana, Ill.: University of Illinois, Graduate School of Library Science, 1977); K. Markey, "Interindexer Consistency Tests: A Literature Review and Report of a Test of Consistency in Indexing Visual Materials," *Library and Information Science Research* 6, no. 2 (April-June 1984): 155-77.

Retrieval using the attribute of what documents are about has been and can be expected to be of primary importance since subject access is difficult, useful, and technically interesting. It has dominated so much that it has, perhaps, hindered clarity of thought about the foundations of information retrieval theory. Retrieval by "aboutness" has to be seen as the use of one attribute among many. Our conceptual framework and definitions should be broad enough to include all attributes not just one.

"Utility"

We define "utility," following usage in economics, as benefit accruing. If reading a document and being informed by it leads to an enhanced state of knowledge which enables one to achieve some goal, then we can describe that process as having been beneficial or useful—as having utility.

We need to note two other outcomes: having a harmful effect, sometimes referred to awkwardly as a "negative utility," "disutility," or "disbenefit;" and having no known effect that could be regarded as useful or harmful— no utility or benefit.

Utility is meaningful only in terms of some objective, explicit or implicit. Giving somebody money has the property of utility if becoming wealthy or purchasing things are goals for that person; if that person were trying to achieve spiritual growth through poverty, then the gift of money would be unhelpful—of negative utility. Utility, then, is in all cases dependent on an objective. People have objectives. Inanimate objects do not. Organizations have objectives only to the extent to which individuals and groups have objectives which they seek to achieve through the organization. Hence, utility is dependent not only on an objective but on the objective of one or more persons. Further, objectives imply values. There are values, implicit or explicit, which make one decide that it is desirable to pursue an objective, and a particular objective in preference over other objectives. Utility and objectives both derive from human values.

We are concerned here with information retrieval and the manner in which it might have utility. In principle, it would seem that being informed might assist in any of the objectives that one or more individuals might have: spiritual, physical, intellectual, professional, or social. These objectives might also be hindered. An obvious example of harmful information would be information that was, in fact, misinformation. The objective of getting from San Francisco to New York is likely to be hindered if one receives inaccurate information about the departure time of the airline flight and, as a result, misses the plane. Even so, although inaccurate information is likely to be the major cause of disutility associated with information retrieval, it is not necessary or proper to equate disutility with inaccuracy since it can happen that accurate information can also hinder the achievement of objectives. It is, after all, not absurd for someone to state honestly: "I would never have undertaken that task had I known more about what was involved, but I am glad that I did it!" Further, it is important to remember that if the utility derived from information retrieval can pertain to any human objective, then it is only to be expected that some of these objectives will appear obscure. They might seem irrational to other people. They might be kept a secret. They might lie deep in the subconscious and not be recognized even by the individuals concerned. They can be expected to reflect values of a very private nature as well as publicly proclaimed ones. There may be inconsistencies between professed objectives and those actually pursued. There will probably be conflicting objectives even for one individual.

The elements of retrieval

We have defined the use of retrieval systems as including three distinguishable stages: the *formulation* of an inquiry; the *retrieval* of signals; and— the topic of the next chapter—the *utilization* of what has been retrieved. The effectiveness of each process can vary:

● The *formulation* of the inquiry may be more or less appropriate to the choice of attributes in the retrieval system. Much depends on the extent to which the person doing the formulation has an understanding of the data sought and of the characteristics of the retrieval system. The phrasing of the inquiry may be unskilful.[25]

● Aside from mechanical failures, the *retrieval* process may be ineffective in two ways: it may respond with data that has been incorrectly retrieved; or it may fail to yield data that should have been retrieved. In conventional terms, these would be referred to as failures in precision and in recall, respectively, For example, using authorship as the attribute for retrieval, "Mark Twain" might be used as the inquiry. The retrieval system might correctly respond with data concerning works written by Mark Twain but fail to retrieve those written by Samuel Clemens—or, if it did, it might also wrongly include data concerning works by Severus Clemens or Susie Clemens.

● *Utilization* might be impaired if the inquirer did not have the necessary abilities (e.g., knowledge, cognitive skills) to become informed by the data retrieved.

From the analysis thus far there emerge several possibilities for things to be related to each other—or to have degrees of relatedness. These include but are not limited to:

---

[25] For a systematic review see N. J. Belkin and W. B. Croft, "Retrieval Techniques," *Annual Review of Information Science and Technology* 22 (1987): 109-45.

1. the inquiry as formulated for the retrieval system;
2. any of a seemingly unlimited range of attributes;
3. data retrieved; and
4. benefit to the user.

Before considering sorts of relatedness, it is important to emphasize again the separateness of the retrieval process from the processes of formulation and of utilization. The difference between retrieval and utilization can be conveniently illustrated by what we might call the case of the disappearing user. Let us imagine that someone formulated and posed an inquiry concerning chocolate, cholesterol, and heart disease to a computer-based retrieval system. The retrieval system responds by yielding a set of data. The user becomes better informed as a result of perusing the data and benefits from a changed state of knowledge. Let us now imagine that, having posed the inquiry, the inquirer loses interest, is unable to await the response, or dies from a heart attack. In this latter scenario, there is no opportunity for utilization of the data, nor, therefore, for benefit to the user. Yet the retrieval system has performed in exactly the same way. The process of retrieval and the data retrieved are indistinguishable, in fact unchanged, from one scenario to another.

We can clarify the distinction between formulation and retrieval by extending this simple case. In some circumstances, the user may modify the formulation of the inquiry if it is thought that the data yielded would not be what is desired. In this case, what has happened is that a *different* search has been formulated, however slight the modification has been. Commonly, the user's knowledge has changed as a result of preliminary indications concerning the set of data that would be yielded. The response by the retrieval system to any given formulated search will not have been changed unless the retrieval system itself has also been altered in some way, e.g., new data added or the indexing modified.

Relatedness

In the evaluation of information retrieval systems, the term "relevance" has been loosely used to denote differing forms of relatedness.[26] A practical approach is to define the most useful relationships and degrees of relatedness first and then give them distinctive names. We shall consider three different relationships for each of which the terms "relevant" or "relevance" has been used.

[26] P. G. Wilson, *Two Kinds of Power: An Essay on Bibliographical Control* (Berkeley: University of California Press, 1968).

Relatedness I: Responsiveness

Responsiveness refers to relatedness of the data retrieved to the inquiry as posed in terms of the attributes used as the basis for retrieval. To what extent *did* the system retrieve all and only the works that it contains by Mark Twain? The quality of the response to the inquiry by the retrieval system will be affected by several factors including the appropriateness and completeness of the data base, the suitability of the attribute(s) used as the basis for retrieval (in this case authorship), and the ability of the retrieval system to identify those data that fit the description offered by the inquiry—or fit it to the desired degree. If one wished to avoid talking of the "relevance" of the retrieved data to the inquiry, one might speak of the *responsiveness* of the system.

Relatedness II: Pertinence

In Relatedness I above, we were concerned with the general term: the relatedness of the retrieval system's response to the inquiry regardless of the attribute(s) being used as a basis for retrieval. We now consider one special case within the general class: when the attribute used as the basis for retrieval is topicality—the subject matter of the data. In ordinary speech one might well speak of one topic as being relevant to another topic. Such relationships (e.g., general to specific, overlap) can be difficult to understand or to define. For example, when retrieving by the attribute of topicality, data on "Freud" are related (relevant) but not identical to the topic of psychoanalysis. We might term this relatedness "pertinence". This sort of relatedness between properties of data within a given attribute could exist with other attributes than topicality.

Relatedness III: Beneficiality

A relationship that is entirely different from either of the above is that between the retrieved data and the benefit of the user. It is in this sense, for example, that Wilson has sought to limit the use of the term "relevance" in *Two Kinds of Power*[27] and it is implicit in all discussions of utility-theoretic indexing. Stated simply, it is assumed that retrieval systems are provided and used in order that their utilization will have beneficial effects. Social values are implied. This raises two questions: (1) Whose values? The users' or those of the providers of the service? and (2) Are we referring to actual benefits or expected benefits? These are critical questions. However, whatever answers are given, it is clear that the relationship is different in kind from both responsiveness and

[27]   Ibid.

pertinence because factors external to the retrieval system affect the outcome: social values and the knowledge and cognitive skills of the users.

Implications for information retrieval

We have defined responsiveness as signifying the extent to which the retrieval system yields data associated with the attribute(s) specified in the formulated inquiry. We have defined beneficiality as the property of assisting in the achievement of objectives. We have noted that these objectives are necessarily the objectives of human beings and relate to human values even though they may sometimes be obscure and even seem irrational to other people. From this discussion the following conclusions would seem to follow.

An ideal information retrieval system would retrieve data and documents that would assist individuals in the pursuit of their objectives, i.e., values. This implies that the information retrieval system should be concerned with the utility of what is retrieved rather than what it is about, since utility, not aboutness, is the goal. In order to achieve utility, the ideal information retrieval system would need to know the objective(s) and value(s) of each user.

Since redundant information does not help achieve goals and may hinder their achievement, the information retrieval system would, ideally, also have to know the state of knowledge of the inquirer—both its extent and its limitations. Avoiding the retrieval of unneeded and unusable data is, after all, a major purpose of information retrieval systems. If a researcher sought material relevant to an inquiry concerning Freud, it is unlikely that it would be helpful to retrieve a document that had been written by that same researcher, even though it may be related to the subject of the inquiry.

It is not practical by any known technique to expect to know all of the objectives of people currently using an information retrieval system. It is still less reasonable to expect to be able to predict what future users' objectives and values might be. Even if one could, the most useful set of retrieved documents is likely to be unique for each inquiry. Further, since each person's mind is unique, even objectives that are ostensibly the same for different people may be different in practice. What is more, since redundant information is to be avoided, subsequent inquiries concerned with the same person's objective would call for different responses since the individual's state of knowledge will probably have changed in the meanwhile. Some things will have been learned, others forgotten. Therefore, an ideal information retrieval system based on utility would have a formidable set of design requirements. It would need to understand objectives that present inquirers might not be willing to admit to or might not consciously understand fully themselves; it would need to predict which persons might use the system in the future and what their objectives might be in that future; and it would in each case need to know not only what the individual's objective is but also that same individual's state of knowledge not at the point in time that the inquiry was made but at the point in time that the data are retrieved. This would have to be true for each and every individual who may come to use the system. What should be retrieved should vary even for different posings of the same question by the same person. All this is quite apart from the fact that the concepts and definitions used may be more or less ambiguous.

Although such an ideal system would seem to be what is needed, the compounding of inherently improbable achievements one upon another means that this ideal system is most likely to remain an inspiring but unrealized achievement. (Not that this might not be helpful. Witness the repeated homage to the inspirational role played by Vannevar Bush's seminal essay, "As We May Think," published in 1945.)[28]

The notion of imagining what future inquiries might be posed may very well be a useful device (cf. W. Cooper[29]), but the combination of needing to know objectives, values, and future states of knowledge—including knowledge not yet known to anybody—casts grave doubt on the achievability of such an ideal system.

In the discussion of "aboutness" above, reasons were adduced as to why complete agreement is not to be expected concerning what documents are about. Nevertheless, within a given cultural and linguistic context, considerable consensus is likely. Indexing and retrieving books according to what they are currently perceived to be about is, therefore, a more practical matter than indexing them in relation to potential future inquiries.

If indexing and retrieval based on aboutness is more practical than indexing with respect to predictions of future inquiries and future knowledge, how does aboutness relate to utility? The answer would appear to be two-fold:

1. If we hold relentlessly to the importance of utility—of being beneficially informed—we can still regard aboutness as a sensible *predictor* of utility to the inquirer. If we seek to reduce our ignorance about Freud, a document *about* Freud is likely to make us more fully informed about Freud. Further, although this process does nothing to minimize the retrieval of knowledge that we already know, this redundancy is at worst inefficient rather than misleading since we can, presumably, ourselves filter out subsequently that which is already known to us.

---

[28] V. Bush, "As We May Think," *Atlantic Monthly* 176 (July 1945): 101-3.
[29] *Cf.,* Cooper, "Indexing Experiments."

2. In our discussion, we have tended to assume that the attribute used as a basis for retrieval would be its subject aboutness. Although a subject retrieval system could operate in isolation, this is a singularly unrealistic and unnecessary assumption, since constant use is in fact made of other attributes of identifying documents which might be useful. A few examples will demonstrate: Contextual attributes such as author, origin, date of creation, and extensions of these can be helpful. Indeed, in the case of archives, the principal means of arrangement and approach for documents is their administrative provenance. In libraries, a common mode of approach is to use the author's name as a means of identifying books on a subject on which it is thought that person might have written. Citations, by means of which an author refers in a document to another document, imply a relationship between the documents—a prima facie indicator that if one document is related to an inquiry, so might the other. The success of the various citation indexes is clear evidence of their value in supplementing subject indexes. Further, a part of the formal information system is the information specialist who operates and may have designed it. Users of archives depend heavily on the archivist for guidance. Librarians have always included in their role the drawing on their experience with bibliography, with their collections and with their users in order to assist users (cf. the "reference interview"). In addition, it is foolish not to include as part of this picture the informal assistance played by friends and colleagues who can and do play a significant role in scholarship and in bureaucracies, to give but two examples.

In brief, information retrieval based on what documents are deemed to be about (as opposed to prediction of what is unknown in relation to future enquiries) can be expected to work moderately well in practice because there is more or less consensus on what documents are about, because "aboutness" can plausibly be regarded as predictive of utility, and because, in practice, subject indexing is supplemented by other indicators of probable utility.

Information retrieval based on "aboutness" lends itself to automatic indexing since the occurrence and more especially the co-occurrence of terms in the text can indicate the apparent subject content of the document. This may be expensive and error-prone, but results likely to be of some use can be achieved.

The very same reasons which make the ideal information retrieval system unlikely also make implausible the concept of an "information counselor" in any sophisticated sense. Any person knowledgeable about sources of information can, in general, be helpful. However, the notion of an information counselor based on an analogy with a dietician, who can diagnose and prescribe information like a change of diet, would have to cope with the same problems as would the ideal information system: in addition to understanding objectives which the inquirer may imperfectly comprehend, the counselor would also need to understand the extent and nature of the inquirer's knowledge, and presumably be able to identify the point at which the inquirer has been beneficially informed to a sufficient extent. The analog of a dietician would be more apt if states of knowledge could be objectively assessed by blood count, encephalograms, and the like.

Summary

The foregoing discussion leads to the following conclusion:

1. The three sorts of relatedness—responsiveness, pertinence, and beneficiality—are different.

2. Since beneficiality (Relatedness III) is rooted in the utilization of retrieved data and in human values, the superficially startling conclusion follows that *relevance in the sense of utility cannot properly be used to evaluate information retrieval processes*. In this, we are using a strict, narrow definition: the ability of the system to yield a set of data responsive to the formulated inquiry. The proper basis for evaluation would be rooted in the responsiveness of the system in terms of the inquiry and the attributes used: "fitting the description" in Wilson's terms.[30] Any use of beneficial effects cannot be an evaluation of retrieval processes only but must be either an evaluation of utilization or some combination of utilization and other processes (e.g., utilization and retrieval and, possibly, formulation, and even other logically prior activities such as identification of need) or concurrent activities (e.g., improvement of cognitive skills in order to improve utilization).[31] Whoever uses benefit or utility in information retrieval evaluation should specify the boundaries of what is being evaluated.

3. It would be helpful if new, distinct terms were to be adopted to distinguish different sorts of relatedness ("relevance"). Confusion might

[30] Wilson, *Two Kinds of Power.*

[31] The difficulties encountered in trying to use beneficiality where responsiveness rather than beneficiality is appropriate is illustrated in a recent discussion of the retrieval of data that are relevant (i.e., beneficial) but not topical. "The material is relevant but not topical. However to expect a retrieval system to respond to an unexpressed need seems a harsh requirement indeed. ... The instance of the relevant but untopical document is unlikely to occur in any test of relevant documents used for system evaluation. ... While it is certainly the case that topicality is not a necessary condition for relevance, it seems that we may comfortably treat it as such without great loss." B. Boyce, "Beyond Topicality: A Two Stage View of Relevance and the Retrieval Process," *Information Processing and Management* 18, no. 3 (1982): 105-9. See Fugman, "The Five-Axiom Theory of Indexing and Information Supply," *Journal of the American Society for Information Science* 36, no. 2 (March 1985): 116-29.

be reduced. Ideally, the terms should be applicable generally to sorts of relatedness and not restricted to specific examples of retrieval activities (e.g., subject-based retrieval as opposed to retrieval on the basis of other attributes) unless such narrower usage is justified and clearly stated.

We shall reconsider the distinction between responsiveness and beneficiality further in our final chapter.

Requisite variety

We can speculate on the consequences of failure to find items. For this it is helpful to invoke a principle from cybernetics—the law of requisite variety—which states, in effect, that a system must have as many different responses as it encounters challenges. Otherwise, the system will fail for lack of being able to respond. In the context of retrieval systems, one might say that, if something appropriate is not retrieved for each and every inquiry, the system will fail. So it will if, for example:

- no signals are retrieved (no suitable books); or,
- if no term in the language of the retrieval system seems promising enough to be worth pursuing; or,
- if, for whatever reason, a promising term does not lead to the retrieval of appropriate signals.

It follows that requisite variety can be increased by attending to one or more of these causes. A more complete collection of retrievable objects (e.g., a bigger collection of appropriate books) will help. (We define completeness as being complete with respect to some range of inquiries.) A wider range of index terms would also help, provided, of course, they lead to appropriate retrieval, as would more extensive and more reliable connections between index terms and retrievable objects.[32]

What are the consequences of failure? They would appear to be two-fold:

- The consequence of an *individual* failure is unlikely to be catastrophic since we are dealing with an open system. If the need is great enough, the inquirer can normally leave the library and try other sources: ask a friend, try another library, etc.
- The consequence of *repeated* failure is that, as the user perceives the *proportion* of failures to be increasing, there is likely to be a reassessment on the users' part of the perceived probable benefits of using the library. Usage is likely to be reduced and to be concentrated more narrowly on those sorts of inquiries which are perceived as being

---

[32] *Cf.* H. Wellisch, "The Cybernetics of Bibliographical Control: Toward a Theory of Document Retrieval Systems," in *Theory and Application of Information Research,* edited by O. Harbo (London: Mansell, 1980), pp. 82-100.

unlikely to result in failure. We consider this sort of reaction more fully in chapter 10.

Competence to use retrieval systems

We have assumed, hitherto, that those who would use retrieval systems are fully competent to do so. This is a most unwise assumption for the following reasons:

1. There are many different retrieval systems. Consider the fact that Sheehy's *Guide to Reference Books* describes more than 10,000 different bibliographies and other works of reference.[33]
2. Typically, several retrieval systems are likely to contain material about a given topic, and many others may well contain at least a little material relating to that topic.
3. Each system is more or less different from the others, even though the differences may sometimes be small and subtle. Further, retrieval systems commonly change. Published works may have new editions and computer-based retrieval systems are continuously being modified.

These are the reasons why a good reference librarian not only knows many reference sources, but also has the familiarity and understanding that come from frequent use, and keeps up-to-date.[34] It is inconceivable that one could know too many sources, could be too familiar with them, or would be unnecessarily up-to-date. This is clearly a major challenge even for the dedicated professional information specialist.

What, then, of the user who is not a professional reference librarian or information specialist? There are, of course, some exceptional individuals, but the general situation is entirely predictable:

1. There is some vague (but generally incomplete) awareness that libraries have considerable potential for the retrieval of information.
2. The number of retrieval systems known to any given user is likely to be small.
3. The expertise that can come only from conscious attention to the complexities of the system is likely to be lacking in most cases.

It is difficult and unreasonable to imagine any circumstances in which this situation could be expected to be otherwise, since such expertise

[33] E. P. Sheehy, *Guide to Reference Books*, 10th ed. (Chicago: American Library Association, 1986).

[34] Lytle, in a study of retrieval from archives, found a significant relationship between search effectiveness and the searcher's familiarity with the retrieval technique. R. H. Lytle, "Intellectual Access to Archives: II Report of an Experiment Comparing Provenance and Content Indexing Methods of Subject Retrieval," *American Archivist* 43, no. 2 (Spring 1980): 191-207. "A searcher experienced in the P method achieved good results with it, as did a searcher experienced in CI using that method," p. 194.

requires opportunity, time, and effort—and not just once but on a continuing basis. It is not at all clear that for everyone the benefits involved in being expert justify paying the price.

The consequence is that the use of retrieval systems is bound to be far less in both frequency and effectiveness of use than is possible and beneficial. But to assert that this is "wrong" would be to forget the price involved (mostly nonmonetary) and to overlook the fact that the use of retrieval systems is a means, not an end. More use of libraries can sensibly be expected to follow—and only to follow—changes in the perceived benefits and perceived costs. What then could or should be done? Three sorts of practical activities would seem sensible:

1. Greater awareness of the existence and of the potential usefulness of retrieval systems would permit *consideration* by the user of more use of them.
2. A lower price—primarily, greater *ease* of use—can be expected to result in an increase of use.
3. More effectiveness in retrieval systems should also help since that should increase the benefit. Yet, caution is in order since use will follow perceptions of *cost*-effectiveness as perceived by the user. (Because we are discussing use, we deliberately listed ease ahead of effectiveness.)

Some of the price (effort) can be reduced by using a competent intermediary (a reference librarian or information specialist). However, it is easily overlooked that using an intermediary may increase the price somewhat unless the user trusts and is accustomed to using the intermediary. Otherwise, for most people, a psychological effort and a change of habit—hence, a price—may be involved in asking for help. The style and demeanor of the reference librarian can increase or decrease the perceived price involved.

In this rather intangible area, the interpersonal skills of librarians become important. So also is instruction (formal or otherwise) in library skills.[35] Major problems include the providing of motivation and the development of good enough instruction. In a university context, a favorable attitude by faculty in the students' area of study and arrangements for credit for bibliographical instruction to count toward their degree

[35] There is a large literature on instruction in library use. See, for example, P. J. Taylor, C. Harris, and D. Clark, *The Education of Users of Library and Information Services: An International Bibliography, 1926-76.* (Aslib bibliography, 9) (London: Aslib, 1979); A. K. Beaubien, S. A. Hogan and M. W. George, *Learning the Library: Concepts and Methods for Effective Bibliographical Instruction* (New York: Bowker, 1982); C. Oberman and K. Strauch, *Theories of Bibliographic Education: Designs for Teaching* (New York: Bowker, 1982); A. F. Roberts, *Library Instruction for Librarians* (Littleton, Colo.: Libraries Unlimited, 1982); I. Malley, *The Basics of Information Skills Teaching* (London: Bingley, 1984).

both help. Pitching the instruction at the correct level and relating the learning experience to the user's personal interests both appear to be important. Unfortunately, skill as a librarian does not, in and of itself, guarantee skill as an instructor.

In the next chapter we shall discuss the *use* of the data and documents that have been retrieved.

9

Becoming Informed

We have departed from the traditional practice of combining discussion of retrieval with discussion of the use made of the data that have been retrieved. Having considered the retrieval process in the previous chapter, we now consider the use of what has been retrieved. We regard it as a quite different sort of process.

Information defined

The term "information" has been widely and loosely used. We would prefer, for present purposes, to follow Fairthorne in adopting a strict definition: Information is not stuff but a process. It is the process of becoming informed.[1] According to this definition, information retrieval systems do not retrieve information: they retrieve physical things, such as signals, data, documents. These physical things *may*, when perceived by somebody with appropriate prior knowledge and suitable cognitive skills, contribute toward a change or increase in that person's knowledge. Here we are concerned with the *process* of becoming informed.

The strict definition of "information" as the process of becoming informed is, intellectually, a satisfying one. Unfortunately, the term "information" has also been used very widely to denote what is, or might be, retrieved—the "physical things" referred to above. In consequence, restricting the use of the term "information" to the process of becoming informed would be substantially at variance with customary usage. (The term "regulation" is also ambiguous in denoting either a process or an entity.) For clarity, therefore, we will use the rather cumbersome phrase "becoming informed" to denote the process. We view this as a two-stage process as depicted in figure 9.1. The first stage in this process is the physiological perception of the signals (can they be seen? ... or heard?).

---

[1] "... information is an attribute of the receiver's knowledge and interpretation of the signal, not of the sender's, nor some external omniscient observer's nor of the signal itself" R. A. Fairthorne, "The Theory of Communication," *Aslib Proceedings* 6, no. 4 (November 1954): 255-67. (Reprinted in R. A. Fairthorne, *Towards Information Retrieval* (London: Butterworths, 1961, pp. 64-79))

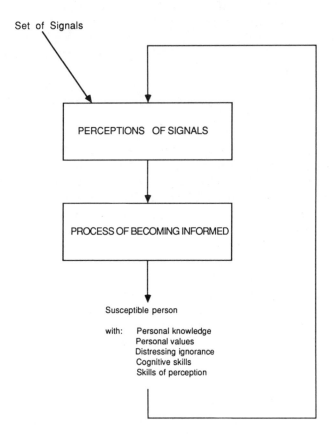

F<small>IG.</small> 9.1   The process of becoming informed

The second stage is the cognitive process of becoming informed. For this, other factors are involved, notably prior knowledge and cognitive skills:

● Can the person *read*—as opposed to merely *see*—the text?
● Is the text in a language that the reader understands?
● Are the concepts involved comprehended by the reader?

If any one or more of these three conditions were not met, then it is unlikely that the individual would become informed.

Some of the paradoxes of becoming informed can be readily explained once variations in the reader's prior knowledge and cognitive skills are taken into account. For example, the very same book can be simultaneously highly informative and not-at-all informative on the same subject area.

A textbook would be uninformative for an expert who is already familiar with the subject matter, but very informative to a novice. A brief note or inscription might be highly informative to the expert who has the necessary background of knowledge and cognitive skills to understand, but not the novice who has not.

The situation is similar in the case of allegories and other literary forms with allusions. The expert reader—one with substantial relevant prior knowledge or insight—will "get more out of" the text than will someone without such knowledge.[2]

The vexing problem of choice of criteria for the evaluation of retrieval systems results in part from this aspect of information. Retrieval can be performed more or less effectively, but only in terms of the attributes assigned to the documents. What can be done, therefore, is retrieval which is more or less accurate with respect to chosen attributes. However, the ultimate goal is to be informative. But, as just noted, the extent to which a document is informative depends largely on the reader, i.e., on factors external to the document.

What results is a troublesome paradox: retrieval systems exist in order that users may become beneficially informed. Yet, strictly speaking, retrieval systems cannot be evaluated on their ability to inform beneficially, because becoming informed depends, in part, on factors external to the retrieval system. We shall return to and resolve this paradox in the final chapter.

Knowledge and opinion as belief

Viewing library services primarily as information services intended to reduce distressing ignorance, risks understating the role of library services in influencing and changing opinions.[3] Influencing opinions and, therefore, attitudes can be a motive in providing library services, as, for

[2] "The early Church fathers sometimes used a threefold method of interpreting texts, encompassing literal, moral, and spiritual meanings. This was refined and commonly believed to have achieved its final form in the medieval allegorists' 'fourfold theory of interpretation.' This method also began every reading with a search for the literal sense of the passage. It moved up to a level of ideal interpretation in general, which was the allegorical level proper. ... Still higher above the literal and allegorical levels, the reader came to the tropological level, which told him where his moral duty lay. Finally, since Christian thought was apocalyptic and visionary, the fourfold method reached its apogee at the anagogic level, at which the reader was led to meditate on the final cosmic destiny of all Christians and of himself as a Christian hoping for eternal salvation." *Encyclopaedia Britannica,* 15th ed., 1977 vol. 7, p. 135, s.v. "Fable, Parable, Allegory."

[3] "The despotic ideal is twofold: to find out what a man is thinking, and to determine absolutely what he shall think. The first has not yet been achieved. Progress has been made with the second by indirect methods, and it is with these that libraries are concerned— methods which do not prevent thinking, but alter its quality." A. Broadfield, *A Philosophy of Librarianship* (London: Grafton, 1949), p. 12.

example, when sponsored by one government in the territory of another.[4] Yet the distinction between knowledge and opinion is not really a fundamental one for our purposes since both are, at root, a matter of belief. Even when considering scientific knowledge, it is well to remember that library collections in past times contained plenty of scientific information no longer believed by scientists on such topics as the orbiting of the earth by the sun, the origin of species (before Darwin), the laws of physics (before Einstein), and much else besides. Indeed, this scientific knowledge is still made available by libraries in the older books in collections. Presumably, some of the contents of the newest books will not find acceptance, or, if accepted, will cease to be accepted in the future. That some of what is believed in one century is superseded by different beliefs in another is the essence of progress in scholarship in science as in other subjects. New history books not only add new assertions concerning historical events, but refute some older assertions and change the way that others are understood. This is even more marked in other areas more concerned with values and less firmly rooted in factual evidence. In brief, we take the view that both people's knowledge and their opinions are elements of what they believe, and that the process of becoming informed is a process that adds to or changes individuals' beliefs.[5]

Barriers to becoming informed

There are different sorts of barriers to becoming informed.[6] In the following discussion, four sorts of barriers will be discussed as they refer to the retrieval of documents.

Let us imagine that someone has an inquiry concerning a specific aspect of Buddhism.

Indicative access

There would be a problem of defining what document, if any, would be likely to contain writing which would probably be helpfully informative with respect to this inquiry. We could well call this *indicative access* since it pertains to the ability of indexing systems to indicate which of the parked documents is likely to be worth retrieving. (It is common in information retrieval circles to refer to this "indicative access" as "intellectual access," which would seem too broad a term and best used only when other sorts of access that we discuss separately below are also included.)

---

[4] See chapter 6, footnote 1.

[5] This rather simplified view should suffice for the purposes of this book. For a broader introduction to this matter see F. Machlup, *Knowledge and Knowledge Production* (Princeton, N.J.: Princeton University Press, 1980), esp. chapters 2 and 5.

[6] This has been discussed in P. G. Wilson, *Public Knowledge, Private Ignorance: Toward a Library and Information Policy* (Westport, Conn.: Greenwood Press, 1977).

Physical access

Having identified a document that will probably be useful, *physical access* is needed to it in order that it can be read. If the only known copy of this document is in Bhutan; if permission is denied for it to be photocopied or sent out of the country on loan, and if access to Bhutan is denied, then the indicative access will not result in any intellectual access—for lack of physical access.

Linguistic access

Even if physical access has been arranged, if it is written in Tibetan, there is likely to be a problem of *linguistic access*. One would have to learn Tibetan or arrange for a translation in order to overcome what would otherwise be an effective language barrier.

Conceptual access

Even when problems of indicative, physical, and linguistic access have been solved, there may remain a difficulty in *conceptual access* if comprehension of the text requires an understanding of concepts of Buddhist metaphysics which the reader simply does not have.

These four sorts of accessibility all pertain to retrieving, and being informed by, documents. As Wilson points out, libraries tend to concentrate on the first two (indicative access and physical access) and to ignore the second two (linguistic access and conceptual access). This uneven attention to the problems faced by people who seek to be informed warrants some discussion.

Libraries do provide *some* assistance. Typically, translations and dictionaries and, commonly, a list of translators are maintained for problems of linguistic access. Introductory texts, directories of experts, and encyclopedias are also stocked so that the would-be reader can, on a self-help basis, work toward an understanding. The selection of books bought emphasizes the language of the library's users even when the language of the original is different. At a more elementary level public libraries have long been concerned with fostering literacy.[7] Similarly, the selection ought also to emphasize the conceptual level expected of the library's users. Generally, however, it is true that the emphasis in libraries is overwhelmingly on the indicative access and the physical access. The wonders of interlibrary loan arrangements are an important feature of

[7] E. G. Smith, "The Literacy Gap: The Involvement of Public Libraries in Literacy Education," *Library and Information Science Research* 6, no. 1 (January-March 1984): 75-94; issue on "Adult Education, Literacy, and Libraries," *Library Trends* 36, no. 2 (Fall 1986): 183-345.

both the practice and the folklore of libraries. Linguistic skills are among the qualifications sought in recruiting library staff, but it is very rare for a translation service to be provided except in libraries of corporations.

As for assistance with conceptual access, a high standard of general education is expected of librarians (their professional training in the United States and Canada begins only after a first general or specialized university degree), and librarians are often encouraged to develop a knowledge of the subject matter dealt with in their libraries. However, this knowledge, for good practical reasons, tends to be wide rather than deep and there are severe limits to the extent to which it can be used to assist users with problems of conceptual access.

The two forms of access that libraries emphasize (indicative and physical) and the two they do not (linguistic and conceptual) also differ in another way. Linguistic access and conceptual access have to do with direct communication. There is no nonintellectual barrier between the document and the eye. Indicative access and physical access involve communication indirectly. Until both of them have been resolved there can be no basis for communication. One can hardly read something if one does not know what it is that one should be reading and, even when that problem has been resolved, one still cannot read it if it is not visible. This distinction between direct communication and the indirect facilitating of communication reinforces the view that libraries are primarily concerned with information retrieval rather than with communication generally.

There is, however, an alternative explanation which has to do with the practical probabilities of people needing help with each of these barriers and with the availability of alternative forms of help. This argument might run somewhat as follows: Library users can, within limits, adapt to and cope with linguistic and conceptual problems, but indicative access and physical access are problems which the library service can handle more effectively than can an individual—and they are problems that can be delegated to the library service with less difficulty. People adapt by tending to direct their reading to texts that are in languages and are at conceptual levels that they can handle. A good library service will provide for some latitude in this matter when selecting and can generally arrange access to other collections of advanced material when that is needed. People tend to confine their attentions to languages they can read fluently. What is more, they tend to confine themselves to the material which happens to be at hand and known to them. However, pursuing this line of argument is likely to be circular. People adapt to situations, therefore it is not clear when behaving one way is the preferred way, or the way that one has to in order to cope with prevailing circumstances. It becomes unclear how libraries might order their priorities differently.

For whatever reason, libraries do presently emphasize—and emphasize heavily—activities that are characteristic of information retrieval rather than those which are not, even within the range of activities which have to do with communication and becoming informed. (Different aspects of access will be examined further in chapter 15.)

The historical features of retrieved objects

In the previous chapter, we discussed the essentially historical aspects of indexing or "signaling through time" in Mooers' words.[8] We now extend that discussion to consider the consequences of these essentially historical aspects for the process of becoming informed.

All communication is somewhat historical in at least the trivial sense that the physical communication of signals must take some time. In direct interpersonal dialog, the delay is so short as to be insignificant. However, when it comes to reading documents, the delay becomes more important.

Setting aside, until later, the special cases of intentional and unintentional inaccuracy in writing, we find that the most that can be said of a text is that it records what was alleged to be accurate as of the time it was written. It is usually assumed that the assertions are still accurate at the time of retrieval. However, two points are fundamental to written statements:

1. They are only descriptions and should not be confused with what they describe. A written statement to the effect that the moon is made of green cheese does not, in and of itself, guarantee that this is so, nor does it cause the moon to become so.
2. Even if the description were accurate at some point in time, it does not follow that the accuracy will continue. Even an accurate statement that, on a given day, the exchange rate for the U.S. dollar was 13.90 Austrian schillings, does not constitute reliable evidence that the exchange rate will still be 13.90 a year later.

The importance of this historical aspect will depend on the changeability of the reality being described. The longitude and latitude of the city of Berkeley do not vary, but the availability of specific houses for sale in Berkeley does. One can, therefore, use an old gazetteer to ascertain geographical coordinates with more confidence than an old list of houses for sale when seeking to buy a house.

The factual data derived from libraries tend to be the reporting of what is printed in the latest edition of whatever book contains data on the matter in question. Crowley's study of the accuracy of public library

---

[8] C. N. Mooers, "Mooers' Law, or, Why Some Retrieval Systems are Used and Others Are Not," *American Documentation* 11 (1960): 204.

reference services was criticized because, although the sorts of questions he asked were reasonable ones (e.g., "What is the name of the Secretary of Commerce?"), they did tend to deal with matters that were volatile relative to the currency of the reference works generally found in libraries.[9] All data and documents yielded by retrieval systems necessarily relate to a past state of affairs.

For some special purposes, the administrative fiction is used that the recorded descripton is to be *deemed* accurate unless it can be proved incorrect. This is to be expected when ascertaining the actual state of affairs is substantially more difficult than referring to retrievable data. The description is, officially, true. This is usually assumed in airline seat reservations. It is also importantly true of ownership, as for example, the ownership of houses. Proving that official records are in error may be a substantial task.

A further consequence of the time interval in retrieval-based information systems is that use of them must necessarily be an historical activity. For some purposes, especially in the study of the humanities, this may be advantageous. One might very well wish to compare what Austrian writers thought before, as opposed to after, the dissolution of the Hapsburg empire. To repair an elderly elevator, one would probably find an elderly repair manual more helpful than a recent one. In the humanities, the range of uses for which records are needed is extremely extensive. Most obviously, this includes biographical data of all kinds: age, attitudes, activities. Further, there are literatures of many genres which reflect the human experience. A proper understanding of the social and cultural contexts that are distant in time or space is important for the proper comprehension of the human experience of people in those places and/or times. The range of circumstances in which people need to use records to reconstruct the past is very large: stage-set design, restoration of houses, appreciation of past literature, and so on.

Logically distinct but similar in practice is the attempt to examine parts of the past in order to examine and, perhaps, explain how the present came to be—or, indeed, how the present is.

In scientific studies, essential features are the statement of hypotheses and the replicability of experiments. These have to be formally recorded. They become historic records to be stored for future critical examination. Without this "archive" or "corpus" denoting the "body" of science, the cumulative development of science through the scientific method as we know it would not be possible.

For the conscious study of the past, the historical nature of records

⁹ T. Crowley and T. Childers, *Information Service in Public Libraries: Two Studies* (Metuchen, N.J.: Scarecrow Press, 1971). Summarized and discussed in F. W. Lancaster, *The Measurement and Evaluation of Library Services* (Washington, D.C.: Information Resources Press, 1977), pp. 91 ff.

seems self-evident. What is less self-evident in practice is that all use of retrieval-based information systems is necessarily historical. Records are descriptions of how something is supposed to be. After the recording process, the record describes what was—or, rather, what was supposed to be. In accounting systems, the record describes how income and expenditures were supposed to be at the time the record was made—or, more commonly, for some even earlier point in time since in accounting it is inconvenient to keep absolutely up-to-date. Weather stations record the temperature and other climatic phenomena at particular points in time. A will records the maker's intentions at the particular date with respect to the transmission of his or her property. Even if one consults such records promptly, one cannot know with certainty that the financial situation indicated in the accounts, the temperature at the weather station, or the desired disposition of property is still as described. Indeed, a change within hours is likely in the first two cases. One may choose to assume that there have been no significant changes, but that is different from knowing with certainty that there have been none. One cannot ascertain by inspection of a record alone whether or not what is recorded is, at the time of inspection, an accurate reflection of the object described. It is, however, sensible to assume that the description is accurate if the probability of change is believed to be low and/or the consequences of being misinformed are not expected to be serious.

A special case occurs when the object retrieved is not a document (i.e, not a conscious description). Museum objects, for example, can be highly informative without being descriptions, e.g., fossil or an obsolete farm implement. However, the difference is superficial. The museum object is regarded as informative about the situation whence it derives, just as a document is. It is possible, in both cases, for the resulting information to be misleading since what is retrieved might be an unrecognized fake, might have been assigned incorrect attributes (of provenance, of nature), and, even if neither a fake nor wrongly attributed, might still be mis- leadingly atypical. Of course, the situation whence it derives is likely to have changed in the meanwhile.

The difference between document and museum artifact would appear to lie more in the assumptions of the beholder than in the signals perceived. That is, we are more likely with documents and data to assume that the information derived describes the present time as well as describing the time of its creation. Indeed, it may sometimes be necessary as a practical matter to make such an assumption. Yet, it remains an assumption of uncertain validity.

Misinformation, harm, and distress

In order that we may later consider the "goodness" and the evaluation of library services, it is desirable to examine two evaluative aspects of becoming informed.

Misinformation

Let us consider the case of misinformation wherein one's knowledge is changed to include "facts" (or rather beliefs) that are false. In simple cases, this is fairly straightforward. If the flight to New York is scheduled to leave San Francisco airport at 9:27 *a.m.* but the travel agent states that it is scheduled to leave at 9.27 *p.m.*, one is being falsely informed.

If one probes more deeply into the question of truth and falsehood, one rapidly gets into difficult philosophical issues which we prefer to leave to others. We simply note that one can be misinformed (intentionally or otherwise) and that even information believed to be correct at the time (e.g., scientific knowledge) may well be regarded as incorrect at some future time.

Harm and distress

Misinformation is generally associated with harm and distress. One may be distressed or harmed (or both) by missing an airline flight to New York because one was misinformed about the the time of departure. However, although misinformation is commonly distressing and harmful, truth is different from benefit. It can happen that one is distressed by information generally accepted as correct, as when learning that there isn't a single "real" Santa Claus. One can even be harmed by correct information. An example of this is the argument that publishing reliable predictions of earthquakes might cause more disruption than would refraining from publishing them. Hence, the phrase "Ignorance is bliss." (*Mis*-information and *lack* of information are not the same, but the distinction does not appear to be important for present purposes.)

On the other hand, it can conceivably happen, even if only exceptionally, that misinformation is beneficial. This would be the case if the flight to New York, which one missed through misinformation, were to crash after take-off.

Our intention here is merely to assert that knowledge is not necessarily always beneficial, nor ignorance (or misinformation) necessarily always harmful or distressing. Yet, in so arguing, we are necessarily asserting social values since beneficial and harmful imply some standard of value. One could make the argument that knowledge is invariably beneficial and lack of correct knowledge is invariably harmful. Yet to do so would imply that one's dominant social value is knowledge. While one could adopt such a social value, it is clear that it is not universally accepted. More commonly, happiness in this world or the next is seen as dominant, with knowledge regarded as normally beneficial because instrumental. As soon as one gets away from the dominant notion of knowledge itself being the supreme social value, then there is scope for knowledge to be at odds with social values. This is seen in censorship. The view is commonly found that the retrieval of pornographic materials is, in at least some circumstances, contrary to human happiness. The view is also commonly found that the unrestricted dissemination of some religious, social, or political views—or secrets of national defense—can be harmful. However, our present purpose is to analyze not to evaluate. We seek only to assert that such social values can be held by people who are involved in the offering of library services. It is important to stress that these attitudes to information and misinformation derive from individuals' social values.

A different but related matter is the assignment of priorities to different sorts of knowledge. Even if some sorts of knowledge are not perceived as being harmful (for example, horse racing results), one might feel that the social benefits derived from such knowledge are trivial compared with other sorts of knowledge, such as home improvements, literary master-pieces, or one's own political or religious point of view. Such views of priorities will affect the relative benefit attributed to being informed in different ways. This may sound paternalistic. It is. Library services *are* normally provided by some for others.

Limitations on the helpfulness of library services

Although library services are, by general consent, intended to be helpful, there are at least two different ways in which the librarian cannot be entirely sure what will be helpful for a given patron because the information is only fully significant in relation to the unknowable inner workings of the user's mind. We have noted above that the process of becoming informed depends on the combination of signals from outside and the cognitive skills and prior knowledge within the user's mind. The librarian cannot fully know what the cognitive skills and prior knowledge of the user are. However, an imprecise estimate may be sufficient for most practical purposes.

A deeper problem has to do with the use of information. In seeking information, it is likely that the user is interested in making a more informed decision in some matter. (The assumption is that becoming better informed will result in a better decision. This is plausible but not certain!) However, decisions are taken on the basis of criteria determined by the decision maker, otherwise the process would be measurement or implementation rather than genuine decision making. The values guiding the decision are necessarily in the mind of the decision maker. Indeed, they may be rooted deep in the subconsciousness of the decision maker who may not be fully conscious of his or her motivating values. It is even less possible for the librarian to know these values; and without a complete knowledge of what the values are, it is not possible to know fully what information would be pertinent.

In brief, the librarian cannot expect to know completely what information is appropriate for decision making even when the decision to be made has been described.

In the last four chapters we have considered why people might want to use libraries, how collections and retrieval systems serve to provide access to data and documents that might be useful, and the process of becoming informed by what has been retrieved. These three processes form a cycle. In the next three chapters we move away from this cycle and look at library services in broader terms. In the next chapter we ask what determines the amount of use that is made of libraries. We then ask how library services come to be provided in the manner and to the extent that they are. In attempting to answer this question we start, in chapter 11, by viewing library services as they are ordinarily provided—as a free public service. In chapter 12 we broaden this discussion to include some consideration of the effects that might result if library services were provided on a commercial basis.

10

Demand

Definition

Various sorts of needs and wants with respect to library service have been discussed in the literature of librarianship. These include:

1. needs that are not recognized as needs—or not recognized as needs for which library services would be useful;
2. needs that are recognized but, nevertheless, no action is taken to use a library service in relation to them;
3. wants (in the sense of desires) to use a library service, whether or not such use is sensible in practice;
4. unsuccessful attempts to use a library service, as when a particular book is sought but is not found;
5. satisfied demand, in the sense that the library was used in a way that was satisfactory to the user.

A variety of terms have been coined in relation to these various sorts of needs and wants.[1] However, we will deal directly only with the last two; both of which represent actual use of a library service. This constitutes the expressed demand (in an economic sense) with which the supplier of library service is dealing. As such, demand is a major determinant of what happens in library services.

However, merely to define demand does not provide much understanding. If we are to have any serious understanding of the structure and functioning of library services, we need to ask: What determines the demand for library services? We also need to know something of the dynamics of the demand for library services.

In exploring the determinants of demand, we take what is basically an economic approach except that we prefer to view "economic man" as being "cybernetic person." Whatever phrase is used, we mean a process with the following characteristics: individuals have desires that, in their own perceptions, could be satisfied by using a library—or, at least, the

---

1.   M. B. Line, "Draft Definitions: Information and Library Needs, Wants, Demands and Users," *Aslib Proceedings* 26, no. 2 (February 1974): 87; N. Roberts, "Draft Definitions: Information and Library Needs, Wants, Demand and Users: A Comment," *Aslib Proceedings* 27, no. 7 (July 1975): 308-13; and T. D. Wilson, "On User Studies and Information Needs," *Journal of Documentation* 37, no. 11 (March 1981): 3-15.

probability is high enough to warrant a try. Individuals weigh the perceived probable "price" of using the library service against the perceived probable benefit of doing so. Library use is likely to follow if the relative price is low enough. "Relative" not only means in comparison with the expected benefits of use but also in comparison with alternatives to that particular library service.

In exploring this theory of demand we will consider two of the paradoxes involved:

1. An economic theory based on price appears inconsistent with the fact that library services are ordinarily free.
2. If library services are provided for free, then libraries would appear to lack the responsiveness associated with market forces. Hence the suggestion that libraries ought to charge in order to become responsive.[2] Then, how is it that libraries exhibit considerable stability and powers of survival, which are characteristics usually associated with systems that are highly responsive to changing circumstances?

The resolution to both paradoxes comes with a reconsideration of the concept of price.

The real price

Economics texts vary in their treatment of the definition of price. Sometimes, price is defined as the monetary exchange value of commodities and services. Sometimes, that definition is implicitly assumed. At other times, a more general definition of price is given and, subsequently, the notion of money as a convenient mode of expression of the price is added as an extension:

> *Price*, measure of the value of a commodity that expresses its worth in exchange for other goods and services. Because it is more convenient to express the relative values of all goods in terms of a common unit of measure. ... In modern economies, the national currency serves this function. ...[3]

Adam Smith was emphatic on price being the sum of the disadvantages accruing to the purchaser: "The real price of everything, what everything really costs to the man who wants to acquire it, is the toil and trouble of acquiring it."[4]

If the "real price" is distinguished from the monetary expression of

---

[2] R. L. Ackoff et al., *The SCATT Report: Designing a National Scientific and Technological Communication System* (Philadelphia: University of Pennsylvania Press, 1976), p. 41. *Cf.* M. Getz, *Public Libraries: An Economic View* (Baltimore: Johns Hopkins Press, 1980), pp. 162-3.

[3] *Encyclopedia Britannica*. 15th ed. 1977. Vol. VIII, p. 204. s.v. "Price."

[4] A. Smith, *An Inquiry Into the Nature and Causes of the Wealth of Nations* (Oxford: Clarendon Press, 1976). Book 1, chapter 5, para. 2.

price, then we can reappraise both the nature of price and the applicability of price mechanisms—and, in particular, any nonmonetary expressions of price—especially in relation to public services. For convenience, the aspects of price will be considered under four headings: time, monetary cost, effort, and discomfort. We shall continue to use the library service as our example, but we do so in the belief that the discussion is of much wider applicability.

Time: delay as an expression of price

Other things being equal, sooner is better than later for anything one wants to have. There is a distinction to be made between waiting for something (during which time one might be able to use the time doing other things) and being obliged to spend much time doing or making it. In both cases, however, an opportunity cost is implicit. Waiting for a book to be made available (e.g., acquired, processed, fetched from the stacks, recalled from another user, obtained on interlibrary loan) is an unwelcome delay. There may be no doubt that a library service in which these delays are short is better than one in which they are long, other things being equal. Best of all is the library service in which books are immediately available, with the necessary tasks of preparation already performed by the time the demand occurs. One prefers not to have to expend the time or incur the delay to get the service.[5] (For a detailed treatment of time as a cost in the use of library services see Van House.)[6]

Money as an expression of price

The use of money as an expression of price needs no explanation. It is included here for completeness. One prefers to minimize (ideally to avoid) the expenditure of money to obtain service. Library services are generally free to those who use them. The exceptions (such as photocopying, online literature searching) tend to be reluctantly imposed, subsidized to keep costs down, and made free when possible. Fines for the late return

[5] *Cf.* "Waiting time does allocate public services, rationing them, as would money prices, according to the tastes, income and opportunity costs of consumers. Time prices differ from money prices, however, since they appear relatively lower to persons with a lower money value of time. ... Thus when two individuals who value their time unequally wait in the same queue, they face different prices." D. Nicols, E. Smolensky and T. N. Tideman, "Discrimination by Waiting Time in Merit Goods," *American Economic Review* 61, no. 3 (June 1971): 312-23.

[6] N. Van House, "Time Allocation Theory of Public Library Use," *Library and Information Science Research* 5, no. 4 (Winter 1983): 365-84. N. Van House *Public Library User Fees: The Use and Finance of Public Libraries* (Westport, Conn.: Greenwood Press, 1983). This monograph is a revised version of her doctoral dissertation: N. V. H. DeWath, "Demand for Public Library Services: A Time Allocation and Public Finance Approach to User Fees." Ph.D. dissertation. University of California, Berkeley, 1979. (Ann Arbor, Mich.: University Microfilms, order no. DEM 80-14651.)

of borrowed materials are better seen as a reluctantly imposed control device intended to sustain the level of service. If books do not come back, they are not available for others. Fines for overdue books are not a price in the normal sense, although they could be viewed as the exchange value for lateness. There is a sizable literature on rationales and techniques for pricing library services but that is not directly relevant here.[7]

Effort and discomfort: inconvenience as an expression of price

Both time and money vary in how they are valued by individuals according to the circumstances. Under these two factors (effort and discomfort), we include a number of considerations that are even less easy to handle than time and money. However, we are primarily interested in the "real price" rather than whether or not its expressions lend themselves to convenient quantitative analysis. Like elephants, inconveniences are easier to recognize than to describe. It is a nuisance to have to travel in order to obtain service. An overheated (or underheated), noisy reading room with a distracting decor makes use of a library service less pleasant. These factors can be cultural and interpersonal as well as physiological. One would prefer not to have to put up with such inconvenience in order to use a library service. If the inconvenience were great enough one would be deterred from using that library. Another library service which was less inconvenient, but otherwise comparable would be preferable.

These aspects of the "real price" invite several comments. It is clear that there can be nonmonetary elements of price in "the toil and trouble of acquiring it." Indeed, the monetary element may be minor or nonexistent.[8]

The question arises as to whether some of these aspects of price ought to be considered as part of the price at all. For example, delay could be viewed as much an attribute of the service or commodity as of the price. From an analytical point of view, there is scope for flexibility here. All of the elements of a cost-benefit relationship are part of the same equation, and it may not matter how one chooses to arrange them. The argument that monetary price is an incomplete expression of price could be countered by the response that, by definition, monetary price is being isolated on one side of the equation and that any aspects not expressed by monetary price can be regarded as attributes of the service or commodity (e.g., a slow service, an inconvenient service). Theoretically, there is a difference

[7] For example, C. A. Casper, "Pricing Policies for Library Services," *Journal of the American Society for Information Science* 30, no. 5 (September 1979): 304-9. See also C. K. Mick, "Cost Analysis of Information Systems and Services," *Annual Review of Information Science and Technology* 14 (1979): 37-64.

[8] Y. M. Braunstein, "Costs and Benefits of Library Information: The User Point of View," *Library Trends* 28, no. 1 (Summer 1979): 79-87.

between using monetary price as a convenient but incomplete representation of exchange value (in which case something has been lost) and asserting that monetary price is what happens to have been isolated on one side of the equation (in which case nothing has been lost).

Each aspect has the same sort of effect in terms of a price mechanism. As the time needed to obtain the service increases, the customer is more likely to give up. This may involve switching to an alternative source of supply or deciding to forego satisfying the need altogether. The elasticity of demand (the extent to which demand changes if the price changes) is well established with respect to monetary price. There are also limits to the amount of inconvenience people are willing to suffer to satisfy their needs. As with monetary price, the point at which people decide that the amount of inconvenience is too much can be expected to vary from one individual to another and from one situation to another. However, there appears to be no reason to doubt that elasticity of demand exists in library use with respect to the nonmonetary aspects of price as well as with monetary prices.[9] The more trouble it is to use a given library, the less one is inclined to use it. Given a choice of sources of service with different degrees of inconvenience, people will tend to choose rationally between them.

These different aspects of price are more or less interchangeable. People may be willing to pay to avoid delay. Others may be willing to save money by waiting, if, in their personal value system, money is scarce relative to time. Similarly, effort and/or discomfort may, for any given situation, be more (or less) preferable to delay or a monetary price. Every competent bureaucrat understands that the choice of process can affect the outcome and that a price mechanism can be invoked to discourage demand even without a monetary price: increased delays, more forms to complete, inconveniently located office, restricted hours of service, redirection from one office to another, instructions that take time to understand are but a few examples. Whether intentional or not, these increases in the nonmonetary aspects of price all have a dampening effect on demand just as the imposition of (or an increase in) monetary price does. If there were complete interchangeabiity between the aspects of price and if there were perfect understanding of what the exchanges were, then all aspects of price could, very conveniently, be related to money. Such a degree of interchangeability appears to occur only in economic theory.

[9] The evidence is slight. Indeed, Casper found grounds for suggesting a lack of elasticity of demand, but that was in rather special circumstances: C. Casper, "The Impact of Economic Variables on the Demand for Library Services," *American Society for Information in Science. Information Choices and Policies. Proceedings of the Annual Meeting, 1979, Minneapolis* (White Plains, N.Y.: Knowledge Industry Publications, 1979), pp. 41-50. Evidence indicating elasticity can be found in M. K. Buckland, *Book Availability and the Library User* (New York: Pergamon Press, 1975).

With this general background, let us return to library services and consider what could happen if the demand for a particular text were to increase.[10] Sooner or later, all copies of that title in the library will be in use and demands for copies will be going unsatisfied. From the library's side there are at least four possible responses:

1. Acquire additional copies. Assuming no increase in the library's budget, this implies some internal reallocation of resources is feasible and acceptable. The price paid by users will include an opportunity forgone elsewhere: a degradation of service in some other respect. (This might well constitute a net improvement in the library service overall, but some disbenefit elsewhere in the library service is ordinarily involved, however slight.)

2. Increased availability could, alternatively, be achieved by faster turnaround. In other words, the librarian could shorten loan periods and/or confine copies to the reading room, so that they will become available for others all the sooner. In this case, instead of imposing a price in terms of a reduction of service elsewhere in the library (as when diverting money to buy extra copies), the service is made less convenient in a different way for the users of that title. Whether they will accept the increased inconvenience and still use the library's copies or decide that they are unwilling to tolerate the reduced convenience, the library has, in fact, responded to regain earlier levels of availability.

3. The library could introduce a monetary charge for preferential treatment. This would be a commercial market response by the library. This move should be expected to reduce demand, and it would bring in some income to improve the service (e.g., by acquiring more copies), and it might make the waiting more tolerable for those who prefer not to pay but realize that they could pay for faster service if they valued their time highly enough relative to their money.

4. A common response is to do nothing. At least, the librarian can decide to adopt no specific response to restore the level of availability. In this, the time aspect of price, the delay, is being increased for the library users.

It is clear that the librarian has more than one possible response. It is also clear that each response improves the service but also increases the real price to the library users, but in substantially different ways. The choice of response by the librarian implies a decision to change the mixture of elements in real price to the library users for using the library.

---

[10] For a detailed discussion see M. K. Buckland, *Book Availability*, summarized in M. K. Buckland, "An Operations Research Study of a Variable Loan and Duplication Policy at the University of Lancaster," *Library Quarterly* 42, no. 1 (January 1972): 97-106.

The response of the user of the library to a change in the real price can be expected to be the same as in any other situation of demand for a commodity or service: the customer can accept the price involved (mainly time and inconvenience in this case), can substitute another source (go to another library, borrow the personal copy of a friend, or buy a copy), can accept a substitute service (a copy of a different title in lieu of the one originally sought), or decide to give up, leaving the need unsatisfied. *Which* decision any given individual will make will depend on the circumstances: the alternatives available; the importance, urgency, and specificity of the need; and the various values held by the individual with respect to time, money, and inconvenience. (See figure 10.1.)

Fɪɢ. 10.1   Determining the demand for library service

Copyright C. Barsotti. Reproduced with permission.

The customers' decisions determine the level of demand for the title. If the increase in demand is dampened enough, the balance of demand and supply will return to where it was originally. In this discussion, we have chosen an aspect of the logistics of library service to provide an example because it seems to illustrate the dynamics of the situation rather well. However, we believe that the same sort of mechanism applies generally.

The double feedback loop[11]

Of fundamental importance to the understanding of the dynamics of library services is the separateness of the responsive behavior of the user and that of the librarian. Let us illustrate this by considering further the example in the previous section of an activity central to library service: somebody looking for a copy of a particular book. Assuming that the library does, in fact, own the desired title and that the user has correctly identified its place on the shelves,[12] the probability of a copy being available when wanted depends on the interaction of three variables: the pattern of demand; the number of copies owned; and the length of time copies are unavailable when being used.

If the librarian knows that the availability of a particular title is low, then availability can be increased by adding extra copies and/or reducing loan periods. Such changes constitute adaptive responses (feedback) by the librarian to improve an unsatisfactory standard of service.

If the user does not find the book, then the user can respond in either of two sorts of ways: by coming back later, in which case the demand remains; or by taking other steps which will have the effect of reducing the demand on the document. One can switch to another library, buy a personal copy, use a friend's copy, or simply give up. This freedom of choice by the user constitutes a second, independent feedback mechanism. The second set of options result in a lowering of demand and, thereby, increased availability.

This double feedback loop (figure 10.2) is of interest from a cybernetic perspective. These two feedback mechanisms are substantially independent of each other in important ways.[13] The librarian's action does not depend

[11] This section is based on insights by Dr. A. Hindle, Department of Operational Research, University of Lancaster, England, during his participation in the work in the University of Lancaster Library Research Unit. For another account of this double feedback loop, see M. K. Buckland, "The Structure and Dynamics of Library Services," in *Progress in Cybernetics and Systems Research*, vol. XI, edited by R. Trappl, N. V. Findler and W. Horn. (Washington, D.C.: Hemisphere Publishing Corp., 1982): 147-51.

[12] For an analysis of the relative importance of different reasons why readers cannot find books on the shelves, see P. Kantor, "Availability Analysis," *Journal of the American Society for Information Science* 27, no. 6 (October 1976): 311-9.

[13] The *double feedback loop* concept presented here could be described as an example of multiple, more-or-less independent primary feedback loops modifying the basic system. This is quite different from the notion of a *secondary feedback loop* (or secondary controller) which modifies the first feedback loop rather than the basic system. If a thermostat is a primary feedback loop controlling a heater, than a secondary feedback loop would control the setting on the thermostat rather than the heater. For a library example of secondary feedback loop, see Buckland, "Structure and Dynamics of Library Service:" "The term variable loan and duplication policy describes policies whereby the length of the loan and the purchase of additional copies are made to vary as a function of pressure of demand. Hence, changes in the level of demand induce an adaptive response by the library. The library service becomes more responsive to demand with respect to the maintenance of standards of service—in this case, the probability of desired documents being available when sought. The librarian's role can move from a primary level of control (responding to needs as perceived) to a secondary level of control adjusting built-in feedback mechanisms to maintain whatever standards of service can be afforded (p. 149)."

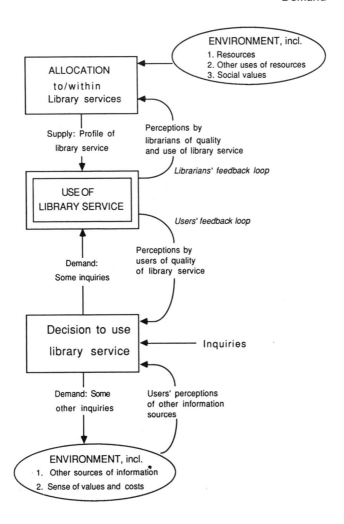

Fig. 10.2   The double feedback loop in library service

on response by the user; and the user's action does not depend on response by the librarian. Further, since library services are normally free, the library's income does not depend directly on the level of demand. Reduced demand, therefore, does not weaken the library as it would a business, where a drop in demand would reduce sales and, therefore, income. Quite the reverse, a reduced demand for a free service reduces the pressure, leaving the existing resources more adequate to cope with the remaining demand. (Similarly, serving increased demand may not be rewarding as it would for a commercial business.)

The dynamics of users' responses to the experience of trying to use library services has hardly been studied and its nature is not yet well known. However, the demand for library services appears to be elastic with respect to a price mechanism based on reliability, delay, convenience, ambience, and, where applicable, money. The adaptive aspects of library demand can be viewed as stabilization by the user with respect to a balance of effort and benefit. If the price of trying to use a library service is perceived by the users as increasing relative to the benefit and/or the alternatives, the frequency of use can be expected to diminish.

Although the librarian *can* respond to improve availability, such response is not very probable because, with present library techniques, evidence about the unsatisfied searches by users commonly does not reach the librarian in any reliable, useful way.

However, the user always knows whether or not the book was found. The user's feedback mechanism will be in effect, whether or not the librarian responds. In other words, it is the responsiveness of the users, more than the responsiveness of the librarians, which serves to restore stability to the library service. This helps to explain a noteworthy cybernetic aspect of library services: Library services can survive with remarkable stability even in the absence of effective library management. Survive, that is, not excel.

As the structure and dynamics of library service have come to be more explicitly understood, it has become possible to make the library's feedback mechanism more effective. For example, variable loan and duplication policies can relate the length of loan and the purchase of duplicate copies more directly to pressures of demand. Hence, changes in the level of demand can induce an adaptive response by the library. The library service can, thus, become more responsive to demand with respect to the maintenance of standards of service—in this case, the probability of desired documents being available when sought. The librarian's role can then move from a primary level of control (responding directly to needs as perceived) to a secondary level of control (adjusting built-in feedback mechanisms to maintain such standards of service as are deemed affordable). Computer-based systems for recording loans can provide, as a by-product, the necessary management information.

However, our present concern is not so much with the mechanics of book availability but, rather, with illustrating the double feedback loop—the separate identities of supply mechanisms from demand mechanisms in libraries where we can assume that the funding of the library service is not derived from charging the user. (When this assumption ceases to be true, the two feedback loops begin to merge into one as will be discussed in chapter 12.)

In the next section we discuss further the ways in which the demand for library services might be sensitive to various factors.

The sensitivity of demand

Historically, research in librarianship has been largely dominated by studies of retrieval and of the history of the book. Study of the dynamics and sensitivity of demand has been seriously neglected. There have been thousands of "user studies," but these have generally been surveys at particular points in time. Hence, as with a photograph, one may get a clear view of the situation at a given moment, but learn little or nothing of the trends, let alone the dynamics of the situation. This is a serious criticism, since applicable research generally involves trying to answer the question: "What would happen if ...?" If it is not at all well known how demand would change if the provision of library services were to be altered, then one knows very little about "What would happen if ...?"

It would be an exaggeration to say that there have been *no* studies leading to models of the dynamics of users and/or of library services. For example, the phenomena examined in bibliometric studies do reflect patterns of user behavior.[14] There have also been a few formal model-building studies of library use.[15] Nor should we ignore the knowledge and "feel" which come with experience of library practice yet may not be reflected in the research literature. What is seriously lacking, however, are models of information-gathering behavior, especially marketing models of consumer preferences in relation to library services.

It is known that *accessibility* is a dominant factor in information-gathering behavior. Perceived convenience influences greatly the choice of source of information.[16] The probability that documents will be immediately available when wanted—itself an index of convenience of accessibility—has also emerged as influential with respect to demand.[17] The opening of a new more congenial library building is known to increase use of library services.[18] The geographical location of a library also

[14] See chapter 16 below. Also F. Narin and J. K. Moll, "Bibliometrics," *Annual Review of Information Science and Technology* 12 (1977): 35-58.

[15] B. S. Nozik, "A Stochastic Model to Predict Demand for Library Services" (Ph.D. thesis, University of California, Berkeley, School of Librarianship, 1974. University Microfilms no. 70-18704); W. M. Shaw, "Loan Period Distribution in Academic Libraries," *Information Processing and Management* 12 (1976): 157-9.

[16] V. Rosenberg, "Factors Affecting the Preferences of Industrial Personnel for Information Gathering Methods," *Information Storage and Retrieval* 3 (1967): 119-27; T. J. Allen and P. G. Gerstberger, *Criteria for Selection of an Information Source* (Cambridge, Mass.: MIT Sloane School of Management, 1967) (PB 176 899); I. W. Harris, "The Influence of Accessibility on Academic Library Use" (Ph.D. thesis, New Brunswick, N.J.: Rutgers University, 1966. University Microfilms order no. 67-5262); E. B. Swanson, "Information Channel Disposition and Use," *Decision Sciences* 18, no. 1 (Winter 1987): 131-45.

[17] Buckland, *Book Availability and the Library User.*

[18] For example, *An Architectural Strategy for Change: Remodelling and Expanding for Contemporary Public Library Needs. Proceedings of the Library Architecture Preconference Institute, New York, 4-6 July 1974,* edited by R. M. Holt (Chicago: American Library

(cont'd. on p.138)

affects the amount of use made of it.[19] All of these effects are to be expected. Using a reasonably planned new library building ought to involve less discomfort for the user than an older one; a site that is conveniently located minimizes travel effort; immediate availability saves time and effort.

These aspects of the real price do not lend themselves to direct quantification, but that fact does not make them any less real. For example, the effect of distance has been studied by various investigators, but the problem emerges as considerably less tractable than might appear at first sight. For example, it is not a matter of actual physical distance but rather of traveling time. Further, since more than one errand can be performed in one journey, the effort of making the journey can properly be shared between different goals, e.g., between going to the library and going shopping. Nor are all modes of traveling equally congenial, nor the same mode at different times, since one can be more or less busy and the weather more or less pleasant. These factors all conspire to make quantification difficult.

As with other human perceptions of value, the appraisal of the "price" of distance is not linear. In other words, an increase in distance from 10 meters to 100 meters is much more significant than an increase from 100 meters to 190 meters, let alone an increase from 10,000 meters to 10,090 meters, even though each example constitutes an increment of the same amount: 90 meters. In terms of perceived and actual impact on behavior, changes from 1 meter to 10, from 10 to 100, and from 100 to 1,000—geometric as opposed to linear progression—are more likely to have comparable effects.[20]

Even though the dynamics of library use are poorly understood and quantitative analysis of the behavior of individual library users is difficult, some general "laws" or patterns have been discovered in information-gathering behavior. In the next section, three general laws that reflect patterns in the demand for library services will be described.

Three patterns of demand: scattering, decay, and inertia

Quantitative studies of the use of library services have resulted in the discovery of three patterns of usage so frequently that each has been

Association, 1976), p. 85; M. E. Veblen, *Giant Strides Since Andrew Carnegie: Creative Architecture in the King County Library System* (Seattle: Shovey Bookstore, 1975), p. 58. See also *American Libraries* 11, no. 10 (November 1980): 623; 13, no. 5 (May 1982); 322; and 13, no. 6 (June 1982); 356.

[19] E. S. Palmer, "The Effect of Distance on Public Library Use: A Literature Survey," *Library Research* 3 (1981): 315-54.

[20] *Cf.* B. C. Brookes, "The Foundations of Information Science. Part III. Quantitative Aspects: Objective Maps and Subjective Landscapes," *Journal of Information Science* 2, no. 6 (1980): 269-75.

referred to as a "law": scattering, decay, and inertia. Between them they do much to define the "shape" of the use of library services.

Scattering: the variation in demand from title to title

It is obvious that some books and articles are used more than others. For every book in a library, there are thousands that the librarian has not seen fit to acquire because the expected usage is deemed too low. Within every library, there are books that have remained unused for years and others that are in heavy demand.

The literature of a subject can be represented by a comprehensive list of articles on that subject. This list can be regarded as representing the literature needed by library users interested in that subject. Analysis of such a list will indicate which periodicals contain a large number of these articles, and it can be presumed that these periodicals will be more useful to this group of users than periodicals that contain very few or none of the articles.

Citations in articles or books can be analyzed on the assumption that an author will refer only to items useful for an understanding of his topic. The totality of such citations can, therefore, be regarded as an approximation of the useful literature of a subject as defined by the group of articles and books whose citations were analyzed—commonly "the ten leading journals on. ..." Periodicals that are relatively heavily cited are likely to be more useful than those that are cited little or not at all.

Actual usage of items as recorded on a library's borrowing records, requisition slips, or other records is relevant in that it reflects the usage made of the stock of a library by its readers. Certainly, the data will lack details of items used inside the library, usage of copies personally owned or borrowed from other libraries, or attempts to use items not found in the library.[21] However, attempts to make explicit adjustments for these factors rapidly become unmanageable and the adjustments for the last two are unnecessary if one is concerned with measuring the actual use of a particular library as opposed to measuring the cosmic importance of a given title.

It should be clearly admitted that all three methods of analysis measure different things, but all three types of data can be treated as approximate guides to the variations in usefulness of specific titles to different groups of users, even though all three methods are open to criticism on theoretical grounds. All three, however, are practical techniques and, what is more important, the literature available seems to suggest that all three give quite similar results.

---

[21] The relationship between recorded use (usually loan records) and unrecorded use has not been adequately studied. There is some indication that the two sorts of usage correlate, e.g., A. Hindle and M. K. Buckland, "In-library Book Use in Relation to Circulation," *Collection Management* 2, no. 4 (Winter 1978): 265-77.

The pioneer of the analysis and description of the variation in demand from title to title was S. C. Bradford, then Librarian of the Science Museum Library in London. He examined the literature of applied geophysics and the literature of lubrication.[22] In each case, he counted the number of references to each periodical title. This indicated the variation from title to title in each subject. He then ranked the titles according to their productivity (the number of references contributed by that periodical to the literature concerned) and created a description of each literature by drawing a graph showing the number of references contributed by the single most productive periodical, the number contributed jointly by the two most productive periodicals, the three most productive periodicals, and so on. Naturally, the additional number of references contributed by successively less productive periodicals became fewer and fewer. However, Bradford noticed that this decreasing productivity followed a recognizable pattern; and, since he had been writing in terms of the "scattering" of a literature over journal titles, this pattern came to be known as "Bradford's Law of Scattering."

The pattern identified by Bradford took on a new significance with the realization that it was, in effect, a law of diminishing returns with respect to the increase in the number of titles in a collection—always assuming that more useful titles are acquired before less useful titles. Seen in this perspective, the pattern that Bradford perceived becomes not so much a statistical curiosity in subject bibliography as a potentially powerful tool in the economic analysis of library provision.[23]

Decay: the variation in demand for a title through time

The demand for library services is characterized by chronological patterns. Most of the research in this area has been concerned with the variation in usage from year to year. It has been found consistently that the annual usage of books declines ("decays") with age.

Although a negative exponential pattern of obsolescence is generally accepted for both monographs and periodicals, rigorous analysis becomes very difficult for reasons that have been stressed in Brookes' lucid treatment of obsolescence[24] and also by Fussler and Simon.[25]

[22] S. C. Bradford, "Sources of Information on Specific Subjects," *Engineering* 137, no. 3550 (January 1934): 85-6. [Reprinted in: *Reader in Operations Research for Libraries*, edited by P. Brophy et al. (Englewood, Colo.: Information Handling Services, 1976), pp. 170-4; and in *Collection Management* 1, nos. 3-4 (Fall-Winter 1976-77): 95-103]; S. C. Bradford, *Documentation* (London: Crosby Lockwood, 1948).

[23] For additional reading on scattering, see E. A. Wilkinson, "The Ambiguity of Bradford's Law," *Journal of Documentation* 28, no. 2 (June 1972): 122-30; Narin and Moll, "Bibliometrics."

[24] B. C. Brookes, "The Growth, Utility, and Obsolescence of Scientific Periodical Literature," *Journal of Documentation* 26, no. 4 (December 1970): 283-94.

[25] H. H. Fussler and J. L. Simon, *Patterns in the Use of Books in Large Research Libraries* (Chicago: Chicago University Press, 1969).

There are two views of the "decay" of demand:

- In a *diachronous* view, one is concerned with the use of a given document in succesive years—"through time"; and
- In a *synchronous* view, one is concerned with the distribution of use made during a given span of time of documents of different ages.

Either way, a similar pattern tends to emerge and, like scattering, can be regarded as a law of diminishing returns with respect to the length of time books are retained.[26]

Inertia: the variation in demand with distance

Earlier in this chapter we discussed effort as being a significant part of the price involved in the use of library services. One particular manifestation of the effect of human inertia—or, more elegantly, economy of effort—may be seen in the decline in the use of libraries as the distance to be traveled increases.[27]

These three empirically found patterns appear to reflect mechanisms that are not yet well understood. Numerous studies have pointed to the existence of such patterns, but very little systematic attention has been paid to the problem of explaining *why* they are found.

The rate of decay in the demand for books with time is generally regarded as varying from one field of discourse to another. So also, it would seem, does the rate of scattering. There is some indication that this variation is associated with variations in the "hardness/softness" of different areas of study, the extent to which concepts can be unambiguously defined. After all, if subject areas do, indeed, vary in their "hardness/softness" and if this does reflect some variation in the definability of concepts, then one should expect "hardness/softness" to emerge as an important variable in the study of information. Further, one should also expect to find manifestations of it in empirical patterns of information use.[28]

---

[26] For further reading on decay, see M. B. Line and A. Sandison, "'Obsolescence' and Changes in the Use of Literature with Time," *Journal of Documentation* 30, no. 3 (September 1974): 283-350.

[27] See Palmer, "The Effect of Distance on Public Library Use: A Literature Survey," *Library Research* 3 (1981): 315-54.

[28] M. K. Buckland and A. Hindle, "Library Zipf," *Journal of Documentation* 25, no. 1 (March 1969): 52-7. This short paper is substantially extended by R. A. Fairthorne, "Empirical Hyperbolic Distributions (Bradford-Zipf-Mandebrot) for Bibliometric Description and Prediction," *Journal of Documentation* 25, no. 4 (December 1969): 319-43. M. K. Buckland, "Are Scattering and Obsolescence Related?" *Journal of Documentation* 28, no. 3 (September 1972): 242-6. Note that D. de S. Price had independently posited a relationship between decay and hardness/softness: D. de S. Price, "Citation Measures of Hard Science, Soft Science, Technology, and Non-Science," in *Communication Amongst Scientists and Technologists*, edited by C. E. Nelson and D. K. Pollock (Lexington, Mass.: D. C. Heath, 1970), pp. 3-22.

Even though the inner workings of the demand mechanism determining the patterns of the use of library services are not well understood, some of the effects can be observed empirically. Three of these effects can be seen in regularities in the distribution of demand from title to title, in the distribution of demand for titles through time, and in the variation in demand with distance. The dismal-sounding trinity of scattering, decay, and inertia warrant attention because they are manifestations of user behavior and, as such, deserve to be central in the design of library services.

In the next two chapters we move from discussion of the *demand* for library services to consideration of the *provision* of library services. How do they come to be provided in the manner and to the extent that they are?

11

Allocation I. Resources, Priorities, and Political Processes

Definition

So far we have examined inquiries, retrieval, becoming informed, and the demand for library services. Apart from occasional remarks, we have not considered what we might well have started with: What sorts of library services are provided, and why? Or, rather, more analytically: What determines what sorts of services are provided? In order to tackle this question we shall adopt the convenient strategy of starting with some simple and naive assumptions in order to reach a simplified explanation. Then we shall gradually discard these assumptions during this chapter and the next in an attempt to match the complexity of reality more closely.

The scale and nature of a library's services are determined by the allocation of resources to and within the library service. We include the setting of priorities as being a part of the allocation process, since determining that support of one activity should take priority over another is tantamount to a preferential allocation of resources. As resources we include anything that could have been used in other ways: money, buildings, effort, equipment, and staff time.

The ability to make and enforce regulations can in itself be seen as a kind of resource. Like other sorts of resources, regulations are used as means for achieving ends. To some extent, regulations are substitutable for other resources. For example, the ability to enforce loan periods of a limited duration has an effect on the availability of library books comparable (though not identical) to the expenditure of additional money to buy duplicate copies. One may even be able to make a very crude estimate of the amount of money saved by specific regulations.[1]

Note that we are discussing what is provided not what is used. One cannot make people use particular library services. Nevertheless, decisions are made as to what particular services are to be provided, to what extent

---

[1] M. K. Buckland, *Book Availability and the Library User* (New York: Pergamon Press, 1975), chapter 7.

they are to be provided, and with what relative priorities. It is essentially a process of allocation of resources and of priorities. The allocation *to* the library determines the overall scale of operations, the allocation *within* the library affects the detailed mixture of specific services, and the mixture of services implies and supports the mission of the library.[2]

We assume that libraries are services provided by some for others. Usually, but not always, the funding for libraries is derived, directly or indirectly, from public funds, i.e., from taxpayers. This is most clearly seen in the case of public libraries and school libraries. The situation is more complicated with university libraries where tuition fees, donations, and overheads on research grants are also sources of university income. Most of the income, however, derives directly or indirectly from public funds. In corporations, library services are commonly offered as a support service and are included in the cost of doing business.

In the next chapter, we shall consider fees as a basis for the provision of library services and some of the implications of moving in that direction. Meanwhile, we start by confining our attention to the limited but typical situation wherein library services are not provided on a commercial basis, but are free in the sense that they are supported by resources which are not derived directly from the users. The users of public libraries do, in effect, pay for the services, by and large, but the connection is indirect: The users may be paying in their capacity as payers of local taxes but not because they are users.

The process of allocation to and within library services—when on a noncommercial basis—is a *political* process. This does not imply that all decisions are made through formal political parties, elections, and the like but, rather, that we regard politics as having to do with who gets what, who controls the decisions about who gets what, and how control is exercised in practice.

Webster's definition of political process is, "the process of the formulation and administration of public policy usually by interaction between social groups and political institutions or between political leadership and public opinion."[3] Although this refers primarily to the affairs of cities, states, and nations, it appears reasonable to follow common practice in extending it to universities, corporations, and other organizations in which resources are allocated.

---

[2] Charles McCarthy, 1873-1921, who allocated resources at the Wisconsin Legislative Reference Library in such a way as to influence what legislation was passed, provides a good illustration. M. Casey, *Charles McCarthy: Librarianship and Reform* (Chicago: American Library Association, 1981).

[3] *Webster's Third New International Dictionary of the English Language,* unabridged (Springfield, Mass.: Merriam Co., 1971).

Diffusion, subversion, and compromise

Having defined allocation as a political process, we now examine the structure of the process more closely and consider some of the factors likely to affect the process in practice.

Diffusion and management

There is a distinction—at least in theory—between those who allocate resources *to* the library (e.g., city council, university president) and the person responsible for administering the library, who allocates resources *within* the library. In theory, this distinction need not matter since the library director might have complete comprehension of and agreement with the intentions of those who allocated the money to the library, and the latter might have adequate technical understanding of what is involved in using the resources to achieve their goals. Such perfection of unanimity and common understanding, however, seems highly improbable in practice, and the director of the library is likely not only to have slightly different preferences but also a degree of latitude and discretion in the allocation within the library. In this way, the allocation process can be said to have been extended downwards.

Six factors make for a further diffusion of responsibility for allocation among those who are employed in the library:

1. Libraries are labor-intensive. In the United States, more than half of a library's budget is ordinarily spent on labor costs.
2. The organizational structures that prevail are largely hierarchical.
3. Larger library services are commonly decentralized geographically for the convenience of users.
4. Some degree of division or, rather, specialization, of labor is normal.
5. Precise, adequate, agreed measures of service are lacking.
6. The effects of providing service are unclear.[4]

This combination of factors means that responsibility for decision making becomes diffused, since many of the decisions concerning details are delegated, often to geographically dispersed areas. (We take "details" to include book selection and the detailed deployment of staff time, e.g., priorities within and between the general areas of helping users directly and of "housekeeping." Although individual decisions may be small in import, we do not wish to suggest that collectively they are unimportant.) Supervision and control by the library director are made more diffuse by the hierarchical levels, by the lack of accepted operational measures of

---

[4] In these and other ways, libraries have the characteristics of 'human service organizations.' For an excellent review of these characteristics see Y. Hasenfeld, *Human Service Organizations* (Englewood Cliffs, N.J.: Prentice-Hall, 1983).

library goodness, and, often, by the superior technical skills or greater local knowledge of those supervised. Since labor is a major part of the allocatable resources, it follows that anybody with any discretion over the deployment of his or her own time shares in the allocation process.

It is clear, then, that the implementation process tends to be widely diffused. In the same sense, insofar as management includes taking decisions which include the deployment of resources and priorities in order to get things done, one could also say that management is also very diffused in library practice. In effect, one can correctly describe the allocation process as a political and managerial process.

Displacement, approximation, and subversion

The diffusion of responsibility for the allocation of resources and priorities make the allocation process vulnerable to distortion in two sorts of ways:

1. The very diffusion places a strain on the communication of the values and goals motivating those who allocated resources to the library. In the communication and interpretation of these values, some distortion is to be expected.

2. Consciously or unconsciously, different people will tend to bias the selection of values and the choice of means of implementation in accordance with their own preferences. They may feel, quite consciously, that the official intentions are unrealistic, and quietly go about interpreting or implementing them in a way that accords more closely to their own sense of values and of the situation, with or without their own self-interest influencing this process. This distortion or adaptation of official intentions may or may not be beneficial from the users' perspective.[5]

A special case of goal displacement can result from concentration on a part of the service rather than on the whole. For example, devoting much expensive labor to very detailed cataloging or to investment in extensive special collections are both desirable when seen in isolation. Yet, at some stage, allocating increased resources to either could interfere with other more central purposes of the library service. This sort of problem can follow from undue emphasis on proximate measures of goodness—those that measure something that is close at hand and relatively easy to measure, rather than distal measures more concerned with the overall, ultimate purpose of the organization.

[5] See P. K. Tompkins and G. Cheney, "Communication and Unobtrusive Control in Contemporary Organizations," in *Organizational Communication: Traditional Themes and New Directions* edited by R. D. McPhee and P. K. Tompkins (Sage Annual Reviews of Communications Research, 13) (Beverly Hills: Sage Publications, 1985), pp. 179-210, esp. 187; Y. Hasenfeld, *Human Services Organizations* (Englewood Cliffs, N.J.: Prentice-Hall, 1983), chapter 4.

In the context of library services, one can think of various possibilities for goal displacement or goal subversion:[6] Fines might come to be treated as a source of income rather than a control device to induce the return of books and, if so, might be set so high as to discourage use of the library; the development of special collections could be beyond (and at the expense of) the reasonable needs of the library's users; one group of users might be given preferential service at the expense of more basic service to other groups of users; perfectionist recordkeeping or time-consuming participation in professional associations could benefit the librarians more than the users.

In any given case, such "goal displacement" might be considered an improvement or a deterioration according to one's perspective. Our present purpose is to analyze, not to evaluate. Hence, we make no judgment as to whether or not the subverting of official goals would lead to a better library service. Indeed, such adaptation is quite likely to be an improvement from the users' perspective since library staff who are low in the hierarchy are often in closer contact with the users. The important point is to recognize that this process of goal displacement is endemic. It can be seen, for example, in the selection of books that are of personal interest to the librarians rather than to the users. To the extent that employees act in accordance with their beliefs, some degree of goal displacement is to be expected.[7] The difficulty in defining and measuring the objectives and performance of library services is unhelpful in this regard.

Compromise

We have assumed, thus far, that there is one set of values and one dominant goal for any given library service. This is inherently unlikely even if only because libraries ordinarily serve groups whose interests do not entirely coincide. A university library service that suits professors best is not necessarily the one that would suit undergraduates best, even though there is substantial overlap. A public library service that emphasized service to local business and industry would not be of most help to local historians or to teenagers. The result is necessarily a compromise involving service to different groups simultaneously. However, it is unlikely to be just any, accidental compromise. Instead, the mixture of services will reflect, albeit rather imperfectly, the values and preferences of those who have been doing the allocation at all levels.

[6] For general introduction to goal displacement, see A. Etzioni, *Modern Organizations* (Englewood Cliffs, N.J.: Prentice-Hall, 1964, esp. p. 10.

[7] For a case-study in which it is implied that the librarians in a public library allowed their own professional values to subvert the use of resources away from the best interests of the users (in the authors' opinion), see F. Levy, A. J. Meltsner and A. J. Wildavsky, *Urban Outcomes: Schools, Streets, and Libraries* (Berkeley: University of California Press, 1974), pp. 165-218.

Mission, objective, and goal

Unfortunately, the terms for describing what one is seeking to achieve are inconsistently used: mission, objective, goal, target, aim, and so on. The best that can be done, if one wishes to use such terms precisely, is to specify explicitly the sense in which one is using each term and not to assume that others will adopt the same definitions.

A serious practical and theoretical problem is how to link or "articulate" the values which guide the initial allocation of resources in such a way that they also guide the detailed day-to-day practical decisions of the library staff. In order to consider this problem of relating decisions concerning what should be done to values and goals, we first present an example of a formal approach using three levels of statement. The example relates to a university library, but examples relating to other sorts of libraries would be similar enough to permit this example to be used as a basis for a general discussion of the problems involved.[8]

Level I: Mission statement

A mission statement is a broad definition of what business the library is in. What is the sphere of activity of the library? This should be a general and generally acceptable, definition of the role of the library, e.g., "To meet the informational requirements of the total university community."

Level II: Objectives

In order to articulate day-to-day work with the mission statement, it is convenient to spell out a list of sorts of activities the library attempts to perform in the pursuit of its mission. This list of objectives should be helpful in perceiving more clearly the best choice of specific tasks in relation to the mission. The list of objectives should be comprehensive, and might include:

---

[8] This material is a revised version of that found in J. Baaske et al., A Management Review and Analysis of Purdue University Libraries and Audio-Visual Center (West Lafayette, Ind.: Purdue University, Libraries and Audio Visual Center, 1973), pp. 34-7. This report was one of several that resulted from the use of the Management Review and Analysis Program (MRAP) in more than twenty large research libraries in North America. The program, developed by the Office of Management Studies of the Association of Research Libraries, is a do-it-yourself kit for studying and improving management functions in large research libraries. The kit itself, the MRAP "manual," is not yet publicly available (March 1982), but for a general description and evaluation see E. R. Johnson and S. H. Mann, Organization Development for Academic Libraries: An Evaluation of the Management Review and Analysis Program (Westport, Conn.: Greenwood Press, 1980). See also D. E. Webster, "The Management Review and Analysis Program: An Assisted Self-study to Secure Constructive Change in the Management of Research Libraries," College and Research Libraries 35 (March 1974): 114-25; M. K. Buckland, ed., "The Management Review and Analysis Program: A Symposium," Journal of Academic Librarianship 1, no. 1 (January 1976): 4-14.

1. To assess the informational requirements of the university community on a continuing basis by formal and informal interaction with all other elements of the university community.
2. To select from available information that portion most applicable to the requirements of the university community.
3. To acquire, organize, and arrange these informational resources in a manner and in a physical setting most conducive to their use.
4. To interpret and publicize an additional range of informational and educative services in order to increase the benefits of the library to all members of the university community.
5. To make available, interpret, and publicize an additional range of informational resources and services by active collaboration with other institutions through interlibrary loan, information networks, and cooperative arrangements.
6. To study the operations and services provided by the library to assure effective use of available resources.
7. To present and interpret to the funders the fiscal and other needs of the library.
8. To provide an environment in which to develop and maintain a capable staff.
9. To anticipate and plan for future developments in the informational needs and services which are likely to affect the university community.

Level III: Performance goals

Levels I and II are related to the library as a whole and deal with general statements. There remains the question of specific goals for individual units (or individuals) within the library. These are usually intended to serve as guidelines for day-to-day decisions concerning priorities for the use of time and other resources. They can also be used as yardsticks with which to assess performance and results. Examples tend to be specific and measurable:

> To check in and distribute all current serials on a same-day basis.
> To reshelve most returned books within four working hours.
> To continue the revision of catalog records, aiming to cover letters D through F by July.

Three problems arise concerning the mission, objectives, and goal of library services:

1. Libraries ordinarily serve a larger organization which supports them, e.g, university, school, corporation, or city or county. Social values and social goals are generally difficult to define in practical ways. Hence, schools, cities, and universities have difficulty in defining their own missions in any other than vague ways. Libraries, in turn, can define their missions as being to support the mission of their sponsoring bodies. If anything, this is likely to be even vaguer than the mission of the sponsoring body since the nature of the support also needs to be clarified. It is to be expected that the mission of the library will be at least as difficult to define as the mission of the sponsoring body.
2. At the other end of the spectrum from mission to goals, there is the endemic problem that the lower-level goals will come to lose their articulation with the upper-level mission and objectives. This is the more likely since, in practice, people tend to develop formal performance goals rarely and to use them even more rarely. The less close

the coordination, the more goal displacement is to be expected. Means may become ends.

3. At any level, there is the likelihood that objectives and goals will be left unrevised as circumstances change. This is not simply a matter of updating written statements which tend to be ignored anyway but, rather, the need to reconsider the continuing appropriateness of the bases for allocation whether they have been written down or not.

The separation of allocation and use

The separation of allocation from use has been repeatedly mentioned, notably in chapter 10. The Golden Rule expresses the situation with respect to allocation very aptly: "He (or she) who provides the gold, makes the rule!" However, this simplistic assertion needs to be qualified in various ways. We have already noted that the rules may be interpreted and subverted in the process of implementation. The use of services can be permitted, but cannot be mandated. The users can influence the allocation in the sense that heavy use of a particular service is likely (though not certain) to result in an increased allocation to that service lest the service collapse under the strain imposed on it. Contrariwise, a service that receives little or no usage is likely (though not certain) to result in a reduced allocation or even discontinuation. This is to be expected when the allocators emphasize the beneficial effects of usage rather than the mere provision of an opportunity to use a service. Users may well be actively involved in the political process that determines the allocation. They can, therefore, be influential. However, this influence arises from their involvement in the political process rather than from the fact that they are users. The fact that they are users, however, is likely to add legitimacy to their statements. The involvement of users in the political process tends to be sporadic and unrepresentative but, commonly, influential. Conscientious allocators are likely to be actively interested in users' views and, indeed, solicit them systematically. And, of course, users may share in the decision making if they contribute "gold." (We consider the effect of user fees in more detail in the next chapter.)

In the next section we consider the values and preferences that influence decisions concerning allocation and, therefore, the provision of services.

On the philosophy of librarianship

J. P. Danton, in his "Plea for a Philosophy of Librarianship," wrote, "The sad truth of the matter is that the profession has not concerned itself with evolving or even thinking about a philosophy."[9] Pleas such as that   of

---

[9] J. P. Danton, "Plea for a Philosophy of Librarianship," *Library Quarterly* 4, no. 4 (October 1934): 527-51. (Reprinted in *American Library Philosophy: An Anthology*,

(cont'd. on p. 151.)

Danton have not met with much response.[10] In this section we consider the notion of "philosophy" in relation to library service and then consider some evidence of its existence.

Webster's *Third New International Dictionary of the English Language, Unabridged* offers a number of definitions of "philosophy." The definition which would seem most meaningful in the phrase "philosophy of librarianship" is: "A system of motivating beliefs, concepts, and principles." This definition is followed by the illustrative quotations:

> The philosophy of a culture determines the general pattern of its ... institutions.
> Three philosophies contending for dominance in contemporary politics.
> The changing philosophy of the courts with regard to many questions.
> Set the ... philosophy and the basic course of the museum.

There is also a closely related definition: "Basic theory concerning a particular subject, process, or sphere of activity ... usually used with (philosophy of religion) (philosophy of education)." This definition has the following illustrative quotations:

> Design philosophy in chemical plants.
> The whole philosophy of the bill is to ignore the realities.
> A chance to prove my philosophy of flying the mail.
> Automation is a completely new philosophy of production.

This second definition is somewhat ambiguous in that it is not entirely clear whether or not the philosophy is deemed to be somewhat value-laden (as the first definition clearly is) or whether it is deemed to reflect a value-free understanding of the processes involved. If it is the latter, then it is synonymous with "theory" as we have used it in chapter 5. If it is value-laden—at least in part—then it overlaps significantly with the first definition.

We shall, therefore, use the first definition: "A system of motivating beliefs, concepts, and principles" to denote the philosophy of librarianship and to distinguish it from the "theory" of librarianship as defined in chapter 5.

---

selected by B. McCrimmon (Hamden, Conn.: Shoe String Press, 1975).) *Cf.*, J. Thompson: "The library profession must establish a philosophy, or philosophies. It must cast off to a large extent the all-pervading emphasis on technical matters, an emphasis which had its origins in the United States. From Dewey onwards we have had a succession of American experts on cataloguing, on library buildings, on storage methods, on circulation systems. We have been bowled over by American expertise and 'professionalism.' This kind of 'professionalism' has its place, but it becomes absurd when it is employed in a philosophical vacuum, and when it distracts attention from considerations of what a library is, what roles it should play, and what a librarian should aim to be." J. Thompson, *Library Power: A New Philosophy of Librarianship* (Hamden, Conn.: Linnet Books, 1974), p. 70.

[10]   A remarkable exception is A. Broadfield, *A Philosophy of Librarianship* (London: Grafton, 1949), which examines the implications for librarianship of adopting a radically liberal point of view. See also J. M. Christ, *Toward a Philosophy of Educational Librarianship* (Littleton, Colo.: Libraries Unlimited, 1972).

There remains a further problem of definition in that "librarianship" can be regarded as denoting either a body of knowledge or a group of professionals. In this case, our definition of philosophy will be seen to impel us toward the latter definition.

Librarianship as value-free technique

A philosopher, asked whether he was for or against a particular invention, replied that he thought the question itself was a curious one. The invention, he declared, was a mere implement—as was a hammer. He would be neither "for" or "against" a hammer, since as an implement it was a neutral object. If the hammer were to be *used*, then his attitude would relate to the intended *use* of the hammer. One might well approve of the use of a hammer to repair a roof but not to commit murder. One might also feel that a given use of a hammer might not constitute the most appropriate choice of the implement for the purpose intended—for example, for driving screws into wood. The use rather than the implement should be the object of moral appraisal.[11]

The technology and skills of librarianship are like a hammer. They are tools of implementation. There would seem no way to view them with approval or disapproval—only their use and their appropriateness to the purpose in relation to other options available.

Librarianship as a value-laden activity

It will be argued that library *service* , the use of technology and skills, is and must necessarily be deeply value-laden, in the sense that uses are involved which relate positively or negatively to social values.

Library services are provided by people who work within the policies and guidelines set by themselves and/or by other people. Since people have sets of values it would seem inherently unlikely that these values do not influence the decisions about the allocation of time and other resources and the priorities in service between the options available.

It is in the context of the present chapter that we need to move a step further and ask *which* (or *whose*) values?—and whose definitions of beneficial effects? In relation to whose goals can the effects be expected to be beneficial? Not everyone will agree that there are universal immutable values which are beneficial, independent of an independent human sense of values. Even if it were so agreed, whose definition or interpretation of

---

[11] For an extended discussion of the evaluation of bibliographical tools using references to hammers by way of illustration, see T. Hodges, "Forward Citation Indexing: Its Potential for Bibliographic Control" (Ph.D. dissertation. University of California, Berkeley, School of Librarianship, 1972. University Microfilms order no. BGD73-16787.) Chapter II: "Factors in Evaluation."

those values is to be adopted? In the absence of agreed interpretations of agreed universal values, we must select. Two very important questions are raised: upon what criteria (i.e., value system) is the allocation to be based? and who gets to do the allocating?

The answer to the first question would seem to depend, in practice, on the answer to the second. The answer to the second is not entirely straight-forward. A simple answer would seem to be that it is the funders: He who pays the pipers calls the tune! But a rather complex situation obtains in practice:

• The funders are not unconstrained: there are laws concerning the use of resources.

• The allocation of resources to the library will depend on the number, needs, and perceived relative importance of other, alternative possible uses of the resources, and the extent to which resources are available.[12]

• In a complex, labor-intensive situation, such as library service, many people may be involved in the allocation of resources, especially as their own time during working hours is one of the principal resources. Anybody working in a library, then, who has any discretion over the allocation of his or her own working time between two or more priorities can be said to be sharing in some part in the allocation of resources within the library service. To take an extreme, but not unthinkable case, a library employee who does his or her own personal work on library time can be said to be allocating (more strictly, perhaps, diverting) resources away from the library as a result of placing a higher value on personal benefits than on the benefits that would derive from the performance of the assigned library tasks.

We can, therefore, answer the question concerning who gets to do the allocating by stating that it is likely to be a lot of people, including: those with the political power to make laws; those who decide how great the resources of the library's parent-body (city, university, company, school, etc.) will be; those who, for any given library service, allocate resources between it and other alternative uses of those resources; and those who manage and suballocate resources within the options available for the detailed employment within the library service.

The set of people who do the allocating, therefore, not only includes those who influence general social priorities and the governing authorities of libraries' parent organizations, but also those who manage and those

---

[12] For a description of how severe the constraints can be see A. Olden, "Sub-Saharan Africa and the Paperless Society," *Journal of the American Society for Information Science* 38, no. 4 (July 1987): 298-304. Also M. Crowder, "The Book Crisis: Africa's Other Famine," in *Africa Bibliography*, edited by H. Blackhurst (Manchester, Eng.: Manchester University Press, 1986), pp. xvi-xxi.

who staff the library service. As in any organization, it is entirely possible for the staff who are ostensibly employed to implement official goals to subvert the goals of those who allocated resources to the library. However, in this context, "subvert" is a value-laden way of referring to the adoption of a different set of values. Hence, what may appear as "subversion" from one perspective may appear to be an improvement from another perspective, being good or bad according to one's choice of values.

In summary, we conclude that the provision of library services necessarily and unavoidably reflects the social values—the "motivating beliefs, concepts, and principles"—of people, and probably of many different people.

Dissension over the choice of values is at a minimum in the case of a private collector using his or her own resources for his or her pleasure. Outside of such purely personal collections, however, library services are provided by some for the benefit of others. Although the librarian (and some of the users) may be able to satisfy some feelings of bibliophily through collecting materials for a university library or other collection, this is likely to be merely incidental to the provision of library services. Recognition that the guiding value is likely to be something more than bibliophily brings us back to consideration of what the determinants of library service might be.

One value is the desire to preserve unique specimens for the future. This value manifests itself in many forms of preservation: museums, archives, historical monuments, nature refuges, and libraries. However, outside of national libraries and the special collections departments of public and academic libraries, this is likely to be a small part of the mission of any given library. The archival role of libraries is generally accepted as being important, but it would be difficult to sustain the argument that more than a small percentage of current expenditures is needed for it.

Institutional pride as a value may lead to the acquisition of choice items but this, again, is unlikely to constitute a major element in expenditures. It is more likely that the library's budget and resources are seen as a suitable means toward some sort of increase in knowledge or in happiness valued by the sponsoring body.

- A school principal can be expected to support a school library to the extent to which it is perceived as improving the education of school children, whether directly or in collaboration with the teachers.
- A university president can be expected to support a university library if the services (and their use) appear to foster learning and discovery by both faculty and students.
- The chief executive officer of a corporation can be expected to be

willing to support a library service if there is reason to believe that employees—engineers, marketing specialists, personnel officer, etc.—would be noticably more effective as the result of becoming better informed through the library service.

● A city council is likely to support a library service if a better-informed citizenry is desired and if it is felt the library is contributing to that end.

However, in all such cases, and other similar cases, the actual choices to be made may be quite specific. It may be felt that professors warrant more support than students, or that some disciplines should have more support than others: or do-it-yourself books and traditional cultural interests may seem to be more valuable than recreational reading and contemporary political controversies. Further, if library services are to be supported for these reasons, then they will also have to be perceived as being cost-effective in achieving those values. Otherwise, the sponsors could—indeed should—allocate their resources away from library services to other means perceived to be more cost-effective, such as increased formal instruction.

It is not, therefore, that philosophy of librarianship is absent but that it is endemic and pervasive.

Philosophy of librarianship in action

In the United States and in the United Kingdom, there is a general, if rather vague, consensus concerning the philosophy of the public library. The public library is seen as serving educational and recreational goals which include the socially desirable goal of a well-informed citizenry.[13] A Western democracy, it is argued in the United States, depends on an informed electorate. The public library, along with newspapers, radio, and television not controlled by the government (and not monopolized by anyone else) are important social institutions in the pursuit of this desired political goal. Another socially valuable goal ascribed the public library is that of being the "poor man's university." Even with the enormous investment in the provision of formal education in the United States and in the United Kingdom, the role of public libraries in facilitating informal education—for free—has been traditionally perceived as important and desirable. (Our present purpose is not to assess the extent of achievement of these goals, but to identify beliefs, concepts, and principles which are held and which are influential.) It should not surprise

---

[13] For a more critical analysis of public library goals see M. H. Harris, "State, Class, and Cultural Reproduction: Toward a Theory of Library Service in the United States," *Advances in Librarianship* 14 (1986): 211-52 and a review of it: D. Bergen, *Library and Information Science Research* 9, no. 2 (April-June 1987): 71-5. Also R. V. Williams, "The Public Library as a Dependent Variable: Historically Oriented Theories and Hypotheses of Public Library Development," *Journal of Library History* 16, no. 2 (Spring 1981): 329-41.

us that surveys reveal that people who do not themselves use their local public library believe that public libraries are desirable, important, and worthy of their own tax-derived financial support. Such apparently altruistic support follows naturally from the prevailing philosophy of the public library and goes beyond the self-interested notion of an "insurance attitude" whereby people support what they themselves might one day want to use. Similar, but less altruistic, is the belief that library services, like education, would make society safer by keeping people out of mischief.[14] Support from tax funds is appropriate, the belief is, because the existence of public libraries helps to achieve a philosophy concerning society.

As a strong contrast in political philosophy, communist countries also tend to be very supportive of libraries. It is not simply that Marx used the British Museum Library to write *Das Kapital*. Lenin and his wife, N. K. Krupskaya, herself a librarian, were ardent supporters of libraries.

> [The library in the USSR is a] cultural institution which helps the reader to understand the philosophy of dialectical materialism and gain genuine scientific knowledge, and assists him in the training of (skilled) manpower for the building of socialism. ... In all phases of construction of the socialist state libraries closely link their work with the most important political and economic tasks. Libraries assist the party in the Communist education of the masses, in arming them with Marxist-Leninist theory, in educating the people with the spirit of Soviet patriotism, loyalty and love for their socialist motherland and of the Communist attitude toward work.[15]

Lenin himself wrote:

> We must use the experience of other countries of capitalist countries, in every way we can; in technical reconstruction, in technical service to readers we must borrow all that we can. But we must build our own library—a library of a different kind, more in keeping with our socialist way of life.[16]

The deployment of resources within public libraries in communist countries can be expected to vary in detail from typical public libraries of the United States and the United Kingdom—notably in terms of what is

---

[14] For a mid-nineteenth-century statement of this belief, see "Imprisonment and Transportation. No. 1. The Increase of Crime," *Blackwood's Edinburgh Magazine* 55, no. 343 (May 1844): 533-45. "Next it was said, that education would lay the axe to the root of crime; that ignorance was the parent of vice; and, by diffusing the schoolmaster, you would extinguish the greater part of the wickedness which afflicted society; that the providing of cheap, innocent, and elevating amusements for the leisure hours of the working-classes, would prove the best antidote to their degrading propensities; and that then, and then only, would crime really be arrested, when the lamp of knowledge burned in every mechanic's workshop, in every peasant's cottage," p. 540.

[15] *Bol'shaya sovetskaya entsiklopediya (Great Soviet Encyclopedia)*, 2nd ed. (Moscow: Gosudarstvennoe Nauchnoe Izdatel'stvo. 1950), pp. 140-1. As quoted in P. L. Horecky, *Libraries and Bibliographic Centers in the Soviet Union* (Washington, D.C.: Council on Library Resources, 1959), p. 2.

[16] Quoted in S. Simsova, ed., *Lenin, Krupskaia and Libraries* (London: Clive Bingley, 1968), p. 46.

included and what is excluded. The basis for the difference can be attributed in large part to the difference in guiding philosophy.

Libraries in educational institutions are deeply influenced by both pedagogical values and political forces. A system which does not emphasize individualized learning in its educational philosophy is unlikely to emphasize the allocation of resources to libraries. Even where an emphasis on school libraries is well established, as in California, the retention of resources in times of retrenchment depends significantly on the educational value placed on libraries and on librarians within the school district, and this tends to reflect the extent to which the librarian has positively influenced the thinking of the principal, teachers, school board members, and other politically influential groups. Whether the influence may have been consciously and deliberately built or whether it followed unprompted from service that was perceived to be beneficial—probably, in practice, a combination of both—the presence or absence of positive concepts, beliefs, and principles with respect to the library can be expected to determine substantially the future resources of the library service.[17]

In universities, a key variable in the provision of library service is the political power of the professors and their beliefs, concepts, and principles. An extreme of this can be seen in some Austrian and West German universities in the allocation of resources for library services to separate "libraries" for each institute, with each professor, (i.e., "ordinarius" or "full" professor) having his or her own institute. Few professional librarians or government officials believe this to be an effective sort of deployment of resources for library service, but the philosophy of the professors differs and the professors have had the political power to prolong this decentralization. More generally, in the United States and in the United Kingdom, the endemic growth of departmental libraries and the (usually) much superior library privileges of faculty can be regarded as reflecting the reality of academic power rather than the orthodoxies of the librarians who usually oppose the growth of departmental libraries.[18]

Clear evidence of philosophy guiding library provision can be seen in selection and censorship issues. Librarians in school and public libraries—like school teachers—are particularly susceptible to attack on the grounds that an item in the collection is at variance with the educational, religious,

[17] A study of the effects on six public libraries in California of severe cuts in local government spending showed that "the libraries that were most active in their efforts to influence their environment suffered the least drastic budget cuts." S. Shoham, *Organizational Adaptation by Public Libraries* (Westport, Conn.: Greenwood Press, 1984).

[18] For an examination of the role of U.S. university library directors in relation to their environment see J. R. Euster, *The Academic Library Director: Management Activities and Effectiveness* (New York: Greenwood Press, 1987).

or social philosophy of somebody.[19] This is only to be expected. Since the offending situation is the result of a political process, political pressures are likely to be used to change it.

Further, it is on philosophical grounds that librarians as a profession tend to be heavily opposed (at least in theory) to censorship. It is the American Library Association that runs what is said to be the only foundation in the United States devoted exclusively to the freedom to read. In practice, it would seem that librarians tend to exert some degree of self-imposed censorship, partly to forestall cruder censorship that might be imposed by others.[20]

Yet another illustration of the influence of philosophy as a guiding influence is the allocation of library resources with respect to the interests of minorities. In California, the development of special collections and services—even separate branches of public libraries—specializing in service to minority groups, such as Chinese and Spanish-speaking communities, is a relatively recent development. It reflects a change in priorities in social values on the part of those responsible for public library services. This, in turn, reflects a change in the general political climate of the communities concerned. Even if it could be demonstrated that such provision may sometimes have been a reluctant concession to political pressures and contrary to the "philosophy" of library administrators and library boards, the thesis that politics and social values drive the allocation of resources for library services still stands. In other cases, the library administration may well have been more in favor of such provision than the community. Either way, the thesis that politics and social values dominate remains; and whose values get priority (and how) tells us something about the nature of the political power and political processes in any given situation.

[19]   There is the practical problem of identifying the materials that one's philosophy leads one to regard as pernicious. Jenkinson gives examples from a list of words and phrases (e.g., academic freedom, inductive method, self-understanding, world view) designed to help parents identify for removal school books that might harm their children by encouraging humanism. E. B. Jenkinson, *Censors in the Classroom: The Mind Benders* (Carbondale, Ill.: Southern Illinois University Press, 1979).

[20]   For a convenient review of intellectual freedom and censorship of library materials see D. K. Berninghausen, "Intellectual Freedom in Librarianship: Advances and Retreats," *Advances in Librarianship* 9 (1979): 1-29. For a discussion of censorship by both librarians ("book burying") and others ("book burning"), see M. P. Farris, "My Client is the Moral Majority," *Barrister* 9, no. 2 (Spring 1982); 12-15. A live recording of a public hearing on August 26, 1968, before the Richmond, California, City Council concerning whether an underground newspaper and like material should be removed from the Richmond Public Library was issued as a phonodisc entitled "What Shall They Read?" (Pacifica Archive Record 024) by Pacifica Foundation (KPFA, Berkeley, California, 1968). For additional material on censorship by librarians, see M.Fiske, *Book Selection and Censorship: A Study of Schools and Public Libraries in California* (Berkeley: University of California Press, 1959); E. Geller, "The Librarian as Censor," *Library Journal* 101, no. 11 (June 1, 1976): 1255-8; K. Donelson, "Shoddy and Pernicious Books," *Library Quarterly* 51, no. 1 (1981): 4-19; and L. B. Woods and C. Perry-Holmes, "The Flak If We Had *The Joy of Sex* Here," *Library Journal* 107, no. 16 (September 15, 1982): 1711-15.

Philosophy as an inexorable feature of librarianship

It used to be fashionable in Great Britain to assert the neutrality and independence of librarians. The slogan "no religion, no politics, and no morals" reflects this stance.[21] What is not always clearly understood is that such an attitude is, in itself, a philosophy. Either it reflects a libertarian, laissez-faire stance or else it indicates a conscious attempt to withdraw from imposing personal values. The latter course is not feasible since librarians are, by the very nature of their work, constantly deciding about priorities. This can only constitute an attempt to opt out of what will remain a continuing activity since, if the librarian is not to make decisions concerning priorities, then he or she must unavoidably be adopting the priorities and values of others which then determine how things are done. Opting out of the determination of priorities is just that: Priorities will still have to be determined by somebody.

A more prevalent event than opting out is the failure to review what the priorities are and to consider whether there may be a mismatch between what the priorities are supposed to be and what is actually happening— and whether either or both ought not to be revised.[22]

It follows inexorably from the definition of philosophy as "a system of motivating beliefs, concepts, and principles" and from the unavoidable necessity of continuously resolving questions of priority that some sort of a philosophy of librarianship informs each library situation whether recognized or not. It follows, further, that anyone interested in library services whether as a provider or as a user would be well advised to examine what sort of philosophy is implied by the actual allocation of resources and how coherently and consistently the prevailing philosophy is effected in practice. In other words, what are the *actual* goals of the organization and how cost-effective is it in achieving them?

[21] D. J. Foskett, *The Creed of a Librarian—No Politics, No Religion, No Morals* (Reference special and information section. Northwestern group. Occasional papers, 3) (London: Library Association, 1962). For a different view, see J. A. Hennessy, "Myths and Alibis: Political Information in Libraries," *Assistant Librarian* 74, no. 10 (October 1981): 126-8: "The rhetoric of librarians must be viewed...with incomprehension if not hostility, a direct result of the refusal or inability of librarians to respond to existing relations of power in society, to accept a political dimension to the ordinary business of handling information.... All information is a fundamental resource and thus a political source; some information is explicitly political within the terms of an allegedly democratic society; other information may become political by virtue of the political values of those who acquire it, use it, control it; librarians claim to have certain skills and objectives in information-handling and thus their work must necessarily assert political values whether explicitly professed or implicitly internalized (p. 128)." See also J. Hennessy, "Guerrilla Librarianship? A Review Article on the Librarianship of Politics and the Politics of Librarianship," *Library Journal* 13, no. 4 (October 1981): 248-55. For a convenient historical overview see A. R. Rogers, "An Introduction to Philosophies of Librarianship," in A. R. Rogers, *The Library in Society* (Littleton, Conn.: Libraries Unlimited, 1984).

[22] For a case study of a public library in which the philosophy of the professional librarians was alleged to be at variance with the values of the community, see Levy, Meltsner, and Wildavsky, *Urban Outcomes*.

The distinctive role of libraries with respect to social values

So far, we have not said anything that could not be regarded as being generally applicable to all sorts of organizations. Libraries, however, do have some distinctive characteristics with respect to their social role. This follows from the combination of their role in providing access to recorded knowledge and the social usefulness of knowledge.

It is an old slogan that "knowledge is power" and certainly knowledge can be an asset. The more one can acquire useful knowledge and reduce one's harmful ignorance, the better one is likely to fare, whether one is developing professional expertise, exercising one's civil rights, acquiring useful skills, or finding out about the activities (actual or potential) of others who may be in a position to influence one's life.

Libraries have no monopoly on assisting in these matters, but, because they are in the business of providing access to recorded knowledge and because they ordinarily do so at no financial charge, libraries do have an opportunity to play a distinctive role in the distribution of knowledge and of benefits in society. How effective this role is and in which direction the distribution is going will depend in large part on the location, nature, and extent of the service being provided—in other words, on the allocation of resources. Further, since political power and knowledge are unequally distributed in practice (in universities and in corporations as in communities) and since different emphases in service are appropriate for different groups, what is beneficial for one group may not coincide with what is beneficial for another and may even be against the best interests of others.[23] Diverting funds for little-used research materials in a university library into multiple copies of textbooks for undergraduates illustrates one such conflict of interest. In a public library, the balance between information services for local businesses and the provision of "survival information" for disadvantaged groups is another. These conflicts of interest exist and need to be recognized but they should not be allowed to obscure the basic issue which is that libraries, like the press, affect the dispersion of knowledge and, as such, have a potentially important role to play in the development of society. The provision of library service is, then, a means of exercising influence. Providing library services in foreign countries is, therefore, a sensible element of national foreign policy, reflecting an interesting mixture of altruism, self-interest, and conscious propaganda.[24]

---

[23] " ... it becomes evident that libraries and educational institutions symbolic of the Western tradition negate in reality all the basic cliches of librarianship: freedom of information or intellectual freedom, the evils of censorship, and the pornographic use of information power, all of which are crucial matters in the ethics and responsibilities of librarianship and education." A. O. Amadi, *African Libraries: Western Tradition and Colonial Brainwashing.* (Metuchen, N.J.: Scarecrow Press, 1981), p. 162.

[24] See chapter 6, footnote 1.

In pursuit of the philosophy of librarianship

Having argued that philosophy—in the sense of systems of motivating beliefs, concepts, and principles—must necessarily pervade the provision of library services, it is reasonable to inquire how one might examine these philosophical bases more clearly. The following approaches would seem worth pursuing.

Political analysis of the motivations and consequences (not necessarily the same!) associated with the present and any proposed patterns of service would seem to be basic. The phrase "political analysis" is used on the grounds that politics is, by definition, concerned with who gets to deploy resources and how. "Policy analysis," "social analysis," and other similar phrases tend to mean much the same sort of thing. Arguably, such analyses cannot be entirely objective since we all have our individual motivating beliefs, concepts, and principles. What follows is not that political analysis should be avoided, but that analyses should be accepted as being less than fully objective.

The study of library provisions, and especially of library management, needs to be recognized as being simultaneously political and technical. It is not only a matter of being involved in the determination of priorities, there are also serious problems in determining how effectively the provision achieves in practice the intended priorities. How consistent are the policies and practices with the objectives and with each other? For this, the deeper our theoretical understanding of how libraries work and how they are used, the more powerful our tools of analysis will be. Preparing professionals with only the techniques of retrieval is clearly to cover only half of what they will be involved in doing.

It is here, perhaps, that the comparative study of library services will really come into a much more significant role than it has hitherto. Danton recognized this: "The major aims and objectives of librarianship as of any constituent of human society, must be derived from the pre-dominating ideals of that society."[25] In consequence, "... how different must of necessity be the organization, administration, functions, aims, and hence philosophical bases of librarianship in, for example, Fascist Italy, Nazi Germany, and the United States."[26]

---

[25] Danton, "Plea for a Philosophy of Librarianship," p. 547. The introduction to the statement on professional ethics adopted by the American Library Association in 1981 seems to include a recognition that the guidelines propounded for librarians to follow derived from a particular political philosophy: "*In a political system grounded in an informed citizenry,* librarians are members of a profession explicitly committed to intellectual freedom and the freedom of access to information...." (Emphasis added.) *American Libraries* 12, no. 6 (June 1981): 325.

[26] Danton, "Plea for a Philosophy of Librarianship," p. 527.

12

Allocation II. Fees, Sponsors, and Stability: Notes on the Political Economy of Library Services

Introduction

The process of allocation of resources and priorities to and within libraries was seen in chapter 11 as being essentially a political process. This is because the resources for libraries do not come from users, at least not in their capacity as users. Resources come from other sources, usually funds assigned to the library from a higher level (e.g., mayor, university or corporation president, school superintendent) and, thus, the claims of other users of the resources are considered with respect to the values and goals of those who do the allocating.

This view is, however, a convenient simplification. Some funds come from private sources on a noncommercial basis, e.g., support from foundations and charitable donations. Other funds come through charging fees. This last is of limited importance at the present time in libraries, but is currently a major point of controversy and it could become a major source of income as it is in some other sorts of information services. Therefore, any theoretical framework which attempts to describe the structure and functioning of libraries—let alone other sorts of information services—would be seriously incomplete unless it included the fee-based provision of services as well as free provision. Before doing so, we need to review some of our assumptions.

We are not here concerned with the technical aspects of calculating actual costs and prices. These are treated elsewhere.[1] We are primarily concerned with exploring how a transition from sponsors to fees would affect the structure and functioning of library services. Hence we note, but do not need to explore, many of the concepts associated with the public financing of public services. We simply note that private and public

[1] S. A. Roberts, *Cost Management of Library and Information Services* (London: Butterworths, 1985). See also chapter 10, footnotes 7 and 8.

162

entities choose (or may be persuaded) to allocate resources to libraries. We do not here consider the specific rationales for doing so—"merit goods," "public goods," and so on.[2]

Critical to our present discussion and different from most other discussions is our treatment of price. Ordinarily, only the monetary price is considered, for which, for clarity, we can use the term "fees." However, as discussed in chapter 9, the fee is only one element in the real price as defined by Adam Smith: "The real price of every thing, what every thing really costs to the man who wants to acquire it, is the toil and trouble of acquiring it."[3] We view the real price as having four sorts of elements: the monetary price (or fee), time, effort, and discomfort. The difference between the monetary price and the real price needs careful attention.

The impact of fees for service

To the extent that fees are charged for the use of services, the political process is supplanted by an economic one whereby the allocation of resources to the service comes at least in part from the user *qua user*. We now review some of the consequences of this: The two independent feedback loops in the double feedback loop characteristic of library services and, presumably, of noncommercial services generally begin to lose their independency. (See figure 10.2 and the discussion in chapter 10.) The allocation of resources begins to depend on demand, even though income from the use of a particular service is not necessarily used to defray the costs of providing that particular service. More use becomes more income, alias more resources. In fully commercial situations, the resources all come from use since the fees constitute the only allocation of resources to the service—its only income. This does not, in and of itself, prevent the manager from reallocating the resources internally in ways which do not entirely coincide with the distribution of demand: the grocer may subsidize a loss-leader; a transport company might subsidize an unprofitable route as a philanthropic gesture. However, such reallocation is conditional upon having a spare margin of resources which permits reallocations.

Pursuing this theoretical analysis further, we consider the point of pure

---

[2] Background reading on financing and fees for libraries can be found in and through W. Schwuchow, "Fundamental Aspects of the Financing of Information Centres," *Information Storage and Retrieval* 9 (1973): 569-75; M. Cooper, "Charging Users for Library Service," *Information Processing and Management* 14 (1978): 419-27; T. J. Waldhart and T. Bellardo, "User Fees in Publicly Funded Libraries," *Advances in Librarianship* 9 (1979): 31-61; D. King, "Pricing Policies in Academic Libraries," *Library Trends* 28, no. 1 (Summer 1979): 47-62; and also see footnote 6 of chapter 9.

[3] A. Smith, *An Inquiry Into the Nature and Causes of the Wealth of Nations* (Oxford: Clarendon Press, 1976), Book 1, chapter 5, para. 2.

competition. Each specific service would have to be priced at the very margin of profitability. If it were set higher, business would be lost to competitors; if lower, bankruptcy would follow. In this situation, no margin remains for reallocation and so the allocation of resources internally also becomes totally controlled, in detail, by the costs of each particular service for which there was a demand at a price marginally above cost. Being controlled by the pattern of demand in a commercial situation means, in effect, being controlled by the users who have economic power. Those without sufficient economic power to pay will cease to be users in such a situation.

The degree of autonomy of the provider of the service is indicated by the relationship between the fee (the price charged) and the cost (the monetary cost of providing it). In a state of pure competition, the fee can only be marginally above the cost: a move up or down will cause loss of business or bankruptcy respectively. In a cybernetic sense, the system has lost its autonomy by becoming controlled in detail by market forces.

Moving away from pure competition through scarcity in supply to monopoly leads, in a commercial context, to the ability to increase fees relative to costs. Users will eventually refuse to pay, preferring to forgo the service, but, up to that point, the provider has a degree of independence to raise prices above costs.

Moving away from dependence on users' fees as noncommercial sources of income are developed is reflected in the ability to reduce fees below costs. At the extreme are services provided at no monetary cost. Indeed, inducements to use a free service could be provided. This represents a very high degree of independence from users. Our use of the terms "autonomy" and "independence" should be viewed cautiously. Resources must come from somewhere: One cannot provide much service if one has neither fees nor sponsor. What we referred to was *economic independence from the user*. However, reducing the dependence on the user only increases the dependence on wherever else the resources do come from. The dependence remains, but its nature shifts from being economic (i.e., commercial) to being political (i.e., whoever is willing to allocate resources without *commercial* return). The library or other institution that provides service for free can, therefore, disregard demand and the level of use just so long as the political origin of its resources remains sufficiently supportive.

Political dependence

For the political source of resources to remain supportive two conditions are required: the source must continue to have resources to allocate; and the library (or other claimant) must remain competitively congruent with the social values of the source.

This notion of being "competitively congruent" takes us staight back to questions concerning library goodness which we posed in chapter 2 and to which we shall return in our final chapter. Let us consider the dynamics of the loss of support by a library. (We use a library as our example. It could as well be a municipal art gallery, a museum, a research institute, a public kindergarten, or any entity that is dependent on appropriations.) Let us consider three sorts of perceptions on the part of those who allocate resources to the library.

1. They may perceive a lack of effectiveness. Do the actual or potential users complain that the service is unsatisfactory or irrelevant to their needs? Or that some other alternative would be more satisfactory? If so, the resources are likely to be reallocated elsewhere. In other words, the service may not be perceived as being satisfactory for the sorts of demands placed upon it.

2. They may perceive that the good being done by the service is no longer sufficiently valuable in terms of their (the allocators') social values to warrant support, especially if there is a reduction in the overall amount of resources to be allocated. How do the intellectual and practical consequences of the knowledge that people can be expected to derive from well-developed public libraries compare with expenditure for the restoration and preservation of historic buildings and clean lakes for the present and future residents and tourists? In other words, the service may be perceived as satisfactory but not very valuable.

3. They may perceive incompetence in performance. Do those who are currently running the service appear not to know what they are doing? If they do know, are they lazy? If either is perceived to be the case, then those supplying the resources may bring pressure to change or otherwise improve the management of the service or, if practicable, shift support to an alternative service. In other words, the library service could be suitable and valuable but not well run.

Later in this chapter we shall consider how these perceptions may be influenced and, in the final chapter, we shall return again to these three aspects of library goodness.

Is political support necessary?

This is a convenient point for a short digression in order to make an important qualification. All the conditions noted above may be met such that the library can be regarded as the most effective means for achieving the sponsor's social values and yet not be a sensible choice. This is when such support is unnecessary in the sense that commercially-based service would provide an acceptable means of achieving the same results. This would be the case if two conditions were both met. First, demand is inelastic. The addition of the monetary element in the price would not significantly change demand, otherwise the beneficial outcomes would cease to be achieved. Since both social values and economic power are differentially distributed across the population, we need to consider not only changes in the overall level of demand but also any change in its distribution. Second, the secondary consequences ("externalities") of the change should not be harmful. For this we need to consider indirect consequences such as the division of users' economic resources from other uses and the alternative uses of the sponsor's resources.

In practice, these two conditions are most unlikely to be met in any strict sense. It is much more likely that the conditions would be partially met insofar as anyone had enough knowledge to predict the consequences. A situation of this sort gives rise to a lot of interest on the part of sponsors in mixed strategies. The general approach is to let commercial processes operate to the extent that they achieve the social values of the sponsors and then allocate resources only for those aspects which would not be achieved through commercial processes alone. This is attractive because it is very economical. It offers the prospect of achieving the social values while conserving as much of the sponsor's resources as possible for other opportunities. There are, however, disadvantages. The dynamics involved may be too little understood to permit confidence in the outcomes, and the mechanics of implementation may prove excessively cumbersome.

In any discussion of means, great alertness is needed since disagreements concerning the means to achieve assumed social values may in fact reflect, consciously or otherwise, differences in preferred social values, i.e., ends.

This analysis merely clarifies the fact that autonomy with respect to the economic power of the user does not mean complete autonomy since economic dependence on the user is merely replaced by political dependence on the sponsor. It is a transition from one sort of dependence to another. The need, in a commercial situation, to promote one's services persuasively among actual and potential users becomes, instead, for the provider of service, a need in a political situation to promote one's services among sponsors. Both sorts of persuasion may be difficult in practice and the intensity of the need for it can be expected, with both sorts, to vary from one situation to another. However, shifting from fees to sponsors does nothing to remove the need—only the nature.

Marketing among sponsors

Having recognized the structure of the relationship with a sponsor, it is not difficult to see what, in theory, needs to be done. We can assert that those in a position to allocate resources to the library are more likely to continue doing so if:

1. They perceive the services to be good. That is, they perceive the services as being capable of satisfying a demand. Is evidence of such satisfaction passed on, directly or indirectly, to the sponsors? Are complaints satisfactorily dealt with?[4]
2. It is perceived that the service is doing good, in the sense of achieving the social values of the sponsors. Is the librarian looking beyond the daily routines and the technology of the service in order to note the beneficial effects of the library service? Even more important, are these effects being made known, directly or indirectly, to the sponsors? The fact that assessing the beneficial effects may be very difficult is inconvenient but, in an important sense, irrelevant, since difficulty in assessment does nothing to reduce the need for assessment.
3. Is it perceived that the librarian is actively and effectively concerned to improve the competence with which the services are provided? Are the difficulties, opportunities, and achievements made known, directly or indirectly, to the sponsors?

Given the structure and functioning of these relationships, the librarian who fails to attend to the persuasion of those who allocate resources to the library cannot be regarded as having accepted the full range of responsibility inherent in the role.

The role of the user in a sponsored service

It is necessary to consider the role of the user in these matters since they share in the political process of allocation directly or indirectly. Particular users may have a formal role in the decisions concerning the allocation of resources to the library. All can be assumed to have at least an indirect role in that their expression of opinions will carry more or less weight with the sponsors in at least three ways:

● Do the users describe the services as being good or bad? How well do the services meet their demands?
● Are they "voting with their feet?" Do they, in fact, use the library? In a noncommercial situation, a reduction in demand can be advantageous in operational terms. The service can cope better with the users who remain. However, reduction of demand is dangerous politically for two reasons: First, reduction is likely to be associated with dissatisfaction among the users; and, second, a service can hardly be regarded as being valuable in the sense of having beneficial effects if it is little used. This dilemma helps explain the ambivalence in attitude

---

[4] Public relations pay off. See P. Berger, "An Investigation of the Relationship Between Public Relations Activities and Budget Allocation in Public Libraries," *Information Processing and Management* 15, no. 4 (1979): 179-93.

found among those who provide service in situations which are not perceived as being commercial and competitive. Emphasis on the social values indicates an increase in use as being desirable; operational considerations provide a motivation to reduce usage.

● It is in the user's best interests to seek to influence the political process.[5] The greater the success that a user has in advocating her or his particular priorities in the political process of allocation, the better the service will be for that user. The techniques of political advocacy are outside the scope of this book, but the importance of such influence can hardly be exaggerated.

Back to price and stability

Discussion of the level of usage brings us back to our earlier concern for the mechanisms that permit the service to maintain an acceptable degree of stability and, indeed, to survive. More specifically, how do free services survive if they lack the responsiveness associated with the market place? We have discussed in some detail the dynamics of the dependence on sponsors as opposed to fees. The relationship is seen as being sufficiently similar to permit the phrase "'marketing' among sponsors." Yet this is only one side of the coin. To achieve stability, the service must not only acquire a viable level of resources, it must also protect itself from excessive demands. The strains imposed by demand must also somehow be kept within bounds that are viable in relation to the resources. How is this to be done in the absence of the traditional control device—fees? The answer lies in the ambiguity of the use of the word "price" which we discussed at the beginning of this chapter. Since the real price includes all the disadvantages and since there are nonmonetary aspects of the real price, there is no obstacle in theory to manipulating the nonmonetary aspects of price and letting the price mechanism continue to do its work. Consider the symptoms of strain on a library's resources and the librarians' responses to such strain: e.g., shorter opening hours, longer delays in processing, fewer new titles and duplicates, lower availability, longer waits at the circulation desk, closure of branch libraries, harassed staff. Each of these sorts of changes represents a degradation of service in the sense that either a service ceases to be available or, more commonly, the service remains available but the price has been raised in its nonmonetary aspects—even occasionally fees are introduced. More time, more effort, and more discomfort are involved in using that library. The user, when pondering the perceived probable costs and perceived probable benefits of using the library will sense that the relative price has gone up. Other

[5] Recommended reading on ceasing to use a service ("exit") and seeking to influence it ("voice") is A. O. Hirshman, *Exit, Voice and Loyalty: Responses to Decline in Firms, Organizations, and States* (Cambridge, Mass.: Harvard University Press, 1970).

sources of information will have become relatively more attractive and fewer inquiries are now worth the "price" of seeking the answer from this particular library service.

We are back to the double feedback loop of figure 10.2. The library service's ability to control the use made of it is largely separate from its dealing with the sponsor. The elasticity of demand on the part of the population of users and potential users means that demand can be effectively regulated. This regulation is only indirectly achieved, aside from attempts to forbid some sorts of use or some sorts of users. There is probably more scope than is usually recognized for the librarian to tune the level and pattern of demand since the librarian can influence the internal allocation of resources and priorities and the effect of this is the determination of where, when, and how severely degradations of service (and, therefore, of price and, therefore, of demand) will be distributed over different aspects of service and, therefore, for different groups of users. For this, however, a detailed understanding of the internal dynamics of the system defined as the services, the users, and the interactions between them is needed.

The seven chapters of Part II: Analysis, have examined separately, five basic processes in the provision and use of library services: inquiry, retrieval, becoming informed, demand, and provision. Part III: Connections and Extensions, will seek to complement Part II by examining how the parts fit together and some characteristics of the whole.

Part III

Connections and Extensions

13

Connections

The basic structure

In Part II we analyzed five response mechanisms which we viewed as determining the provision and use of library services: inquiry; the demand for library services; retrieval; becoming informed; and the provision of library services. Part III examines library services as a whole from various perspectives. In the present chapter we shall examine connections and interactions between the parts. The area with which we are concerned—the provision and use of library services—is a highly complex area. In particular, it involves a variety of different and complex sorts of human behavior: economic, political, cognitive. In consequence, it is not to be expected that any very simple model would be able to reflect reality. However, it is proposed that a model based on three connected systems constitutes an economical representation of the true complexity. These three connected systems have the following characteristics:

- The three systems are quite different from each other in nature;
- The three systems are connected to each other, but only to a very limited extent; and
- Each of the three systems is dominated as much or more by inter- action with the external environment as it is by other features of the library service.

We shall consider each of these three systems separately, and then together.

Provision: a political and managerial system

The allocation of resources to and within a library service has been discussed in detail in chapters 11 and 12. The process can be briefly summarized. The external environment (society) possesses resources, some of which are allocated for library purposes. There are also, in this environment, other potential uses for these resources. The library service is in competition with these other possible uses of the resources.

There are, in any given social environment, social values that guide the allocation process. There is variation from one individual to another, from one time to another, and from one place to another in these social values. Consensus is likely to emerge but is liable to change. There are also changes with respect to who gets to do the allocation of the resources. Resources may be more or less plentiful; other uses may be more or less pressing; social values vary; and the balance of influence on the political processes may change as power structures evolve. Nevertheless, the combination of these factors dominates the allocation of resources to and within the library service, and this allocation determines in detail what sort of service is provided.

The allocation of resources is, then, a political and managerial process within the limitations imposed by the library technology available at the time and place. It is tempting to try to be logical and to distinguish the allocation of resources *to* the library from the allocation *within* the library. However, it is unreasonable to do so because the distinction is imperfect in practice. Those who allocate *to* the library ordinarily do so with specific expectations concerning the allocation of resources *within* the library as part of their intentions, even though managerial discretion concerning details is ordinarily left to the library administrator.

The detailed allocation of resources determines the profile of services provided:

- how many of what sorts of titles are acquired
- how many of what sorts of titles are discarded
- regulations of access and use; shelf access, duplication, borrowing, etc.
- the availability of space and its use
- type of arrangement of books on the shelves
- catalogs and retrieval services
- readers' advisory and reference services.

These aspects of service are not, in practice, independent of one another, as we shall consider further in chapter 14 below.

Perceptions of the quality of service by those who allocate (including the library staff) provide an element of feedback which can affect future (re)allocations of resources and, thereby, modify the profile of service. However, this feedback mechanism has tended historically to be rather weak, mainly on account of difficulties associated with knowing what is actually happening in the use of library services. It is important to remember that the quality of a service is perceived and judged in terms of the social values derived from the environment and held by those who do the perceiving. However, the "goodness" of the service is seen in relation to the use (hence, the benefits) as well as to the nature (or quality) of service. In other words, resources may be reallocated away from even an excellent service if little or no use is being made of it—or away from a

Screen 001 of 001

PURCHASE ORDER.	0034019-0001	STATUS.	ON ORDER
FORMAT.	E-BOOK	MEDIA CODE.	010
COPIES.	01	COPIES RECEIVED.	00
PARTS PER COPY.	001	PARTS RECEIVED.	000
VENDOR NAME.	0038738 SCHOLARLY BOOK CENTER
ISBN/ISSN.	008035755
AUTHOR.	BUCKLAND, M. K.
TITLE.	LIBRARY SERVICES IN THEORY AND CONTEXT
DATE/HOLDING.	E2Y1988
CATALOG NOTE 01.	WE HAVE THE 1983 EDITION: Z665.B916 1983

ACQ-MSU>

ZDAIC *** ACQ ITEM CHECKIN PO# 0034019-0001 I?

```
3Barcode                                    3
3Barcode                                    3
3Barcode                                    3
3Barcode                                    3
3Barcode                                    3
3                                           3
3<Page 1 of 2>                              3
@DDDDDDDDDDDDDDDDDDDDDDDDDDDDDDDDDDDDDDDDDDDY
```

[PROCEED]
[QUIT]

F1 = HELP info ------ Esc = QUIT ------ F9 = show previous / do online sear

cost-effective service if it is perceived as having little relevance to the mission of the sponsoring body.

This political and managerial system which determines the pattern of library service is shown schematically in figure 13.1. It can be seen that it is the "library feedback loop" in chapter 10. In our final chapter we will consider in more detail how and why the profile of library service varies from one situation to another.

F<small>IG.</small> 13.1   The provision of library services:
a political and managerial system

Information through retrieval: a cognitive system

In chapter 6, we considered inquiries as the driving force behind the use of libraries as information systems. Inquiries, we speculated, derived from "distressing ignorance," which, in turn, we attributed to the combination of particular states of personal knowledge (notably gaps and incongruencies) and of personal values that alone make important (and, therefore, distressing) particular portions of our ignorance.

Some inquiries reach the library and, by a combination of collection development and a retrieval process which is rooted in logic, linguistics, and technology, a set of signals is retrieved. This process is examined in chapters 7 and 8.

If the signals are perceived by the user, then through a cognitive process, which is dependent on the individual's prior personal knowledge and cognitive skills, a learning process takes place—a process of becoming informed, of changing the state of the individual's personal knowledge. This was considered in chapter 9.

Here, again, the external environment dominates. Even though library services can be regarded as being of great actual or potential importance, it should be recognized that, for any individual, most personal knowledge by far, derives from sources of information other than library services.[1] The environment is also the dominant source of personal values, cognitive skills, and factors that spark the desire to do things for which library services are appropriate. This cognitive system is summarized in figure 13.2.

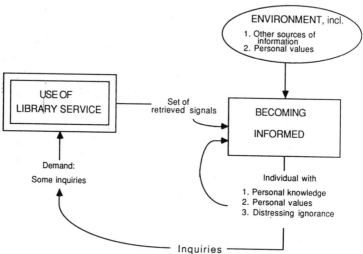

Fig. 13.2   Information through retrieval: a cognitive system

Deciding to use a library service: an economic system

The mere fact that distressing ignorance has engendered an inquiry in somebody's mind does not mean that an action will in fact be taken to resolve the inquiry—and even less that a library service will be utilized to reduce the distress.

As discussed in chapter 10, there is a decision process whereby the perceived probable benefit of using the library is compared with the perceived probable cost. The benefit derives from the personal values of the individual and the perceived chances of successful reduction of the distress through use of the library. The cost—the "real price"—is mainly nonmonetary, having elements of time, effort, and discomfort.

Significant, therefore, in the decision whether or not to use the library is the perceived quality of the library service from the perspective of the potential user. How beneficial—and how costly—previous experiences in using the library services have been are likely to influence heavily the potential user's perceptions of the quality of library service—and of the cost of using it. The decision to use a particular library service for a particular inquiry is likely to be taken only if it seems likely to be worthwhile. More formally, all of three conditions would need to be met:

[1]   See footnote 5 of chapter 4.

1   the perceived probable benefit exceeds the perceived probable cost;
2. alternative sources of information are perceived as less attractive in terms of probable cost and benefit; and
3. the individual has not decided to discontinue—temporarily or permanently—the attempt to resolve the distressing ignorance. This is liable to happen at any point.

Here, again, the external environment dominates because there are so many alternative sources of information—other people, other libraries, other books—in addition to any given library service. Most people, most of the time, resolve their inquiries by means other than the use of library services. In that sense, using a library service is an unusual, atypical activity. The challenge, for all parties, is to determine what sorts of inquiries library services are most appropriate for. Anyone eager to increase library use would be well-advised to seek to reduce the perceived costs and to publicize probable benefits.

We describe this process as being "economic" even though the monetary element is mainly absent. We summarize this system in figure 13.3, which can be seen to be the same as the "user feedback loop" described in chapter 10 as one part of the double feedback loop which characterizes library services.

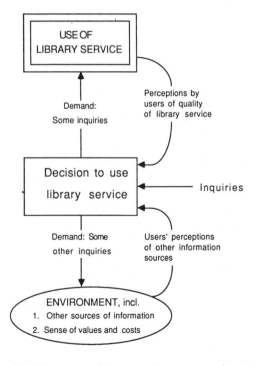

F<small>IG.</small> 13.3   Deciding to use a library service: an economic system

How are the three systems connected?

The one and only element that connects all three systems is the act of using the library service.

- In the *cognitive system*, using the library service generates the set of retrieval signals that leads to the user becoming informed and acquiring new knowledge.

- In the *political and managerial systems*, use of the library provides principal justification for allocating resources to the library and also generates the perceptions of use which constitute a feedback loop to those who allocate.

- In the *economic system*, the experience of using the library provides part of the basis for the user's future decisions whether or not to use the library. The other parts are the potential user's assessment of the alternative sources of information and of the importance (and urgency) of the inquiry itself.

The other, separate interaction by two of the systems (the *cognitive system* and the *economic system*) is the role played by the demand decision in determining whether an inquiry will be directed to the library service or whether it will be directed at some other source of information in the environment. The critical importance of this decision-point in determining library use can hardly be exaggerated.

Each system is dominated by the external environment which determines the resources for provision of library service; the values and preferences of allocators and of users; most of the communication to and, hence, the knowledge of individuals; and alternative sources of information. The provision and use of library services are deeply rooted in their social contexts.[2] This aspect can be easily overlooked when one is concerned with the study of libraries and especially of the techniques of library services. Aside from surveys of actual or potential users there has been remarkably little research and writing on the relationships between library services and their social contexts.[3]

---

[2] In systems theory one would say of an open system that the output of the system is exchanged in the environment for renewed input and that the value of the output is decided in the environment. See M. P. Marchant, *Participative Management in Academic Libraries* (Westport, Conn.: Greenwood Press, 1976), chapter 2, "The Library as an Open System," pp. 13-28.

[3] Useful starting points include: *Libraries in Society: A Reader,* edited by D. Gerard (London: Bingley, 1978); *Information and Society: A Collection of Papers,* edited by M. Barnes (Leeds: School of Librarianship, Leeds Polytechnic, 1981); A. O. Amadi, *African Libraries: Western Tradition and Colonial Brainwashing* (Metuchen, N.J.: Scarecrow Press, 1981); B. Landheer, *Social Functions of Libraries* (New York; Scarecrow Press, 1957). See also footnote 13 of chapter 11.

The relationships between these three different systems can be visualized by superimposing figures 13.1, 13.2, and 13.3, which represent the three systems. This is done in figure 13.4.[4]

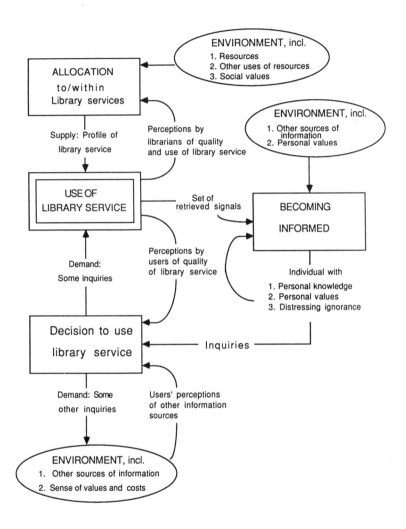

FIG. 13.4   The three connected systems determining the
provision and use of library service

[4] For a similar approach see N. A. Van House, "Public Library Effectiveness: Theory, Measures, and Determinants," *Library and Information Research* 8, no. 3 (July-September 1986): 261-83.

14

Coherence and Consistency

In previous chapters we have made frequent references to the detailed allocation of resources and to the profile of services provided. It is clear that the pattern of services offered can vary greatly. In this chapter, we take a closer look at the profile of services offered. What would be the right blend of services for a given situation? What internal budget allocation would be most effective in avoiding internal inconsistencies?

Introduction

The lack of a single, unifying measure of effectiveness for the evaluation of library services makes it difficult to relate the parts to the whole. The challenge for the librarian is to make decisions that are consistent and coherent in relation to each other and to the goals sought, even though the individual decisions are concerned with disparate matters.

This problem can be seen in the logistics of library provision: One can buy books, but have they been cataloged and processed in a timely manner? Is it sensible to acquire so few copies of a title that users are unable to find a copy when they want one? Loan periods may be unnecessarily and, therefore, inconveniently short if there are ample copies—or, if only few copies are bought, then it is inconsistent to permit very long loan periods if convenient availability is desired. Sending books to be bound may strengthen them for future use, but that is of limited benefit if the binding process is lengthy and coincides with peak demand. Money saved in acquisition procedures permits more books to be bought, yet this economy is likely to result in delays in getting books to the shelves. To what extent would it be worthwhile spending extra money for prompter acquisition, or for speedier binding? How can one make duplication and lending policies mutually consistent?[1]

There is, however, a wider problem since these logistical aspects are only part of library service. In this chapter, we consider the wide problem of coherence and internal consistency in library service.

---

[1] These logistical issues are examined in M. K. Buckland, *Book Availability and the Library User* (New York: Pergamon Press, 1975). See also P. Kantor, "Availability Analysis," *Journal of the American Society for Information Science* 27, no. 6 (October 1976): 311-19.

Searches as determinants of library services

Our starting point was the need to relate library services to demand in a coherent, consistent manner. In this section we speculate on the implications for the planning of library services of the four dimensions of searches considered in chapter 6.[2]

- *document specificity*: the extent to which one or a limited number of documents is wanted;
- *information specificity*: the extent to which the data sought are precisely defined;
- *importance*: the importance of resolving the search; and
- *urgency* of the search.

Searches of high document specificity

Since the emphasis is on obtaining specific, known documents, a premium should be placed on author and title catalogs. Tools of subject access serve a minor, auxiliary role. Reliable document delivery is at a premium because the requests are specific and, by implication, the substitution of alternative titles is likely to be inappropriate. A high level of immediate availability on open-access shelves would seem desirable for convenience but, in fact, open access does not seem essential. Lengthy loan periods are tolerable if a particular item can be recalled from loan on request. Good service would be possible from closed stacks (even with shelving by size and accession number in compact storage) if documents are to be kept secure and in good order. Urgency permitting, interlibrary loan could serve this type of demand better than any other kind of demand. High document specificity calls for investment in union catalogs and finding lists. The need for expert reference staff would appear to be at a minimum. ("I know what I want, please get it!")

Searches of high information specificity

For searches of high information specificity there would be a premium on subject access, including both a subject arrangement of documents and subject indexes that provide additional points of access to them. The indexes might be purchased bibliliographic tools or locally produced. In such circumstances, one might expect special emphasis on computer-based reference services and on local indexes on account of the additional power each can bring. In-depth indexing of parts of documents would

---

2 For a fuller discussion see chapter 6, and M. K. Buckland, "Types of Search and the Allocation of Library Resources," *Journal of the American Society for Information Science* 30, no. 3 (May 1979): 143-7.

seem, in general, to be desirable, though not necessarily affordable. Experienced subject specialist reference staff or information officers can play a substantial role. To the extent that one document may be substitutable for another, low levels of immediate availability and lengthy loan periods become tolerable. Large but not necessarily exhaustive local collections within the subject area concerned are desirable to provide a large array for browsing. Access to large holdings is also likely to be needed because the result of a search of high information specificity might become a search for one or more highly specific documents. ("I want something on the history of Glasson Dock in the Lune estuary.") However, interlibrary loan would suffice unless urgency is a major concern. The collection, even if large, ought to be on open access and arranged by subject in order to facilitate browsing even though one can also browse in subject indexes.

Searches of low document specificity

In general, the requirements for searches of low document specificity tend to be the reverse of those for high document specificity. Since not one but several documents are likely to meet the searcher's needs, lower immediate availability, smaller collections, and higher discarding and loss rates can be tolerated with less difficulty. Widely read library staff, thoroughly familiar with the collections, are likely to be helpful. Since the searches are of low document specificity, open access is indicated. Stored material in closed access is probably of very limited value unless the unlikely assumptions can be made that users will ask for the help of the staff and that the staff are very familiar with it. Interlibrary loan is likely to be little used.

Searches of low information specificity

In the case of low information specificity, the requirements appear to be a less specialized version of the case of high information specificity. A general interest, open access collection with helpful, stimulating intermediaries is likely to be most suitable. Good readers' advisors and interesting displays are likely to be beneficial. Although we do not wish to imply that this is the only type of search they handle, the image evoked is that of a small public library, large bookshop, or (disregarding the reserve collection) an undergraduate library.

Budgetary implications

Internal interactions within libraries need to be considered in terms of the probable effects of different resource allocation decisions on various

library "outcomes." (see figure 14.1) The combination of resource allocation decisions and the interactions inherent in library provision determine
the characteristics of the service provided. How, then, do we decide
which profile of outcomes would be most appropriate for any given
service situation?[3]

Note: Some of the stronger interactions are indicated by lines. The impact of
emphasizing any given feature can be traced by following the lines. For
example, if *Collection completeness* is to be stressed, then more *New titles*
are required. This drains the *Budget* so, assuming no supplementary funding,
it will require less investment in other areas, such as *Duplication; Reference
staff;* and/or *Catalogs, Guides, and indexes.* Less *Duplication* will affect
Availability and *Browsability*, unless compensating adjustments are made to
Loan policies. Any impact on *Availability* is likely to affect *Circulation* and,
in turn, the amount of *Reading* depending on what has happened to *Loan
policies.* The lack of a line between two items indicates that the interaction
is weak or indirect. The outcomes are also influenced by the characteristics
of the users.

FIG. 14.1   Some interactions in library provision

Source: M. K. Buckland and A. Hindle, "Acquisitions, Growth, and Performance Control Through
Systems Analysis," in *Farewell to Alexandria: Solutions to Space, Growth and Performance Problems of
Libraries*, edited by D. Gore (Westport, Conn.: Greenwood Press, 1976).

Even though the outcomes are interrelated and depend in large measure
on the characteristics of the user population, management decisions will
still determine which are given greater emphasis than others. In the
preceding paragraphs we have speculated concerning which outcomes
are more important for different types of searches.[4] These are summarized

---

[3]   This section is based on M. K. Buckland and A. Hindle, "Acquisitions, Growth and
Performance Control Through Systems Analysis," in *Farewell to Alexandria: Solutions
to Space, Growth, and Performance Problems of Libraries*, edited by D. Gore (Westport,
Conn.: Greenwood Press, 1976), pp. 44-61. "Browsability" is defined as the extent to
which the array of books available to the browser tends to be systematically biased in
favor of the less popular and the less recommended.

[4]   See also F. W. Lancaster, *The Measurement and Evaluation of Library Services*
(Washington, D.C.: Information Resources Press, 1977).

in figure 14.2. In theory, this begins to formalize the connections which would indicate cost-effective relationships between patterns of need and management decisions. Practical implementation of this knowledge may not be easy, not least because any given library is likely to be serving differing levels of document specific and information specific searches at the same time. However, the relative frequency of different types of search and their perceived relative importance could reasonably influence the style of library services provided.

Outcome	High Document Specificity	High Information Specificity
Collection completeness	Importance depends on urgency. Selection should be influenced by expected level of future usage.	Subject coverage as needed in areas of of interest
Immediate availability	Depends on urgency	Moderate importance depends on substitutability
Collection bias	Not important	High importance
Circulation	Not relevant	Not relevant
Reading	Not relevant	Not relevant
Awareness		
—of documents	High	Low
—of data	Low	High

Fɪɢ. 14.2   Importance of outcomes according to type of search

Reflecting on the conclusions reached above concerning the appropriateness of differing emphases in relation to different types of search, it does not seem entirely fanciful to see in this analysis at least a partial explanation of the distinctive features of service in different types of libraries. Academic libraries, special libraries, and public libraries do appear to reflect the attributes ascribed to libraries serving users whose searches tend to be characterized by tendencies to emphasize high document specificity, high information specifity, and low levels of both, respectively.

Consider, for example, the differing attitudes toward discarding between academic libraries and public or special libraries. Note also the higher investment by academic libraries (even when financial crises mandate the cancellation of serials subscriptions) in circulation systems that enable specific documents to be promptly recalled from loan—an option often forgone in public libraries.

This is not to suggest that the patterns of information specificity are, or should be, the sole determinants of priorities in the planning of library services. What is suggested is that there appears to be a practical need for a deeper and more rigorous analysis of information-gathering behavior. Furthermore, this analysis needs to be explicitly linked to the decisions that librarians have to make concerning the allocation of resources. Information specificity, document specificity, importance, and urgency are suggested as elements to be included in such an analysis.

Just as one can hardly design equipment unless the design requirements are well known, so likewise libraries and information services are unlikely to be cost-effectively provided unless the characteristics of the people to be served are known in terms that can be related to the decisions that the designer or planner can make.

There have been innumerable "user studies," some including potential as well as actual users. However, while such studies unquestionably give some insight, it seems unlikely that substantial improvement will follow unless the information-gathering behavior can be categorized according to more or less standardized taxonomy *and* related to budgetary and planning decisions in some practical manner.

15

Access

Introduction

The previous two chapters examined how parts of library services relate to each other to form a whole. We now address the same theme, but use a different approach. This time we step back from examination of mechanisms and responses and, instead, review the conditions that have to be satisfied if people are to become informed through the use of library services.

We noted in chapter 9 that the emphasis on library service is on retrieval rather than on communication. This is consistent with the frequent references to the notion of "access" in the literature of librarianship. Each individual library has its own special focus with respect to mission, groups of users, and sorts of materials collected. Nevertheless, *access* is clearly a common and central concept in library service. The term "access" is used by different people in relation to quite different bits and pieces of the whole, as in "subject access," "open access," "restricted access," and "knowledge access systems." However, each refers to one or more aspects of providing means of access to information, of enabling users to *accede* either to a source of information or, in a fuller sense, to knowledge, to understanding. Occasionally two or more different sorts of access are considered at the same time.[1] In this chapter we *start* with the assumption that *all* of the provision and use of library services is concerned with access to knowledge and proceed to categorize, in top-down fashion, the different aspects or dimensions of access.

Inquiry, resource, user

As a basis for proceeding we restate some points examined in earlier chapters:

1. In considering inquiries (chapter 6), we noted the very varied range of inquiries that can arise: they can be simple or very complex.

---

[1] The "Lacy Report" covered several sorts of access including changes in information technology, libel, censorship, illiteracy, preservation, and the future of libraries: American Library Association, Committee on Freedom and Equality of Access to Information, *Freedom and Equality of Access to Information: A Report to the American Library Association* ("The Lacy Report") (Chicago: American Library Association, 1986).

2. The personal knowledge and the cognitive skills of the individual determine whether or not the individual *will* become informed by the books or other material (chapter 9). Insufficient linguistic skills and lack of comprehension were noted as examples of powerful barriers to knowledge. For simplicity we shall refer to personal knowledge and cognitive skills as that person's *expertise*. The individual's expertise defines the sorts of sources that individuals can learn from.

3. In discussing collections (chapter 7), we observed that although collections can be large and wide-ranging they can never be fully complete. Each collection reflects more or less conscious selection to match local needs. Library materials also have many different attributes, any one or more of which might be useful in identifying material likely to be useful. Any map of scholarship would surely be very complex and of many dimensions. The customary dimensions of subject content, authorship, date, and form need not be repeated here. One dimension relevant to this discussion is the extent to which materials have been interpreted, using a broad sense of the term to denote explanation and summary, as well as interpretation from one language to another. Education, scholarship, and debate—and library collections—are permeated with processes of interpretation and summarizing. Articles and books explain, cite, refute, and build upon earlier work.

In the interpretation and the summarizing there is a trade-off: the new version may be more convenient and require less expertise to be understood, but some of the details and nuances of the original are always lost in the process. A large proportion of book usage, in or outside of libraries, is of books that include a significant measure of "popularization" in the respectable sense of the term, meaning explanation that is understandable to many people. Individual documents vary greatly in the extent to which they can be regarded as interpretations or summaries. Each library collection has a greater or lesser emphasis on interpretive material. It is not argued that this would be a simple, linear dimension, only that it is helpful, at least for the sake of discussion, to recognize that library materials and, therefore, library collections do vary in this regard.

The relationships between these three factors are central to effective library use. They can be viewed as paralleling each other in that:

(a) The degree of interpretedness of the library's material needs to match the inquiry itself. Evidence is lost in interpretation and summary: details, fine points, and subtle features are eroded. Hence too simplified an account may simply be *inadequate* for the purpose at hand.

(b) The expertise of the library user needs to match the complexity of the material. An explanation that assumes too much expertise on the inquirer's part is ineffective.

In brief, for learning to be effective and efficient the source should be at a degree of interpretedness that matches both the nature of the inquiry and the expertise of the inquirer. Otherwise an over-interpreted source will have lost too much of its capacity to be informative and an under-interpreted source will be imperfectly intelligible.

Language is only one aspect of this, as can be seen in the example of an explanation that is at the right cognitive level but is unintelligible because it is in a foreign languge that the user does not understand.

Six aspects of access

We have defined "access" as the means to enable an inquirer to learn from—become informed by—a source pertinent to an inquiry, to *accede* to the evidence that will yield the knowledge desired.

It may not always be possible to provide access: no pertinent source may exist for some inquiries; with some obscure inquiries the source may exist but understanding it might be beyond anybody's expertise, as with fragments of lost languages.

In simpler cases suitable, intelligible, credible sources exist and the problem of access reduces to bringing a source and the inquirer together. However, six types of barrier have to be overcome to enable access to be achieved:

1. Identification

A suitable source needs to be identified. This "indicative" access is the realm of bibliography and of information retrieval, as discussed in chapters 7 and 8. Ordinarily this is thought of in terms of finding a pertinent document "about" the topic of the inquiry, but, more generally, the retrieval system may need to be responsive to requests for retrieval on appropriate attributes, commonly, but not necessarily, including subject content. (Strictly speaking, this is usually at least a two-stage process: deciding where to look ("channel-selection") as well as identifying a specific book, record, or other source.)

The best source that can be identified might still be insufficient to answer the inquiry: it might lack sufficient detail or it might deal with only one part of the inquiry. It might then be acceptable to change the inquiry to make it more compatible with the sources that can be identified. Such inquiry modification is not, logically, the same as "question negotiation" as used in the literature of reference service, which in its pure form is concerned with establishing a *clearer definition* of the inquiry in terms that the information system (reference librarian, index, classification system) can handle.[2] It is reasonable to assume that, in practice, question negotiation also includes some inquiry *re*definition intentionally or otherwise.

2. Availability

The inquirer needs to be able to inspect the source or a copy of it. This "physical" access, "document delivery," is a matter of logistics and technology. If a source that has been identified cannot be made physically available in an acceptable fashion, then another will have to be identified and made available.

3. Price to the user

We use "price" to denote what the would-be user must expend to use the service (*cf.* chapter 10). The price may include, but is not restricted to, money. "The real price of everything, what everything really costs to the man who wants to acquire it, is the toil and trouble of acquiring it" (Adam Smith).[3] The "real price" includes time, effort, and discomfort as well as money. ("I was too embarrassed to ask ... "). In particular, price includes the effort of learning to use difficult, "user-unfriendly" systems.[4] The price (as discussed in chapter 10) must be acceptable to the inquirer. To the extent to which it is not, price is a barrier to access.

4. Cost to the provider

Not all expenditure is borne by the inquirer, least of all in library services which are traditionally free, in the sense that monetary charges are not usually made. In this context we use the term "cost" to denote what has to be expended by the *providers* of service. To the extent that the sponsors or providers of service may incur expenditure of effort, money, or inconvenience, the arrangement would have to be acceptable to or, at least, not incompatible with, their view of their role, mission, and values. Meeting the need may encroach on values of a social, cultural, or political nature.

---

[2] See, for instance, G. Jahoda and J. S. Braunagel, *The Librarian and Reference Queries: A Systematic Approach* (New York: Academic Press, 1980); B. C. Vickery and A. Vickery, *Information Science in Theory and Practice* (London: Butterworths, 1987), chapter 7: Intermediaries and Interfaces.

[3] A. Smith, *An Inquiry into the Nature and Causes of the Wealth of Nations* (Oxford: Clarendon Press, 1976), Book 1, chapter 5, para. 2.

[4] See, for instance, M. J. Culnan, "The Dimensions of Perceived Accessibility to Information: Implications for the Delivery of Information Systems and Services," *Journal of the American Society for Information Science* 36, no. 5 (1985): 302-5.

As discussed in chapter 11, library service is largely defined by the allocation of resources, and this allocation is based on the resources and social values of those who allocate. Providing access to appropriate evidence might in some cases be regarded as an unacceptable challenge to these values: to national security, to private or corporate vested interest, or to social values as in the case of indecent or irreligious materials.[5] These nonmonetary values have a long history of restricting access in a manner similar in nature to restrictions caused by financial shortages.[6]

5. Cognitive access

Once physical access to a suitable source has been achieved, another condition for successful access is that the inquirer has sufficient expertise to understand it (chapter 9). If not, then some combination of two remedies are possible:

(a) *Explanation* would involve additional interpretation of the source—a translation, perhaps, if the existing source is in a foreign language, or an explanation by someone with more expertise, either on an informal ad hoc basis or by the creation of a new summary.

(b) *Education* is another solution in that the inquirer may be able to acquire more expertise, for example by consulting a dictionary, an encyclopedia, or someone who has the requisite expertise, and may then be able to understand the book.[7]

There is one further aspect involved in "acceding to knowledge," which has not traditionally been thought of as having to do with access, yet

---

[5] See, for instance, *Library Trends* 35, no. 1 (Summer 1986): 3-183. Issue on Privacy, Secrecy, and National Information Policy.

[6] "How strange it is that for most liberal thinkers—academics as well as statesmen—knowledge is almost always 'good' and worthy of wide diffusion, although history is full of attempts by governors—political, moral, and religious leaders; and well-meaning parents—to discourage the spread of 'dangerous' or 'unwholesome' knowledge." F. Machlup, *Knowledge and Knowledge Production* (Princeton, N.J.: Princeton University Press, 1980), p. 12.

[7] Mention of the need to increase expertise invites speculation on the scope for using artificial intelligence or "expert systems" to supplement human expertise. In the terms of this chapter, expert information systems would appear to be useful, in principle, for four different tasks of increasing probable practical difficulty: question negotiation—translating inquiries into the language of the retrieval system; education—augmenting the user's expertise to understand what has been retrieved; inquiry modification—negotiating a different inquiry that the retrieval system can respond to in lieu of one that it cannot; and explanation—interpreting, summarizing, and/or simplifying evidence that is unclear to the user. *Cf.* L. C. Smith, "Artificial Intelligence and Information Retrieval," *Annual Review of Information Science and Technology* 22 (1987): 41-77. *Advances in Intelligent Retrieval: Informatics 8; Proceedings of a Conference, Oxford, 1985* (London: Aslib, 1985); *Information Processing and Management* 23, no. 4 (1987): 244-382 (Special issue: Artificial Intelligence and Information Retrieval).

plays the same kind of role in practice as the other aspects discussed above, and so can reasonably be included in the discussion of access.

6. Acceptability

We use the term "acceptability" to denote two related issues: (i) inquirers may be reluctant to accept a particular source as credible, regarding it as having inadequate "cognitive authority" in Wilson's term;[8] and (ii) the inquirer may be unwilling to accept the evidence of the source because it is unwelcome in what it signifies and conflicts with other beliefs, a matter of "cognitive dissonance."[9] Everyone will agree that some sources *should* be denied credibility. The problem is in deciding which.

Summary

The variety of ways in which the term "access" has been used is symptomatic of the several ways in which library services are concerned with providing access. The notion of "access" can provide a unifying concept for the field as a whole so long as "access" is viewed in terms of a broader, multi-dimensional way.

In a narrow sense of a library as a *document* retrieval system the notions of (1) identification, (2) availability, (3) price to the user, and (4) cost to the provider constitute a useful categorization of conditions that must be met. For a broader view of library services as providing access not just to documents, but to *knowledge*, becoming informed, the addition of requirements for (5) cognitive access and (6) acceptability constitutes a necessary and sufficient expansion of that categorization. Each one of the dimensions constitutes a type of barrier to access; each one must be satisfied if access is to be effected.

The very diverse nature of the different aspects of access means that quite different sorts of actions are needed to remedy difficulties on each. For example, the remedy may be technical (better retrieval systems for identification, better document delivery for availability), additional time, effort, or money (price), an increase in resources or a change in social and political values (cost), instructional (remedying inadequate expertise for identifying materials or for understanding them when they are made available), or altered attitudes (acceptability).

---

[8] P. G. Wilson, *Second-hand Knowledge: An Inquiry into Cognitive Authority* (Westport, Conn.: Greenwood Press, 1983).

[9] L. Festinger, *A Theory of Cognitive Dissonance* (Stanford, Calif.: University Press, 1986); A. G. Greenwald and D. L. Ronis, "Twenty-five Years of Cognitive Dissonance: Case Study of the Evolution of a Theory," *Psychological Review* 85, no. 1 (1978): 53-7.

16

Measurement and Quantification

Introduction

So far we have largely ignored problems of measurement. We did so because we were primarily concerned with the *theoretical* task of defining a conceptual framework rather than the *practical* difficulty of doing things. In day-to-day activities, however, it is very helpful to be able to measure things: doing so can add a sense of proportion. In this chapter we shall review the progress that has been made in measurement with respect to library services. We shall also consider some of the problems.

Although there were some earlier examples of measurement and quantification in libraries, the late 1960s mark a convenient turning point. The first serious monograph on the subject was published in 1968[1] and it was around then that the literature begins to reflect the results of quantitative techniques being applied to libraries by different groups in different places. By the mid-1970s this activity was no longer novel.[2] By the late 1980s it has been broadly absorbed and diffused.

Reflecting on this corpus of literature, on the topics which have been selected for study, on the weaknesses and gaps, and on the significant but limited extent of practical implementation, one suspects that progress in this field is probably very similar to progress in to other areas of social service. The conditions, at any rate, would appear to be similar:

- staff strive to provide a range of different services to multiple constituencies with differing interests;
- service, not profit, is the objective, and there is no single measure of overall effectiveness;
- intangible benefits and externalities abound;
- there are role uncertainties for personnel concerning professional as opposed to administrative roles; and

---

[1] P. M. Morse, *Library Effectiveness* (Cambridge, Mass.: MIT Press, 1968).

[2] A bibliography published in 1976 listed 700 items: M. K. Buckland and D. H. Kraft, "A Bibliography on Operations Research in Libraries," in *Reader in Operations Research for Libraries*, edited by P. Brophy et al. (Englewood, Colo.: Information Handling Services, 1976), pp. 355-92.

● political control over service priorities is unevenly distributed among the segments of the population being served.

A labor-intensive, not-for-profit activity in which intangible benefits are provided to individuals is necessarily a complex system even though it may not be a large one.[3]

The approach of this chapter will be to review those areas in which most work has been done, then to identify some areas in which more work needs to be done.

Bibliometrics: the structure of published literature and of its usage

"Bibliometrics" is the term used to denote the quantitative study of phenomena of "documentary discourse," such as authorship, publication, reading, and citation.[4] This area includes studies of: the growth of the literature on a given subject;[5] patterns in the distribution of publishing productivity by individual authors ("Lotka's Law");[6] how articles on any subject are dispersed across journals ("Bradford's Law of Scattering");[7] the "obsolescence" of literature;[8] the epidemiology of ideas as reflected in technical literature;[9] and the study of networks and patterns in scholarship as evidenced by analyses of who cites whom.[10]

[3] Library services are not alone in these characteristics; see Y. Hasenfeld, *Human Services Organizations* (Englewood Cliffs, N.J.: Prentice Hall, 1983).

[4] D. H. Hertzel, "Bibliometrics, History of the Development of Ideas," *Encyclopedia of Information Science and Technology*, vol. 42 (New York: Marccl Dekker, 1987), pp. 144-214; F. Narin and J. K. Moll, "Bibliometrics," *Annual Review of Information Science and Technology* 12 (1977): 35-58; R. N. Broadus, "Early Approaches to Bibliometrics," *Journal of the American Society for Information Science* 38, no. 2 (March 1987): 127-9; *Collection Management* 2 (Fall 1978): 195-261: Special Issue on Bibliometrics.

[5] M. R. Oliver, "The Effect of Growth on the Obsolescence of Semi-Conductor Physics Literature," *Journal of Documentation* 27 (1971): 11-17.

[6] A. Bookstein, "Patterns of Scientific Productivity and Social Change: A Discussion of Lotka's Law and Bibliometric Symmetry," *Journal of the American Society for Information Science* 28, no. 4 (1977): 206-10; M. L. Pao, "An Empirical Examination of Lotka's Law," *Journal of the American Society for Information Science* 37, no. 1 (January 1986): 26-33.

[7] M. G. Kendall, "The Bibliography of Operational Research," *Operational Research Quarterly* 11 (1960): 31-6; M. G. Kendall, "Natural Law in the Social Sciences," *Journal of the Royal Statistical Society* (Series A) 124 (1961): 1-18; E. A. Wilkinson, "The Ambiguity of Bradford's Law," *Journal of Documentation* 28 (1972): 122-30.

[8] M. B. Line and A. Sandison, "Obsolescence and Changes in the Use of Literature with Time," *Journal of Documentation* 30 (1974): 283-350; B. C. Griffith et al., "Aging of Scientific Literature," *Journal of Documentation* 35, no. 3 (September 1979): 179-96.

[9] W. Goffman, "Mathematical Approach to the Spread of Scientific Ideas—The History of Mast Cells," *Nature* 212, no. 5061 (1966): 449-52.

[10] D. de S. Price, *Little Science, Big Science* (New York: Colombia University Press, 1963); D. de S. Price, "Networks of Scientific Papers," *Science* 149 (1965): 510-15; K. W. McCain, "Cocited Author Mapping as a Valid Representation of Intellectual Structure," *Journal of the American Society for Information Science* 37, no. 3 (May 1986): 111-22.

There is almost endless scope for mathematical modeling in this area. The data—usually the references at the end of articles—are readily available to all and, increasingly, in machine readable form. Hence, experiments can be replicated or extended indefinitely. Hitherto, the precise formulation of the distributions found, and whether they are really the same as each other, has been a fertile area.[11]

It is convenient to identify two principal sorts of modeling:

1. *Descriptive analysis.* The identification and explication of patterns is an area in which the foundations of librarianship merge with the foundations of other social sciences. There are affinities with mathematic linguistics and, seemingly, broad tracts of quantification pertaining to human behavior. This area was advanced and popularized by Derek de Solla Price and others interested in the science (and sociology) of science. Notions such as the "invisible college" (clusters of mutually citing scholars),[12] and "technological gate-keepers" (individuals through whom a disproportionately large amount of communication flows),[13] and the use of citation analysis to write history[14] and to predict Nobel Prize winners[15] can hardly fail to intrigue.

Since this work is primarily descriptive, it is of questionable usefulness. We cite it, however, on the grounds that it provides insights and that mathematical modeling of parts of what is a very complex area could form the basis for applied research.

2. *Prescriptive models.* Some researchers have examined bibliometric studies and endeavored to explore their implications for library management decisions. The principal example of this concerns scattering, obsolescence, and the determination of optimal library size.

Bradford's Law of Scattering, which is a measure of the dispersion over all available journals of articles on any given subject, is normally formulated as a cumulative, ranked distribution. The few journals which contribute most of the articles on a topic constitute the "core" or "nuclear zone." Other titles which contribute less are ranked and added, individually or in clusters ("zones"), in order of decreasing number of

[11] R. A. Fairthorne, "Empirical Hyperbolic Distributions (Bradford-Zipf-Mandelbrot) for Bibliometric Description and Prediction," *Journal of Documentation* 25 (1969): 319-43; B. C. Brookes, "Towards Informetrics: Haitun, Laplace, Zipf, Bradford and the Alvey Programme," *Journal of Documentation* 40, no. 2 (June 1984): 120-43; L. Egghe, "Consequences for Lotka's Law for the Law of Bradford," *Journal of Documentation* 41, no. 3 (September 1985): 173-89.

[12] D. Crane, *Invisible Colleges: Diffusion of Knowledge in Scientific Communities* (Chicago, Ill.: University of Chicago Press, 1972).

[13] T. J. Allen, "Roles in Technical Networks," in *Communication Among Scientists and Engineers,* edited by C. R. Nelson, and D. K. Pollock (Lexington, Mass.: Heath Lexington Books, 1970), pp. 191-208.

[14] H. Small and E. Greenlee, "Collagen Research in the 1970s," *Scientometrics* 10, nos 1-2 (1986): 95-117.

[15] E. Garfield, "Citation Indexing for Studying Science," *Nature* 227 (1970): 669-71.

articles contributed. Expressed this way, Bradford's Law of Scattering can properly be regarded as a law of diminishing returns with respect to the number of titles held in a given subject area.

Obsolescence, the fall-off in use of materials as they age, can similarly be regarded as a law of diminishing returns with respect to the length of time material is retained in a library's collections. (For this and scattering see chapter 10.)

A significant breakthrough in library operations research was the realization that, taken in conjunction, these two laws of diminishing returns provide some insight into the elusive concept of optimal library size. Making important assumptions about the degree of scattering, the rate of obsolescence, the behavior of library users, and the value of users' time, one can, in theory, prescribe the least-cost journal collection capable of meeting any given percentage of the demands on a given subject. Priority in this area (sometimes referred to as "the $p\%$ library") appears to belong to Cole,[16] but a number of other researchers have rediscovered or refined this and related approaches.[17] The same problem occurs in the case of file size in computer-based bibliographical information storage and retrieval systems. What combination of range of titles and range of years should be stored for computerized literature searches to provide what percentage of completeness of coverage? What combination should be retained in primary storage for the initial search as opposed to secondary storage (or manual systems) for extended searches?

There are three principal difficulties in this approach: (a) An unrealistically homogeneous demand is generally assumed. Overlapping, non-homogeneous subsets of demand are difficult to handle; (b) The models remain incomplete and optimization impossible until one can determine the *impact* on the user population of different values of p. What proportion of demand *should* we endeavor to satisfy and how does the choice of p influence the demand? (c) An entirely probabilistic solution may be politically unsatisfactory for the librarian who may prefer instead to minimize the regret which could result from irate library users seeking material that was either not purchased or, worse, discarded because future demand had been *expected* to be negligible.

On account of the incompleteness of our knowledge of library-user interactions, it seems likely that bibliometric analysis will come to be useful not so much in *prescribing* what should be done but rather in

---

[16] P. F. Cole, "Journal Usage Versus Age of Journal," *Journal of Documentation* 19 (1963): 1-11.

[17] B. C. Brookes, "Optimum $p\%$ Library of Scientific Periodicals," *Nature* 232, no. 5311 (1971): 458-61; M. K. Buckland, *Book Availability and the Library User* (New York: Pergamon Press, 1975); B. Houghton, "Cutback on Periodicals," *New Library World* 73 (1972): 210; B. K. Sinha and R. C. Clelland, "Modelling for the Management of Library Collections," *Management Science* 22, no. 5 (1975): 547-57.

helping us to understand the dynamics involved; in *predicting* the probable consequences of decision-making; and, by helping identify atypical situations, in identifying malfunctions and interesting anomalies in operational systems.

Far less developed are explanations of the *causes* of the patterns that are observed.

Logistics of documentary delivery

The study of the logistics of library services may be less elegant than bibliometrics, but the results can and have been implemented with success. The aspects most commonly studied are: the distribution of demand over a collection;[18] the growth in collection size;[19] the distribution of lengths of time involved in book usage and inter-usage intervals; standards of service, for example, "immediate availability," which usually signifies the probability of library users finding what they want when they want it;[20] the impact of policy variables, for example, how many different titles should be provided? How many copies of each? How long should they be retained? How long should the loan period be? Should overdue books incur fines? How far is photocopying a reasonable substitute for lending? How far is dependence on interlibrary loan an acceptable substitute for acquisition? How should a network of back-up interlibrary loan facilities be organized?

This area contains two documented examples of implemented operations research studies.

Example 1: National Lending Library, U.K.

The design and development of the National Lending Library for Science and Technology at Boston Spa, Yorkshire, England (now known as the Document Supply Center) is a classic case of the use of common sense and simple quantification.

The British government, inspired by the progress of Russian technology in the form of Sputnik, decided to build a new national library, not a conventional library but a library for libraries. This was to be a back-up

---

[18] A. Kent et al., *Use of Library Materials: The University of Pittsburgh Study* (New York: Marcel Dekker, 1979); K. W. R. Brownsley and Q. L. Burrell, "Library Circulation Distributions: Some Observations on the PLR Sample," *Journal of Documentation* 42, no. 1 (March 1986): 22-45.

[19] R. E. Molyneux, "Patterns, Processes of Growth, and the Projection of Library Size: A Critical Review of the Literature on Academic Library Growth," *Library and Information Science Research* 8, no. 1 (January-March 1986): 5-28.

[20] D. H. Revill, "'Availability' as a Performance Measure for Academic Libraries," *Journal of Librarianship* 19, no. 1 (January 1987): 15-30; J. Mansbridge, "Availability Studies in Libraries," *Library and Information Science Research* 8, no. 4 (October-December 1986): 299-314.

facility which would collect British and foreign scientific literature and make it available by interlibrary loan. The whole enterprise was aggressively unconventional. Few people agreed that a modern science and technology library should be set up in a remote rural location; should prefer manual to computerized methods; and, for the most part, have no catalog. The design and development were, however, based firmly on the collection and analysis of factual data. The result was rapid and spectacular success. It now also serves as a back-up facility for libraries in North America and worldwide.[21] Central to the whole plan was the elementary use of queuing theory. In a concise and lucid paper, Urquhart and Bunn summarized the best available data on the interlibrary loan demand in Britain and demonstrated that, for the great majority of journal titles, there was no statistical justification for interlibrary loan provision separate from the main national reference libraries.[22] They then used queuing theory to calculate the number of copies needed to maintain at least 95 percent availability on demand with either regionalized or centralized provision.The inescapable conclusion that centralized provision was not only more economical at low levels of demand but increasingly more economical at higher levels of demand ran entirely contrary to the conventional wisdom of the British library profession at that time.

Example 2: Variable loan policies, University of Lancaster

In 1968, the University Librarian at the University of Lancaster, England, was worried by complaints that users could not find the books they sought. The library had its own small in-house research unit to which the problem was referred. The study proceeded by adopting "immediate availability when needed" as a measure of service and by identifying the relationship between the four variables associated with the availability of any given title: pattern of demand; number of copies; loan period; and probability of a copy being available.

For any given level of demand, the probability of a copy being available is directly related to the number of copies and inversely related to the length of loan period. Hence, the loan period and the duplication policy should be related both to the level of demand and to each other. As with the National Lending Library, it is essentially a queuing problem. At Lancaster, however, analytical solutions based on queuing theory were

---

[21] For a history of this library, see B. Houghton, *Out of the Age of Dinosaurs: The Evolution of the National Lending Library for Science and Technology* (London: Bingley, 1972). See also D. J. Urquhart, *The Principles of Librarianship* (Metuchen, N.J.: Scarecrow Press, 1981).

[22] D. J. Urquhart, and R. M. Bunn, "A National Loan Policy for Scientific Serials," *Journal of Documentation* 27 (1959): 21-37. Also reprinted in *Reader in Operations Research for Libraries,* edited by P. Brophy et al. (Englewood, Colo.: Information Handling Services, 1976).

abandoned in favor of programming a computer to simulate the borrowing and returning of books.

It was estimated that users could find the books they wanted about 60 percent of the time. Three alternative strategies were compared for increasing this success rate to about 80 percent: selective duplication of popular titles; shortened loan periods for undergraduates; and a "variable" loan policy whereby the loan period depended directly on the demand for the document not the status of the borrower. The last was deemed superior in cost-effectiveness and was implemented.[23] The expected improvement in service resulted but also provoked a dramatic and largely unanticipated increase in demand which the adaptive properties of the system helped meet. This work has been replicated in detail at Case Western Reserve University[24] and implemented elsewhere. A by-product has been the use of the modeling to create library management games for professional education in librarianship, though their impact has been small.[25]

Morse's pioneering treatise, *Library Effectiveness: A Systems Approach*,[26] was largely concerned with the logistics of book availability and drew heavily on queuing theory and on a Markov model of book obsolescence in analyzing book availability at the Massachusetts Institute of Technology Science Library. His work has since been extended by Chen.[27] Meanwhile, Kantor has clarified and extended the analysis of factors interfering with book availability by explicitly incorporating the adequacy of the library's collections and users' failures to find items which were in their correct places as additional factors.[28]

Another topic in library logistics is the use of mail delivery of books as an alternative to bookmobiles. A treatment of this topic by Hu et al. serves to illustrate the problems of externalities, the secondary consequences of library use.[29] Children may be the majority of the users. Fostering the use of books by children is generally agreed to be good for

[23] M. K. Buckland, *Book Availability and the Library User* (New York: Pergamon Press, 1975); M. K. Buckland, "An Operations Research Study of a Variable Loan and Duplication Policy at the University of Lancaster," *Library Quarterly* 42, no. 1 (January 1972): 97-106.

[24] W. M. Shaw, "Library-User Interface: A Simulation of the Circulation Subsystem," *Information Processing Management* 12 (1976): 77-91.

[25] J. Daly et al., The Use of Gaming in Education for Library Management: Final Report on a Research Project (Lancaster, England: University of Lancaster Library, Occasional Papers, 8, 1976).

[26] Morse, *Library Effectiveness*.

[27] C.-C. Chen, *Applications of Operations Research Models to Libraries* (Cambridge, Mass.: MIT Press, 1976).

[28] P.B. Kantor, "Availability Analysis," *Journal of the American Society for Information Science* 27, no. 5/6 (1976): 311-19.

[29] T. Hu et al., A Benefit-Cost Analysis of Alternative Library Delivery Systems (Westport, Conn.: Greenwood Press, 1975).

their education in general and their verbal skills in particular. These benefits clearly ought not to be ignored, yet nobody seems to know how to incorporate them. This remains a major problem in planning library services in a society that is very highly dependent on verbal skills.

Telecommunications

The rise of networks of hundreds of libraries interconnected on-line with bibliographical data bases (outstandingly, with OCLC in Dublin, Ohio) has inspired a new interest in modeling multilibrary relationships.[30] For the most part, the structure of the problems remains substantially the same as before computerization. What is new is the greater formality, the increased availability of data, and the emphasis on telecommunications. One can expect this to be a fertile area for quantitative analysis.

Hierarchies and networks

Libraries almost unavoidably tend to fall into formal or informal networks—with hierarchical structures being especially common. In universities it is normal to have main and departmental libraries. In the public library systems there is generally a hierarchy of two or three levels with headquarters, regional centers, and neighborhood branches. In all cases, other libraries as a source of interlibrary loans constitute an additional layer. Inside each library there is generally a three-stage hierarchy: reserve and/or "ready-reference"; main shelves; and storage.

Four types of work are relevant here:

1. Studies in weeding—discarding or relegation to secondary storage—are generally based on estimates of the frustration caused by the diminution of the collection by weeding.[31] Considerable time and ingenuity have been devoted to developing, testing, and predicting the consequences of various quantitative decision rules for weeding. Unfortunately, the inexpensive rules (e.g., those based on date of publication) tend to be low in effectiveness and those that are more effective tend to be uneconomically expensive. Since there is no doubt that the distribution of demand on library collections is highly

[30] R. E. Nance et al., "Information Networks: Definitions and Message Transfer Models," *Journal of the American Society for Information Science* 23, no. 4 (1972): 237-47; W. B. Rouse and S. Rouse, *Management of Library Networks: Policy Analysis, Implementation, and Control* (New York: Wiley, 1980).

[31] W. C. Lister, "Least Cost Decision Rules for the Selection of Library Materials for Compact Storage," Ph.D. thesis, Purdue University, Lafayette, Ind., 1967; H. H. Fussler and J. L. Simon, *Patterns in the Use of Books in Large Research Libraries* (Chicago, Ill.: University of Chicago Press, 1969); S. J. Slote, *Weeding Library Collections* (Littleton, Colo.: Libraries Unlimited, 1975); J. C. Urquhart and N. C. Urquhart, *Relegation and Stock Control in Libraries* (Stocksfield, England: Oriel Press, 1976).

skewed, that large quantities of books receive very little use, and that the continued expansion of conventional library buildings is expensive, we can confidently expect economic pressures to result in more, not less, research on weeding and associated problems.

2. The design of interlibrary loan arrangements becomes highly relevant because, insofar as the delayed supply of documents and a diminished scope for browsing are acceptable, dependence on interlibrary loan is a temptingly inexpensive alternative to local expenditure on library collections. The problems are basically technical and the literature includes studies of transportation systems,[32] the routing of inter-library loan requests between libraries,[33] and special interlibrary loan facilities (e.g., National Lending Library, described above). However, decision-making is hampered by disagreements concerning the impact on users of increased dependence on remote resources and by uncertainties concerning the financing, control, and dependability of interlibrary loan facilities.

3. Overlap studies have been made to consider the problem that many but not all of the titles held in one library are also held in other nearby libraries. By collaborating in the processing of titles held in common, operational economies might be achieved. By sharing access to uniquely held titles, the range available to each library's users is greatly extended.[34] Similar methodological and practical concerns arise in planning and evaluating abstracting and indexing services covering the literature in different areas.

4. The design of hierarchies of collections has also been studied.[35] Even the most unitary library is part of a two-stage hierarchy with interlibrary loan resources constituting the second stage. This has taken on a new significance in recent years as some library researchers, drawing heavily on earlier operations research studies, have been propounding a revisionist view of library size. The argument, stated briefly, is that since the distribution of demand over the collection is highly skewed, continued emphasis, even in academic libraries, on maximising library size is likely to continue a decreasingly cost-effective

---

[32] A. Reisman et al., "Timeliness of Library Materials Delivery: A Set of Priorities," *Socio-Economic Planning Sciences* 6, no. 2 (1972): 145-52.

[33] W. B. Rouse and S. H. Rouse, *Management of Library Networks: Policy Analysis, Implementation, and Control* (New York: Wiley, 1980).

[34] W. S. Cooper et al., "The Duplication of Monograph Holdings in the University of California Library System," *Library Quarterly* 45, no. 3 (1975): 233-75; M. K. Buckland et al., "Methodological Problems in Assessing the Overlap Between Bibliographical Files and Library Holdings," *Information Processing and Management* 11 (1975): 89-105; W. G. Potter, "Studies of Collection Overlap: A Literature Review," *Library Research* 4, no. 1 (September 1982): 3-21.

[35] B. C. Brookes, "The Design of Hierarchical Information Systems," *Information Storage and Retrieval* 6 (1970): 127-36.

use of resources.[36] In several ways, discussions of the controversial question of optimal library size epitomize rather well both the progress and stimulating effects of operations research applied to libraries and also the serious incompletenesses that remain.

Storage methods

For multimillion volume libraries, physical storage is a major problem. Various strategies for economy are possible including sorting and shelving books by size, shelving books on their fore-edges, compact shelving, and remote storage on low-cost sites. However, the marginal gains in economies of space are counterbalanced by reduced accessibility for both staff and users, and increased transportation costs. A whole series of analyses of this problem, dealing with height, physical accessibility, principles of arrangement and cost, has been conducted under the leadership of Leimkuhler at Purdue University.[37]

Performance of indexing systems

It is important to distinguish clearly between the "information theory" (or "communication theory") associated with Shannon and Weaver and "information storage and retrieval theory." Both are concerned with signaling, but there is a fundamental difference. "Information theory" is concerned with the direct transmission of signals from A to B regardless of meaning. With information storage and retrieval, the communication is indirect in that the message may have been generated by A but it is not known who, if anyone, would be interested in the signal. In this case, however, the meaning of the signals is of great importance. Each potential B needs to determine which signals generated by each A might be of interest.

The performance of indexing systems is concerned with analyzing what has been retrieved in comparison with what should have been retrieved and also with the costs involved. Traditionally, this has been measured by means of a two-by-two contingency table: Relevant/Not relevant; Retrieved/Not retrieved. For a more detailed discussion see chapter 8 above. In general terms, "precision" (retrieval of relevant items but not nonrelevant items) can be improved only at the expense of

---

[36] D. Gore, ed., *Farewell to Alexandria: Solutions to Space, Growth and Performance Problems of Libraries* (Westport, Conn.: Greenwood Press, 1976). For library size, see footnote 5 of chapter 20.

[37] For example, F. F. Leimkuhler and J. G. Cox, "Compact Book Storage for Libraries," *Operational Research Quarterly* 12 (1964): 419-27; F. F. Leimkuhler, "On Information Storage Models," in *Planning Library Services,* edited by A. G. Mackenzie and I. M. Stuart (Lancaster, England: University of Lancaster Library Occasional Papers, 3, 1969).

"recall" (retrieving *all* relevant items even though some nonrelevant items are also retrieved) or vice-versa. This is awkward because one ends up with a play-off rather than a single measure. There are two others problems: (1) the assessment of retrieval performance tends to be a subjective, arbitrary, and inconsistent activity—as is the assignment of descriptors by indexers and catalogers;[38] and (2) a retrieved item may be relevant but of no utility to the inquirer since it may be redundant or incomprehensible.

The literature on information retrieval makes extensive use of logic, set theory, probability, and statistics, especially in the work on experimental computer-based retrieval systems[39] and on tests of retrieval performance.[40] It is a relatively self-contained area, characterized by powerful tools and considerable talent. The problem is not in the manipulation of the measurements, or even that the results suggest that there is relatively little to choose between different systems, or that laboratory tests on small-scale experiments may not always yield the best insights. The real problems are at the borders with the rest of the world. The point of departure is the sorting of records between those that are relevant and those that are not. Yet it is not really understood what relevance is, or what it signifies, what the consequences of retrieval are, or when to stop doing it. As with citation analysis, the sophistication of the manipulation of the measurements is far ahead of our understanding of what is being measured.

Underdeveloped areas

Users and potential users

It would be an exaggeration to say that there have been *no* studies leading to mathematical models of the users and potential users of library services. For example, the phenomena examined in the bibliometric studies reflect patterns of user behavior. Also there have been a very few

[38] T. Saracevic, "The Concept of 'Relevance' in Information Science: A Historical Review," in *Introduction to Information Science*, edited by T. Saracevic (New York: Bowker, 1970), pp. 111-51.

[39] For an introduction see G. Salton and M. J. McGill, *Introduction to Modern Information Retrieval* (New York: McGraw-Hill, 1983); G. Salton, "Mathematics and Information Retrieval," *Journal of Documentation* 35, no. 1 (March 1979): 1-29; A. Bookstein, "Probability and Fuzzy-set Applications to Information Retrieval," *Annual Review of Information Science and Technology* 20 (1985): 117-51.

[40] See *Information Retrieval Experiment*, edited by K. Sparck Jones (London: Butterworths, 1981); *Information Retrieval Research*, edited by R. N. Oddy et al. (London: Butterworths, 1981).

model-building studies of library use.[41] What are seriously lacking, however, are models of information-gathering behavior. Models of marketing or of user preferences in a library context would seem appropriate.

It is known that *accessibility* is a dominant factor in information-gathering behavior. People are likely to choose a source that is convenient rather than one that is particularly likely to provide the information sought but is difficult to obtain. It seems likely that the demand for library services is quite elastic with respect to a "price" in terms of perceived accessibility (see chapter 10). However, our knowledge of what demand is sensitive to—and how elastic it is—remains very incomplete. Improving the physical ambience (as when a new library is opened), reducing travel effort, and increasing the probability of finding what users seek are all known to increase library usage. Financial charges are unusual in libraries. When instituted they decrease demand. There have been endless studies of library use but not of the dynamics of how library services come to be used (or not used). The reasons for this neglect would seem to be that it is a dificult area to tackle, and the traditional research techniques of neither operations researchers nor librarians lend themselves at present to resolving these problems. Unfortunately, serious limitations to the usefulness of *quantification* in libraries will remain until further progress is made in this aspect.

Analytical cost models

Libraries provide a variety of different services to a variety of different user groups. Typically, the same titles and the same staff serve more than one purpose. Attempts have been made to generate analytical cost models, usually for the purpose of charging for services, for program budgeting, and/or for estimating the library component in overhead charges on research contracts.[42] Predictably, much depends on the accounting conventions adopted as the basis for attributing costs to cost centers. Particularly in academic libraries, the results are dominated by the attribution of costs of books and serials between research and instruction when both functions are being served simultaneously. The choice here dominates the outcome because it affects not only the books and serials expenses but also a large portion of the labor costs which are directly related to book and serial acquisitions and processing.

[41] See, for example, B. S. Nozik, "A Stochastic Model to Predict Demand for Library Services," Ph.D. dissertation, University Microfilms no. BCD75-08029 School of Librarianship, University of California, Berkeley, 1974; W. M. Shaw, "Loan Period Distribution in Academic Libraries," *Information Processing Management* 12 (1976): 157-9.

[42] F. F. Leimkuhler and M. D. Cooper, "Cost Accounting and Analysis for University Libraries," *College and Research Libraries* 32, no. 6 (November 1971): 449-64.

Library "goodness"

Older operations research textbooks were apt to imply that one should meet with top management to ascertain the objectives of the organization, identify the options available, then use mathematical techniques to compute the optimal solution. Such a simplistic approach is of little use for library services because the most difficult task is identifying what the problem is and then in structuring it in a form that is both tractable and acceptable. It is *here* that help is most needed.

Consider the situation. A library serves a variety of different groups with different values, with different behavior patterns, and expressing different needs. A chemist urgently needs to know the thermophysical properties of a compound; a historian is inquiring about an obscure document whose name has been forgotten and which may not, in fact, exist; a bedridden senior citizen may be lonely, bored, and wanting a novel; a disadvantaged citizen wants to know whom to contact about food stamps; a student is sitting in a library carrel with a book. It may not be a library book. The student may be asleep.

Strictly, one cannot determine optimal decisions in library management unless one knows what all these wants are, how effective (and how costly) alternative types of service arrangements are in each case, *and* what values should be assigned to the generally rather intangible outcomes. It is likely that this will remain impossible to do in any strict manner. Yet, library administrators are continually making decisions based on assumptions, explicit or implicit, on precisely these matters.

Lancaster has provided a very convenient review of progress in the development of measures of library service and in analyses of the often conflicting relationships between them.[43] Of the measures discussed in the literature, "immediate availability" and related measures of document delivery are clearly measures of a library's *capability*. Circulation (borrowing) counts and measures of actual reading ("document exposure") are measures of the *utilization* of library services. There has been a growing interest in measures of performance, and in the interactions and budgetary relationships between them. We shall return to issues of library "goodness" in chapter 20.

Synthesis

Most studies addressed specific topics. Hamburg and others at the University of Pennsylvania endeavored to provide a coherent and complete

[43] F. W. Lancaster, *The Measurement and Evaluation of Library Services* (Washington, D.C.: Information Resources Press, 1977). See also B. C. Vickery and A. Vickery, *Information Science in Theory and Practice* (London: Butterworths, 1987) and N. A. Van House, "Public Library Effectiveness: Theory, Measures, and Determinants," *Library and Information Science Research* 8, no. 3 (July-September 1986): 261-83.

approach for a university library and for a large urban public library.[44] The unifying measure of performance was "document exposure"— basically a measure of the number of hours of reading. Considerable ingenuity was applied to transforming all library activities into this one measure of output. However, "document exposure" seems to have found little acceptance in the library community.

A RAND Corporation study entitled *An Economic Analysis of Public Library Services* examined Beverly Hills Public Library and endeavored to make recommendations that would maximize the net economic benefit to the community of having a free public library service.[45]

A different approach was derived from studies by De Prospo et al.,[46] extended in Altman et al.,[47] and further developed in the well-known *Output Measures for Public Libraries*.[48] Here a variety of measures of performance are developed without attempting to blend them explicitly into a single objective function, but with systematic attempts to relate them to each library's own planning processes.[49]

Conclusions

The use of measurement and quantification in libraries is probably quite typical of social services. The logistical aspects have proved relatively tractable and some progress has been made. The statistical analysis of observable phenomena of the use of documents (e.g., citations and recorded use of documents) has also progressed—as has analysis of properties of retrieval systems.

The fundamental problem is that the sophistication of the manipulation of what is measured is in great contrast with—and, unfortunately, distracts attention from, the fundamental weakness of our understanding of the significance of what has been measured. Citation analysis provides an excellent example: the mathematics can be done, but the significance of acts of citing is not well understood.[50] After a period of enthusiasm in

[44] M. Hamburg et al., *Library Planning and Decision-Making Systems* (Cambridge, Mass.: MIT Press, 1974).

[45] J. P. Newhouse and A. J. Alexander, *An Economic Analysis of Public Library Services* (Lexington, Mass.: Lexington Books, 1972).

[46] E. R. De Prospo et al., *Performance Measures for Public Libraries* (Chicago: American Library Association, 1973).

[47] E. Altman et al., *A Data Gathering and Instructional Manual for Performance Measures in Public Libraries* (Chicago: Celadon Press, 1976).

[48] N. A. Van House et al., *Output Measures for Public Libraries: A Manual of Standardized Procedures* , 2nd ed. (Chicago: American Library Association, 1987); *cf.* P. B. Kantor, *Objective Performance Measures for Academic and Research Libraries* (Washington, D.C.: Association of Research Libraries, 1984).

[49] Specifically C. R. McClure et al., *Planning and Role Setting for Public Libraries: A Manual of Options and Procedures* (Chicago: American Library Association, 1987).

[50] See footnote 7 of chapter 8.

the late 1960s and early 1970s, the use of operations research techniques began to lose favor in librarianship. Bommer summarized the criticisms rather well: too much emphasis on mathematics (perfect solutions to hypothetical problems); too little attention to implementation; too little emphasis on the process of investigation and too much on the product (model); and too little attention to the strategic problems of libraries.[51] Yet, in a sense, mathematical approaches went underground in the sense that a steady flow of activity continued, increasingly by librarians and by faculty of schools of librarianship, in quantitative approaches to decision-making and planning.

The expansion and diffusion of quantitative approaches bodes well for the future, and the widespread adoption of computers in library service is likely to provide much easier access to data on, for example, the use of catalogs. Nevertheless, some areas, such as those concerned with library objectives and the dynamics of user behavior, are likely to remain difficult to address.

Bibliographic postscript

The intent of this chapter is to discuss briefly the nature and unevenness of measurement and quantification in relation to library services. There are general introductions to quantitative techniques written for librarians[52] and, more recently, review articles.[53] For operations research in libraries there are reviews[54] and tutorials,[55] but these are now dated. As quantitative

---

[51]   M. Bommer, "Operations Research in Libraries: A Critical Assessment," *Journal of the American Society for Information Science* 25, no. 3 (1975): 137-9; see also M. Elton and B. Vickery, "The Scope for Operational Reseach in the Library and Information Field," *Aslib Proceedings* 25, no. 3 (1975): 305-19.

[52]   See, for instance, K. F. Stock, *Grundlagen und Praxis der Bibliotheksstatistik* (Munich, F.R.G.: Verlag Dokumentation, 1974); I. K. Ravichandra Rao, *Quantitative Methods for Library and Information Science* (New York: Wiley, 1983).

[53]   M. T. Kinnucan et al., "Statistical Methods in Information Science Research," *Annual Review of Information Science and Technology* 22 (1987): 147-78.

[54]   *Planning Library Services*, edited by A. G. Mackenzie and I. M. Stuart (Occasional Papers, 3) (Lancaster, England: University of Lancaster Library, 1969); A. G. Mackenzie and M. K. Buckland, "Operational Research," in *British Library and Information Science 1966-70s*, edited by H. A. Whatley (London: Library Association, 1972), pp. 224-31; *Operations Research: Implications for Libraries*, edited by D. R. Swanson and A. Bookstein (Chicago, Ill.: University of Chicago Press, 1972). Also issued as *Library Quarterly* 42, no. 1 (1972); Hamburg et al., *Library Planning; Reader in Operations Research for Libraries,* edited by P. Brophy et al. (Englewood, Colo.: Information Handling Services, 1976); P. B. Kantor, "A Review of Library Operations Research," *Library Research* 1, no. 4 (Winter 1979): 295-345; P. Oswitch, "Modelling Information System Dynamics: A Perspective," *Library and Information Science Research* 5, no. 2 (Summer 1983): 129-55.

[55]   Elton and Vickery, "The Scope for Operational Research," *Aslib Proceedings* 25, no. 3 (1973): 305-19; D. H. Kraft, "Library Operations Research," in *Larc Institute on*

(cont'd. on p. 207)

techniques have been absorbed, the literature has become large, diffuse, and less isolated. The references in this chapter, therefore, should, for the most part, be viewed as illustrative examples and not as a guide to the state-of-the-art. To find material on any particular aspect, reference should be made to secondary sources such as the *Annual Review of Information Science and Technology, Library and Information Science Abstracts, Library Literature,* etc.

Library Operations Research, edited by H. W. Axford (Tempe, Ariz.: Larc Association, 1973), pp. 19-62; D. H. Kraft and D. H. McDonald, "Library Operations Research: Its Past and Our Future", in *The Information Age: Its Development, Its Impact*, edited by D. P. Hammer (Metuchen, N.J.: Scarecrow Press, 1976), pp. 122-44; A. Hindle, M. K. Buckland and P. Brophy, "The Techniques of Operations Research: A Tutorial," in *Reader in Operations Research for Libraries*, edited by P. Brophy et al. (Englewood, Colo.: Information Handling Services, 1976), pp. 3-27; F. F. Leimkuhler, "Operations Research," *Encyclopedia of Library and Information Science* vol. 20 (New York: Marcel Dekker, 1968), pp. 412-84; A. Bookstein and K. Kocher, "Operations Research in Libraries," *Advances in Librarianship* 9 (1979): 143-84.

17

Technology

The role of technology

Libraries are concerned with knowledge, culture, information, facts, and beliefs.[1] The purpose of a library, in the words of Frederick Kilgour, "is to actively participate in the evolution of those profoundly human creations: beauty, faith, justice, and knowledge."[2] However, as a practical matter, libraries and librarians deal with physical objects, with *representations* of knowledge, culture, information, facts, and beliefs. Libraries deal with texts and images—or, more strictly, with text-bearing objects and image-bearing objects, with millions of these objects on miles of shelving. It is reasonable to expect, therefore, that any significant change in the nature or characteristics of these physical objects could have profound effects for library services.[3]

Technology has to do with the handling of physical objects and, for that reason, should be of extraordinary interest to librarians for good practical reasons. (We use "technique" to denote a *way* of doing something and "technology" to denote a useful physical resource that can serve as a *tool* or a means to accomplish something. Any given technique will make more or less use of different technologies.)

Each tool, each technology, has its capabilities and its limitations. Improvements in technology bring changes (usually increases) in capabilities and changes (usually, but not necessarily, reductions) in limitations. In other words, the general effect of improvements in technology will be to reduce practical constraints. This is not to imply that the adoption of new technology may not involve practical difficulties and false starts

[1] For a discussion of facts, knowledge, and beliefs as the scope of library service see D. Bergen, *Issues of Access in the New Information Age* (Kingston, R.I.: University of Rhode Island, Graduate School of Library and Information Studies, 1984) (ERIC Report ED 271 119).

[2] F. G. Kilgour, "The Impact of Technology on Libraries," in *The Information Society: Issues and Answers,* edited by E. J. Josey (Phoenix, Ariz.: Oryx Press, 1978), pp. 12-19. Reprinted in F. G. Kilgour, *Collected Papers of Frederick G. Kilgour: OCLC Years* (Dublin, Ohio.: OCLC, 1984), pp. 393-7.

[3] This duality of culture on the one hand and physical objects on the other as the realm of libraries may explain some ambiguity in the status of librarians. An individual who fosters knowledge and culture can reasonably be viewed differently from someone who (merely) stores physical objects.

when attempts are made to implement it,[4] but, in general terms, improved technology has the effect of diminishing constraints and, in this sense, has a liberating effect. In this chapter we address possible liberating effects consequent on the use of new technology for library service.

Our concepts and understanding are based upon what we know and are familiar with. Library technology was very stable for a century, until recently. Library technology has been firmly based on the technology of paper and of cardboard. Our views of library services derive from, and are deeply rooted in, those technologies. Small improvements are relatively easy to grasp; large changes are not. The implications of any radical change in technology are unlikely to be understood or appreciated for a long time, except, perhaps, by a few visionaries who are able to concentrate on key underlying principles, but whose visions could prove to be seriously erroneous. As a general rule, the more radical the change, the greater the need to go back to first principles. As noted in our discussion of collections in chapter 7, the development of electronic digital computers and associated technology has constraints quite different from those of the technology of paper and of cardboard. There is a massive literature on how computer technology could, should, or might be used in library services and elsewhere. Much of it is heavily technical and practical; some of it attempts to predict changes and to forecast the future,[5] a topic that we shall consider in the next chapter.

Considering a new technology, and thinking about its possible applications, are not easy. One understandable tendency is to think of the new technology in relation to the uses of the current technology. Such uses are, however, necessarily based on the capabilities and limitations of the current technology and this, in turn, is a constrained and distorted interpretation of what ideally needs to be done. Ideally one would like to be able to consider new technology in relation to first principles, to a theoretical definition of what would constitute ideal library service. (It may very well be prudent to *implement* technological changes in a gradual manner but that is a matter of tactics rather than of principle or strategy.)[6]

Unfortunately, thinking in abstract terms about practical matters is not only difficult but also remote from our experience with library provision

[4] For a good review of what can go wrong when using computers in libraries see S. R. Salmon, *Library Automation Systems* (New York: Marcel Dekker, 1975), chapter 9: "The Problems of Library Automation Systems."

[5] E.g., "Fifteen years from now there will be a microchip in your telephone receiver with more computer power than all the technology the Department of Defense can buy today. All the written knowledge of the world will be one of the items found in every schoolchild's pocket." H. Reingold, *Tools for Thought: The People and Ideas behind the Next Computer Revolution* (New York: Simon & Schuster, 1985), p. 16.

[6] For librarians' responses to technological change see S. F. Fine, "Technological Innovation, Diffusion and Resistance: An Historical Perspective," *Journal of Library Administration* 7, no. 1 (Spring 1986): 83-108.

and use, especially where library technology is concerned. However, it can often be helpful to examine problems backwards or upside-down. In addition to studying the potential of new technology, it can be useful to examine the capabilities and limitations of past library technology. (In this we summarize and continue our discussion in chapter 7.)

The technology of paper and cardboard

It is difficult, in practice, to analyze objectively that which is familiar. What one needs is the proverbial "Man from Mars". What would an extraterrestrial find interesting about traditional library technology? We shall assume that an extraterrestrial with sufficient technology to visit earth would take for granted the technology of computers, especially mass storage, online retrieval, and telecommunications. The extraterrestrial might be more intrigued by the properties of an information technology that would not exist on a planet without vegetation, and is certainly different from computers: that is, paper. The extraterrestrial might observe that paper has two properties that differentiate it markedly from computer technology:

1. Paper is a strictly localized information technology. Unlike computer technology the paper and the would-be reader have to be in the same place at the same time. If they are not, one or the other has to move. This may sound trivial, but the consequences are not. Some years ago in a large and decentralized university library system there were twelve subscriptions to *Chemical Abstracts*. It was felt by some to be rather extravagant to have so many subscriptions, but no group of users was willing to give up their own and have to walk across the campus to use some other copy. In the event it required the personal attention of the university president to achieve a reduction in subscriptions. The moral is that the localized nature of paper (and, it would seem, of library users) is a powerful factor. In this, paper as an information technology differs from computers. How many of the worldwide users of the Lockheed DIALOG information retrieval service know where the information is stored? Or even where their local telephone exchange is located? Does it matter whether they know or not?

2. Paper is also an isolated technology. Books lend themselves to being used by only one person at a time. Again, this differs radically from computer technology. When using an online catalog one does not even know how many other people, if any, are using the catalog at the same time.

Microform would presumably be viewed by the extraterrestrial as paper with bad habits: it is even more local in that a reading machine must also be in the same place; again it is suited for use by only one person at a time; and one cannot even scribble on it.

Some implications of technological change

Both the nature of the limitations of traditional library technology and some consequences of the introduction of new technology can be briefly illustrated by reviewing some aspects of current library service.

Collections: access and local holdings

In chapter 7, which discussed library collections, the "localized" property of library collections in traditional media, such as paper and microform, was identified. It leads naturally and reasonably to an enormous emphasis on assembling collections of copies of materials *locally*, since holding material locally is, in effect, a necessary (though not a sufficient) condition for prompt and convenience access to it.

With machine-readable texts and images, prompt and convenient access no longer depends on the materials being stored locally, though it may well be sensible to store a copy locally depending on size, cost, usage, telecommunications, and other technical considerations.

In brief, the new technology removes the constraint of localness that dominates the technology of paper. In this alone, the whole function and mystique of local collections begins to evaporate to the extent to which paper is supplemented by the less-localized media of databases.

Catalogs: back to bibliography[7]

Chapter 8, which examined retrieval, did so in general terms. We now consider library catalogs in relation to changing technology. Library catalogs are defined in the Anglo-American Cataloging Rules as a "list of library materials contained in a collection, a library, or a group of libraries, arranged according to some definite plan."[8] As a listing of material, a library catalog is a special form of bibliography defined by the intersection of two subsets:

1. Library catalogs use one particular level of description: the edition of the monograph and the title of the periodical. More detailed

---

[7] For a fuller discussion see M. K. Buckland, "Bibliography, Library Records, and the Redefinition of the Library Catalog," *Library Resources and Technical Services* (forthcoming).
[8] American Library Association, *Anglo-American Cataloging Rules*, 2nd ed. (Chicago: American Library Association, 1978), p. 564.

("analytical") cataloging is possible and can be found, especially in small, specialized libraries, but is not customary.[9]

2. The set of records in a library catalog is further defined geographically: the records that pertain to the particular collection, library, or, in the case of a union catalog, two or more libraries.

Catalog records are composed of two elements: (i) a bibliographical element describing a title or an edition, a description that is common to all copies of that title or edition; and (ii) local holding information, such as the call number, specific to the individual copy or copies.[10]

Both are needed. However, the bibliographic access provided by library catalogs (i) is substantially inferior in detail, extent, and quantity to that available through bibliographies—as was pointed out when modern library catalogs were developed in the late nineteenth century.[11] The technology of paper and of cardboard does not, however, lend itself to the combining of entries from bibliographies with individual library holdings statements (ii above). The solution adopted when modern librarianship was defined in the late nineteenth century was, in effect, the creation of a new, *third* file, the catalog, containing elements from each. However, computers have now replaced the paper and cardboard as the technology of choice. Computer technology, in contrast to that of paper and cardboard, lends itself well to the linking, merging, and rearrangement of files. As widespread, convenient access comes to be provided to bibliographies, and as libraries' internal operations are computerized, it is to be expected that a more direct, online, linking will be provided, enabling the user to start with the power of published bibliographies and then refer directly to local library holdings information, in effect augmenting or bypassing the catalog.

As noted above in our discussion of collections, the long-established relationship between "locally held" and "conveniently available" can be

---

[9] The limitation by level of description is a matter of standard practice, not of principle. Indeed there is explicit provision in the rules for more detailed description. American Library Association, *Anglo-American Cataloging Rules*, 2nd ed. (Chicago: American Library Association, 1978), Rule 13.5A and examples, pp. 271-2. Two good examples of published library catalogs containing entries for articles in periodicals and individual contributions within books are: *Index-Catalogue of the Library of the Surgeon-General's Office, United States Army*, 1880, and *Catalogue of the Library of the Peabody Institute of the City of Baltimore*, 1883-92. However, the high cost of analyticals had led to its general abandonment and recourse to published bibliographies.

[10] In terms of the MARC format for the communication of bibliographic records, the fixed fields and those with tags numbered through 899 describe an edition of a work or the record describing that edition. Fields 900 and above refer only to individual copies or to individual's records associated with those copies.

[11] For an excellent review see R. C. Swank, "Subject Catalogs, Classifications, or Bibliographies? A Review of Criticial Discussions, 1876-1942," *Library Quarterly* 14 (1944): 316-32. Reprinted in R. C. Swank, *A Unifying Influence: Essays* (Metuchen, N.J.: Scarecrow Press, 1981), pp. 1-27.

expected to weaken. Much that is conveniently available will *not* be held locally, but can be conjured up in a virtual copy on the glowing screen. What then of the role of a library catalog that is, *by definition*, limited to locally held material? To emphasize what is *locally stored* as opposed to *locally accessible* would be an irrelevant and unhelpful approach to providing library service. Some redefinition of the nature and role of the library catalog is indicated.

Information technology and library use

Chapters 7 and 9 above explored the nature of collections and the purpose and manner of their use. The process of becoming informed involves a combination of mental effort and mechanical process. Circumstances vary greatly but, as one example, we can envisage a scholar who might read a text and then produce a summary, rebuttal, or commentary, perhaps in a different language. As another example, numbers might be copied into a calculator and statistical summaries generated automatically. The former case is largely cerebration, yet a variety of mechanical aids might prove useful: paper, pencil, and cards are traditional aids; a dictionary, perhaps, or photocopies of the originals; a word processor might be helpful in the preparation of the summary or in preparing a concordance or other mechanical analysis of the text.

The technology used to assist in these processes is, by and large, that referred to as "information technology." It seems reasonable to expect that information technology will continue to make progress in supplying more powerful and cheaper tools. For this reason alone, one should expect that there will be more options available. In the meanwhile texts, images, and sounds are increasingly available in digitized form. The more these materials are available in machine-readable form, the more scope there is to use information technology to aid in the reading, copying, excerpting, analyzing, inferring, and adding to the resources—to the processes of learning and of scholarship. Examples of studies that have been transformed, such as mathematical linguistics, are not hard to find and, at least among the users of academic libraries, personal computers are already common.[12]

The amount and range of resources that are in machine-readable form is increasing and requires or, at least, lends itself to machine-assisted use. The number and power of technological aids to handling texts, images, and sounds continue to increase. The consequence appears to be a significant change in library use in the form of a significant increase in

---

[12] By 1986, 45 percent of U.S. faculty in the humanities and social sciences reportedly already had personal computers. H. C. Morton and A. J. Price, "The ACLS Survey of Scholars: Views, Publications, Computers, Libraries," *Scholarly Communication* 5 (Summer 1986): 1-16.

machine-assisted use of library materials. What help will library users receive in the future with the interaction between library resources and the user's personal computing environment? And from whom? Such help would appear to be a logical development of the role of reference librarians, but has hardly been addressed yet in the literature on information technology in libraries.

Conclusion

Librarians and library users are concerned with the search for intangibles: knowledge, information, entertainment. Nevertheless, the situation is dominated in practice by the sheer mass and complexity of physical objects needed to support these concerns. Different technologies have different capabilities and limitations and, therefore, technological change alters the constraints upon effective library service. Specifically, new technology improves the physical storage and handling of records. However, the fact that a record has been stored in some place does not mean that you know that it exists, that you could find it if you wanted it, that you could understand what it signified, that you should believe it, that it is not contradicted by some other record, or that just those who should have access to it do have access to it. Therefore, paradoxically, we may expect that the liberating power of the new technology will (and should) induce renewed attention to these traditional nontechnological concerns of librarianship—so long as librarianship is a service profession, concerned with ideas as well as with records.[13]

Planning for libraries and statements of mission and objectives are understandably influenced by what is known to be feasible. Improvements in technology change some of the constraints on what is feasible. A natural consequence is that ideas, plans, and policies tend to reflect obsolescent understanding of the possibilities. In the next chapter we shall explore the nature of change in library service.

[13]   J. H. Shera, "Librarianship and Information Science," in *The Study of Information: Interdisciplinary Messages*, edited by F. Machlup and U. Mansfield (New York: Wiley, 1983), pp. 379-88.

18

Change

Introduction

So far the various aspects of the provision and use of library services have been analyzed. Relationships between the parts, and between parts and the wider environment, have been noted. These relationships have been seen as defining library services in any given situation. The motivations of the users, the pattern of their inquiries, and the levels of demand are the basis of the usage of the library's services. The allocation of resources to and within the library defines the intended pattern of provision. What sorts of services *can* be offered depends on the techniques and technologies available to the librarian. It was implicit in the preceding chapters that a change in any part could be expected to have some effect upon the whole: additional resources; changes in the social values of those allocating resources; changes in the motivations of those seeking to use libraries; changes in the environment which offer more (or less) by way of alternative sources of information; changes in technology; and so forth. Each of these can be expected to result in an altered situation.

In this chapter we take the opportunity to consider *change* in library services, not in terms of the minor, short-term changes in equilibrium of the sorts just noted above, but in the longer term. There has been continuing concern about the future of libraries. Given the extent to which the provision and use of libraries are influenced by the social environment, and given possibilities for the use of new information technology, it would be unreasonable to expect libraries to remain static. But, if not, then what will be the nature of the change? The issue is not whether there will be change but what will be the nature of the change. If we are to make any claim to understand the nature of library services then surely we ought to have notions, some forecasts, about how library services might change.[1]

A book by J. C. R. Licklider, entitled *Libraries of the Future*,[2] appeared in 1966 and provides a convenient point of departure. Licklider

[1] This chapter is based on M. K. Buckland, "Education for Librarianship in the Next Century," *Library Trends* 34, no. 4 (Spring 1986): 777-87. The advice of John Ober is gratefully acknowledged.
[2] J. C. R. Licklider, *Libraries of the Future* (Cambridge, Mass.: MIT Press, 1965).

described how the digital computer and associated technology could be used to provide sophisticated access to recorded knowledge. He outlined an online catalog enriched with additional indexing, access to full text, and a good deal of what would now be called "expert systems." The library user and the system engage in dialogue, negotiating heuristically answers that are a compromise between what the user wants and what the system can supply.

Licklider described what he called a "procognitive system," that might now be described as a "smart" retrieval system. A library user is envisaged as sitting at a console using a typewriter and typing in a request for information on the topic "computer comprehension of semantic relations."

It is not that this vision is not plausible. It was and it still is, within limits. But what are the likely limits? What can be said of the completeness or potential distortion that this vision represents? Exploring the answers illustrates some of the difficulties inherent in such forecasting.

1. How complete is the forecast in its own terms?

The extent to which the "procognitive system" could work depends on the effectiveness of descriptions or "representations" of recorded knowledge. Consistent, unambiguous representation (e.g., indexing and abstracting) is more feasible in some fields of discourse than in others, in the "hard sciences" than in the "soft sciences," in descriptions of the physical world than of intellectual and social worlds. The problem does not appear to be a matter of inexpert indexing or abstracting. The linguistic ambiguities of, for example, some social sciences literature, appear to be symptoms rather than causes, which seem to lie in the nature of the knowledge itself.[3] Even though the system would be able to draw inferences and to make suggestions, the feasibility of Licklider's vision would vary by subject area, as he himself recognized. In this regard the vision appears to be applicable to a part rather than to the whole of recorded knowledge.

2. Is the forecast incomplete, covering only one aspect of the area being forecasted?

Essentially Licklider was concerned with techniques of retrieval. The vision in *Libraries of the Future* is incomplete—or the title is too broad. In projecting what may happen an author will tend to focus, consciously or otherwise, on an aspect of librarianship that has interesting possibilities and to extrapolate its development. Changing one aspect while keeping

---

[3] M. Bunge, *Scientific Research I: The Search for System* (Berlin: Springer, 1967), pp. 97-8. See also above, chapter 8.

others more or less stable is a standard technique in science fiction writing.[4] It can be used in reverse, to project anachronisms into the past for humorous effect, as in Mark Twain's *A Connecticut Yankee in King Arthur's Court*. In this case, projecting backwards into the past, the incongruity is obvious. With projections into the future, selective and uneven extrapolation can be difficult to detect.

3. How complete is the extrapolation in terms of its effect?

In Licklider's case the computer and its associated technologies were seen as a means of easing the problem of access to recorded knowledge through the creation of a smart information retrieval system. With hind-sight we can now see that the computer and its associated technologies are also exacerbating the problems that Licklider's procognitive system was intended to relieve, since, in other contexts, computers enable a great increase in the quantity of recorded knowledge through word processing, teleconferencing, and the recording and accumulation of vast stores of data. In other words, they aggravate the problem as well as offering a remedy. This discussion of Licklider's book is not intended as a criticism of his work but as a means of stressing the problem of completeness in forecasting.

Some assumptions

At this point it may be convenient to review some assumptions:

1. The most that we should attempt is to make some forecasts of what seems likely, not to make specific predictions.
2. A major concern (here as elsewhere) is to view the field as a whole and, therefore, to seek to avoid creating visions based upon the uneven extrapolation of one aspect or another.
3. Although it would be desirable to depict the future as it seems likely to be, such prediction is rash and a probable source of embarrassment if, in later years, anyone bothers to review the foolhardy predictions that have been made. There is, however, an additional motivation relating to the purpose of this book as a whole: the best basis for a good prediction would be a deeper understanding of the nature of things—and if we can understand better the nature of things then we can hope to be more effective in the present and near future regardless of the merits of long-range forecasts.

---

[4] "The science fiction writer's task is both more crucial and more difficult because he is extrapolating, speculating. The historical novelist has a solid and readily accessible framework of known fact to fall back on; the man who speculates about the future has only his knowledge and his reason to guide him." R. A. Heinlein, "Science Fiction: Its Nature, Faults, and Virtues", in B. Davenport et al., *The Science Fiction Novel: Imagination and Social Criticism* (Chicago: Advent Publishers, 1959), pp. 17-63.

4. Not all options are considered here. A nuclear holocaust, for example, could change things a great deal. For present purposes we concentrate on the development of what we take to be long-term trends.

Some examples of stability

A basic question is: what *could* change? The introduction of computer technology into library practice is good evidence that there has been, and is likely to continue to be, *some* change, but how extensive will that change be? It seems unrealistic to expect to know how extensive change will be, but it is possible to derive some insight by looking back and seeing how changeable different aspects of librarianship have been.

Consider, for example, the following topics: copyright; public access to government documents; education for librarianship; preservation and conservation; reduction of catalog costs through cooperative cataloging arrangements; and improved subject access. These are thoroughly contemporary issues, yet each of them is discussed in the *Library Journal* for 1886, where there is also discussion of women in librarianship and the lack of comparable pay—and a plea that the emphasis on library technology needs to be complemented by more bibliographical instruction. It is clear that not everything has changed in a century and, on that basis, there is an initial presumption of only moderate change in the next century. Perhaps this list of topics should be noted as a prediction of the contents of the *Library Journal* a hundred years hence.

Consider the following comments on the importance of having a collection development policy that includes selection of works by dissident writers who challenge the establishment:

> Moreover, all those who have written most successfully against any science, or those who have opposed with most learning and force ... the books of some of the most famous and renowned authors (should be included) ...
> Neither may all those who have introduced or modified anything in the sciences be omitted, for it is merely flattering the bondage of man's feeble wit if the scanty knowledge that we possess of these authors is buried under the disdain to which they are inescapably subject for having set themselves up against the ancients and having learnedly examined what others were accustomed to accept by tradition. For this reason, since of late more than thirty or forty authors of reputation have declared themselves against Aristotle; since Copernicus, Kepler, Galileo, have altered astronomy; Paracelsus, Severinus the Dane, Duchesne, and Crallius, medicine; and since many others have introduced strange and unheard-of reasoning, such as had never been foreseen, I affirm that all these authors are requisite to a library ...

The examples are, of course, dated and the wording sounds quaint, but the argument is still relevant and cogent in terms of the Western liberal tradition of librarianship. With the substitution of more contemporary examples, this text could still be used in a policy statement or course on collection development. The quotation is from Gabriel Naudé's *Advice on Establishing a Library*, first published in 1627, not one mere century ago but three and a half.[5] This represents an element of stability in librarianship that contrasts markedly with the rapid change that Licklider sketched.

Three sorts of change

The stark contrast in degrees of change in the two examples—Naudé on collection development and Licklider on retrieval—suggests new questions. How far are various aspects of librarianship capable of change? How far are different aspects of librarianship differentially prone to change? If we had some sense of how different aspects for library services appear to be susceptible to change, then we might hope to consider them separately and then aggregate the results. The rates of change in the past century should provide some basis for assessing the probable rates of change in the future.

Contrasts and similarities between librarianship in the 1880s and in the 1980s suggest that, as a first approximation, aspects of library services can be sorted into three categories with respect to change: (1) library values; (2) library technology; and (3) library science.

Library values

Library values include social values as they influence library policy and professional issues, as discussed in chapters 11 and 12 above. These library values determine the mission of the library service, the librarians' attitude toward readers, and the role of the librarian.

It should be stressed that the concern here is with values which underlie day-to-day priorities and decisions. We are not concerned here with the practical techniques used to implement those decisions. One might well commend Naudé's principles of books selection today, but not all of his advice on book procurement. His recommendation that one rummage around bookshops looking for printed sheets not yet folded and bound is no longer sound practical advice.[6]

In general, library values appear to have changed rather little since the 1880s, at least as regards mainstream librarianship in the United States. There are variations in, for example, the relative emphasis on outreach from time to time.

Consideration of selection and censorship (both book-burning and book-burying) helps to clarify the issues. The specific titles that a librarian

---

[5] G. Naudé, *Advice on Establishing a Library* (Berkeley: University of California Press, 1950), pp. 23-4. Originally published as *Avis pour dresser une bibliotheque* in 1627.

[6] Ibid., p. 54.

is willing or allowed to include clearly change with time. Where the line is drawn between acceptable and unacceptable—to the librarian or to the community—will vary with respect to individual titles and categories of material as society's standards and social, political, and religious values change. Yet there will always be a line drawn somewhere, and the arguments concerning where the line should be appear to vary little over time. In other words, a good discussion of selection and censorship in the 1880s is likely also to be a good and valid discussion in the 1980s and, probably in the 2080s—even though the specific titles and examples can be expected to change.[7]

This is not to imply that library-related values are universal or unchanging. They are not. What would be acceptable in San Francisco today may not be acceptable in Teheran or Beijing. What is acceptable in Massachusetts now might not have been acceptable in colonial times—and vice-versa. Although there can be change over time in a given place, such changes are based on *cultural* forces rather than the mere passing of time.

Library technology

"Library technology" as used here means technology available for use in library services. Further, technology is concerned with the handling of physical things: paper, cardboard, microform, and magnetic, optical, or other recording media.

Technology is of particular significance for library services because libraries are concerned with *recorded* knowledge. Librarians and library users are concerned with ideas and assertions represented in texts and images, but can only do so through text-bearing and image-bearing objects, such as books made of paper, sound recordings on magnetic tape, numbers on cathode ray screens, and so on. These are the principal text-bearing objects.

Carbon paper, microfilm, and typewriter were all available a century ago. The telephone, teletype, punch cards, and electronic computers have added to the options available. Currently there is interest in optical digital disks to record texts and in radio waves to carry them.

While it cannot be known what technology will be available a hundred years from now the trend is clear: additional media for bearing text; more powerful technologies for handling text; and, unlike value-related aspects of librarianship, a clear line of progress with time. In this case we can be very confident that the *technological* tools available for library service will be very much improved in the future.

---

[7] "Basically, the issues involved in censorship cases do not change. All that changes is what society considers acceptable and unacceptable." A. Curley and D. Broderick, *Building Library Collections*, 6th ed. (Metuchen, N.J.: Scarecrow Press, 1985), p. 145.

Library science

There is, however, a third category of aspects of librarianship that is distinguishable from library values and from library technology. This third category has to do with our *understanding* of library services and so is different in kind from either of the others. (This book is intended to be about the understanding of library services, rather than library technology or library values.) We use the term "library *science*" to designate this third category, but in doing so we are using the term in a narrower, stricter sense than is customary in, for example, the phrases 'School of Library Science' or 'Master of Library Science' where the term library science is used to denote the entire field.

Our narrower approach would, in general, exclude library automation as being more properly included in library technology, but it would include the following:

1. Information retrieval theory, including the broad areas of the description and representation of the contents of pieces of recorded knowledge: indexing, cataloging, classification, abstracting.
2. Information gathering behavior: user studies, bibliometrics, social epistemology, and the utilization of knowledge.
3. Historical studies of books and of communication.
4. Analysis and description of bibliographical control in general.
5. The understanding of the nature and workings of libraries and related information services.[8]

Of these parts of librarianship it can be said that there has been some progress in the past century but not very much. Because the central issues—that is, information retrieval theory and information-gathering behavior—are, or should be, rooted in truly obscure aspects of human behavior, progress will be slow and difficult. Scholarly explanation will tend to lag behind the intuitive understanding of those intimately involved in the activities. Unlike library technology we cannot claim that there has been much progress, or that there is likely to be much in the foreseeable future. Much of the progress of the past century in these areas has been the refinement of earlier progress (e.g., cataloging principles) or concerned with relative superficial symptoms of deeper phenomena (e.g., bibliometrics and citation analysis).

Assistance may come from related disciplines such as cognitive psychology and artificial intelligence. Librarians have voiced hopes for the interdisciplinary insights available from sociology, psychology, philosophy, and linguistics, but, over the past century, the contributions of

---

[8] This outline draws on that of P. Wilson, "Bibliographical R&D", in *The Study of Information: Interdisciplinary Messages,* edited by F. Machlup and U. Mansfield (New York: Wiley, 1983), pp. 389-97.

these disciplines to the understanding of librarianship have been modest and more relevant to context and background than to central concerns. One might wish that the intellectual history of librarianship and of library schools—the effects of different disciplines and strands of thought—had some of the attention devoted to the institutional history of libraries and library schools.

A critical assumption here is that the contribution of artificial intelligence will be modest and/or concentrated on the simpler problems of library service. What we might expect would be different if one were to assume that artificial intelligence will have a massive effect, or that it will solve the more intractable problems of indexing, interpreting, and explaining.

The extent and academic context of librarianship

In recent years there has been a broadening of the scope and extent of librarianship, often using an expanded name, such as "library and information studies" or "library and information management." The contexts of "library and information management" are clearly very extensive: libraries of many kinds, obviously, but also online retrieval services, archives, data bases, records management, and documentation of many kinds in engineering, litigation, and bureaucracies. Whether or not the activity is labeled librarianship is hardly relevant. Library service can sensibly be viewed as one member of a family of retrieval-based information services and schools of librarianship could and probably will become, by merger or by expansion, colleges of broader scope—with the Master of Library Science (MLS) degree an important speciality within a range of programs. There is currently some movement in that direction, largely fueled by practical considerations of enrollment and placement.

There are plausible theoretical arguments why this trend could be expected with the gradual maturing of the academic side of librarianship and the evolution of library schools as academic departments. Although library schools are ordinarily viewed in relation to libraries, they also need to be viewed in their own right—as academic departments in an academic setting.[9]

A more conceptual academic perspective is possible. For example, one can take the view that information science has to do with representations of knowledge both in the abstract sense ("texts") and the physical manifestations of these representations ("text-bearing objects"). Within that broad area, a plausible conceptual definition—as contrasted with an

---

[9] For further discussion of the maturing of library schools as academic departments see M. K. Buckland, "The School, Its Faculty and Students," in *Changing Technology and Education for Librarianship and Information Science*, edited by B. Stuart-Stubbs (Greenwich, Conn.: JAI Press, 1985), pp. 117-27.

institutional definition (i.e., *library* schools) of the scope of schools of "library-and-information-studies" as they mature would be that they specialize in the analysis, description, storage, arrangement, retrieval, and use of representations of knowledge. Arrangement, description, and retrieval imply representations of the texts and images. The library card catalog, composed of brief descriptions of books and journals, is a familiar example of the representation of representations of knowledge.[10]

Information retrieval may be regarded as central because it includes principles of indexing, cataloging, classification, content analysis and description, techniques of storage, strategies for retrieval, and similar sorts of activity. Yet retrieval, though central, cannot be the only concern. In order to see retrieval in context, information studies in the broader sense need to be examined. Such studies concern representation of knowledge, knowledge itself, and, indeed, people and their needs insofar as their needs are related—through knowledge and representations of knowledge—to retrieval.

Pragmatic and theoretical views that argue for more broadly based schools are reinforced by considerations both of economies of scope and economies of scale. Hence the forecast is that the presently prevailing pattern of "library school" with the primary or sole mission of awarding a "library degree" will soon survive only in isolated cases of arrested development.

Curriculum

Any given curricular content can be packaged many different ways, and any particular forecast of the future curriculum is as likely to be criticized for the way it is packaged as well as for its contents. The content of the Master of Library Science degree and its successor program is likely to resemble current programs in broad outline. If the mission of library programs is to bring information to people then that mission itself will be unaffected by changes in the media used to bring information and people together. Therefore, the curriculum of the future can reasonably be expected to continue to contain a few basic overlapping elements:

1. The role of information and of library services in society.
2. The needs, information-gathering behavior, and institutional contexts of groups to be served—e.g., students, researchers, children, the aged, and so on.

---

[10] Arguably the emphasis on text and text-bearing objects is too narrow and "signal," "signal-bearing object," or even "information" and "informative objects" would provide definitions that are more complete. Probably so, but for present purposes we use "text" and "text-bearing objects" without wishing to imply that we exclude anything other than written language.

3. The theory and practice of information retrieval—cataloging, classi-
    fication, indexing, bibliography, etc.
4. The managerial, political, and technological means most likely to be
    useful in developing and providing good library service.

The least amount of change can be expected in those parts of the curriculum that deal with library values. It is not that these values cannot
change, but rather that, in the United States at least, there is no obvious
reason to expect the major cultural and political changes that would
move us from the Western liberal tradition of library services. Librarians
may well seek to resist such changes.

Librarians can hope for, expect, and should actively seek to effect
improvements in their understanding of the provision and use of library
services in library science, as narrowly used in this chapter. It is not clear
that substantial progress should be forecast, however. Forecasters can
confidently predict dramatic changes in information technology, changes
that will offer capabilities that are currently unavailable.

The prospect of having catalogs, bibliographies, and texts all online is
already beginning to overcome some of the major barriers to good service
imposed by the constraints inherent in the technology of cardboard and
paper. One such barrier is the historic separation between catalogs and
bibliographies;[11] another is the physical separation of the catalog from
the text; a third is the need for the user to travel to the library or for "hard
copy" to be transported to the user in order for the human eye to see the
text. Information technology is beginning to remove these three familiar
physical impediments to good service. Currently there is a fundamental
move from providing library services in libraries to providing library
services wherever people happen to be. Online catalogs, online reference,
and telephone service from reference desks are steps in that direction.

Librarians and their schools are likely to be preoccupied with the
excitement of changing technology, at least for the next few decades. Yet
paradoxically, if the technological change is so great it may in some sense
be trivial. If *storage* problems diminish, problems of *access* become
dominant. Yet what information technology contributes best is physical
storage and physical access. There remain the problems of deciding what
should be retrieved, of language barriers, of comprehension, and of the
politics of access to information. The control of access to any resource is
properly viewed as a political matter.

The excitement of library technology provides a line of rapid change;
one may hope for library science—the understanding of library service—
to change too; and one may hope for library values to change but little.

---

[11] R. C. Swank, "Subject Catalogs, Classifications, or Bibliographies? A Review of
Critical Discussions, 1876-1942," *Library Quarterly* 14, no. 4 (October 1944): 316-32. Reprinted in *A Unifying Influence: Essays* (Metuchen, N.J.: Scarecrow Press, 1981), pp. 1-127.

19

Other Sorts of Information Service

Our intention has been to develop a conceptual framework for considering library services. Nevertheless, it seems justified to try to extend this, or any similar framework, in two ways. The first sort of extension has to do with similarities between library services and other retrieval-based information services. If, instead of insisting that library services are entirely unique, we were to explore the notion that library services could be viewed as examples of information services based on retrieval, then perhaps the conceptual framework developed for library services might also serve as a conceptual framework for one or more other members of this family—or, indeed, for retrieval-based information services as a class. The second sort of extension is different in kind. How could this, or any other framework that might be developed, accommodate or mesh with other sorts of information services that are not retrieval based? These issues need detailed consideration well beyond the scope of this chapter, but we shall speculate briefly concerning these two sorts of extension in this chapter.

Retrieval-based information services generally

What if we had set out to write a similar but different book developing a conceptual framework for considering some other retrieval-based information service such as archives instead of libraries, with a title such as *Archival Services in Theory and Context?* The mere act of defining a class of activities by the two criteria that (1) they must be information services, and (2) they must involve retrieval already ensures a significant degree of commonality among the activities included in the class. To the extent that a conceptual framework is developed for one, a basis is provided for a conceptual framework for all—"Retrieval-based information systems in theory and context."

We begin by noting a few candidates for inclusion in the class of retrieval-based information services.

Archives

Archives constitute an obvious choice even though the practices and traditions of archivists differ importantly from those of librarians. Archives are ordinarily the files of documents assembled in the conduct of the affairs of an organization and no longer in routine use. A difference from libraries is the choice of attribute by which documents are physically arranged: library collections are usually arranged by subject content; archival collections are arranged "by provenance," in the same series and chronological sequence that they were originally assembled. One might envisage subject and/or name indexes to them, but not their rearrangement by subject or author. In other words, the attribute by which they are arranged (administrative provenance) differs from the subject arrangement of library practice. Other characteristics are that each record is liable to be unique, that the juxtaposition of the records within each series is in itself likely to be meaningful, that the number of records tends to be very large indeed, and that the frequency of use of individual records tends to be very low. There has been a tendency to stress the differences between archives and libraries rather than the similarities.[1]

Records management

Records management is concerned with maintaining an organization's systems of files, especially those records whose usage has not yet reached a frequency so low that they can be discarded or relegated to archives.[2] Although records managers are generally regarded as being concerned with paper records in folders, there is extensive use of microfilm and, increasingly, of records in machine-readable form. Even if this were not the case, it is not clear that the choice of text-bearing medium would be any more relevant for a conceptual framework for records management than it is for library services. It could be argued that current records management practice is primarily preoccupied with the logistical aspects of handling records, storage, microfilming, the preservation of vital records, and the destruction of others, rather than the content of the records. Yet there seems to be no reason why this should not be seen as an incomplete stage of development and why sophisticated techniques for intellectual access should not be developed as the trend to machine-readable

---

[1] *Journal of Library Administration* 7, nos. 2/3 (Summer/Fall 1986). Special issue: Archives and Library Administration.

[2] See, for example. W. Benedon, *Records Management* (Englewood Cliffs, N.J.: Prentice Hall, 1969. Available from Trident Bookstore, 5153 State University Dr., Los Angeles, CA 90032). W. O. Maedke, M. F. Robek and G. F. Brown, *Information and Records Management*, 2nd ed. (Encinio, Cal.: Glencoe, 1981).

records continue and as records management practice becomes more sophisticated.[3]

Management Information Systems

Management Information Systems (MIS) are formal computer-based information services designed to help managers to make decisions. So far, there has been remarkably little interaction between librarians and those who develop and operate Management Information Systems. At least a partial explanation can be found in differences in the records used. Traditional MIS has been concerned primarily with numerical data derived from inside the organization whose managers are to be informed. Being internally derived, some control is possible over what data are collected and the form in which they are collected. The organization of these data is likely to be fairly well structured, and they are relatively easy to handle in a computer. Such data are relatively "tidy." There may well be problems in defining and documenting the data, but for the most part, formulating a search is not likely to involve significant difficulties of indexing and retrieval. The specification of the search is likely to tend to reduce to simple logic. Since the data are numerical there is plentiful scope for using mathematical models to predict possible future situations.

This is all quite different in appearance from what librarians do, yet it seems likely that there will be some convergence. One reason is that the sort of data that MIS can handle best tend to relate to internal, operational decisions. This is needed, but managers also need to take strategic decisions concerning their organizations' relationships with the environment with which they must deal. Becoming informed concerning the environment is likely to be based mainly on conversations, reports, and the scanning of data derived from outside the organization. These sorts of data are "messy" in the sense that they are mainly textual and commonly composed by people outside the organization who had quite other purposes in mind. If the data are numerical, the definitions are likely to be inconsistent. Even if these data were in machine-readable form, they would still be difficult to organize and to retrieve. Indexing is a serious problem for data to be used for strategic decision making. Handling them requires skills that librarians have developed over the years. Hence, extending the range of decisions to be supported by Management Information Systems from operational problems to include strategic

---

[3] J. M. Pemberton, "Records Management Courses in Accredited Library Schools: A Rationale and a Survey," *Records Management Quarterly* 16, no. 3 (July 1982): 10-12, 14-16; M. K. Buckland, "Records Management in its Intellectual Context: Experience at Berkeley," *Records Management Quarerly* 16, no. 4 (October 1982): 26-8, 30.

problems can be expected to include greater attention to textual records and to techniques more closely resembling those of librarians.[4]

Other plausible candidates for membership in the same family as library services are not difficult to find: museum documentation involves particularly difficult problems of classification and indexing;[5] litigation support systems use computer-based retrieval to help marshal evidence in law suits;[6] office information systems generate large, complex data bases of mostly textual records that need to be retrieved in various ways; data base management systems facilitate the creation of information storage and retrieval systems for all sorts of purposes. The contexts vary, the attributes used as a basis for retrieval vary, and those involved are likely to be more conscious of their differentness. Nevertheless, in each of these examples there appears to be a profound structural similarity to library services in the five types of processes that we have been using:

Inquiry

In each case inquiries arise. There would seem to be no reason to expect any change in the processes that generate inquiries, since these processes are external to the information system. Significant differences can be expected from one situation to another in the users' perceptions of the sorts of inquiries regarded appropriate to particular information services, but that is also the case among library services.

Retrieval

The scope for variation in the nature of retrieval-based information services would appear to be quite limited when considered at a theoretical rather than a technical level.

What is to be retrievable? If we are to deal with retrieval-based information services generally, then we must be able to consider anything

---

[4] See J. V. Hansen, L. J. McKell and L. E. Heitger, "Decision-oriented Frameworks for Management Information Systems Design," *Information Processing and Management* 13, no. 4 (1977): 215-225. For additional discussion of text processing in relation to MIS see M. J. Culnan, "Information Science and the Automated Office: Challenges and Opportunities," in *American Society for Information Science. Proceedings of the 44th Annual Meeting, Washington, 1981* (White Plains, N.Y.: Knowledge Industries Publications, 1981): 139-42; and M. J. Culnan, "Document Processing in the Automated Office: Implications for MIS Research and Education," in *First International Conference on Information Systems, Philadelphia, 1980. Proceedings* (Chicago: Society for Management Information Systems, 1980): 165-73.

[5] For fuller treatment of museum documentation, see E. Orna and C. Pettit, *Information Handling in Museums* (New York: Bingley, 1980); and D. A. Roberts and R. B. Light, "Museum Documentation," *Journal of Documentation* 36, no. 1 (March 1980): 42-84.

[6] See, for example, *Legal and Legislative Information Processing,* edited by B. K. Eres (Westport, Conn.: Greenwood Press, 1980), chapters 9 and 12.

that might be made retrievable with the expectation that subsequent perception of it would be informative. It is this restriction to things which could be informative that defines present interests within storage operations generally. We are interested in information services, not in stores of munitions, food, or other sorts of supplies. It is this restriction to those things that can be informative that enables us to use the term "signals" in a loose way to include such concrete but informative objects as books, statistical summaries, and museum objects.

What attributes are to be used as a basis for retrieval? Indexing or arranging books according to their bindings would be an extravagant waste of money for almost (but not quite) all library users. For the rare student of book-binding it would be very useful. The choice of attributes to be used for retrieval is largely a problem of prediction because one must necessarily deal with future inquiries. A good understanding of current inquiries should serve as a fairly reliable predictor for the near future. Beyond that, the uncertainty increases since the determinants of future interests are not knowable in any reliable way. Judgment concerning the choice of attributes needs to be based upon consideration of the sorts of inquiries that the providers of the service will handle and also the nature of the retrievable objects and/or the representations of those objects. Objects vary in their attributes: dinosaur bones do not have authors. Some attributes may be well worth using in theory, but technological and economic considerations inhibit their use in practice.

As an instructive example we can consider archives where retrieval is customarily based on the attribute of "provenance": the administrative source of documents or "fonds." Provenance is an attribute not ordinarily used in libraries and is different from the subject arrangement typical of library practice. Nevertheless, the power of provenance to convey information through context alone is significant and should be supplemented, not replaced by other attributes of descriptive cataloging and subject indexing.[7]

There may be brief descriptions of the nature and contents of classes ("series") of documents and occasionally a brief description ("calendar") of individual documents within a series. Detailed indexes of the mention of specific names or topics within the archives, however, are rarely affordable luxuries. The expression of the inquiry in the language of the retrieval system is, in general, a matter of expressing the inquiry in terms of the series generated by a specific administrative body for a specific period of time, such as: "May I please see the correspondence of the Secretary of the Academic Senate for 1925-26?" The hope is that the array of documents defined in this way will contain the material desired. Within the

[7] R. C. Berner, "Archival Management and Librarianship: An Exploration of Prospects for their Integration," *Advances in Librarianship* 14 (1986): 253-83.

conjunction of series and time span, one browses. Of course, detailed indexing with respect to a wide variety of attributes would permit the formulation of more explicitly detailed searches, but this would require an enormous investment of resources since archival holdings, unlike library holdings, tend to be individually unique as well as extremely numerous.[8] For detailed indexing of archives to become prevalent, there would have to be dramatic (and highly improbable) changes: a reduction in the costs of indexing; increased funding for archive administration; and/or a radical increase in the importance assigned to the value of indexing archives relative to the value of acquiring them.

Museum documentation provides an interesting challenge. Unlike books in libraries, museum objects generally lack such convenient attributes as author, title, publisher, and International Standard Book Number. It is, presumably, more difficult to catalog dinosaur bones than a book about dinosaur bones—not to mention storing them and making them accessible. More than with library materials, the age, composition, cultural context, purpose, and mode of creation of museum objects may be difficult to establish even when they are not fakes. Future inquiries are hard to predict. A recent indexing system for museum collections of human artifacts takes the original, principal intended use of the object as the major attribute for retrieval.[9]

Situations vary, then, with respect to the range of attributes that can be sensibly used for retrieval. In an airline seat reservation system, it can be confidently predicted what the sorts of questions will be. Also, in that case, the terms used in the search can easily be expressed in useful, unambiguous ways, in contrast to a query such as "What do you have on symptoms of stoicism in Western culture?" in which each of the principal terms is only vaguely definable. However, in library service there is also a wide range in the definability of inquiries, so we have a situation that parallels what is found in library services.

Retrieval systems have several aspects, notably the notation, the syndetic structure, the form of coordination of the indexing language, and the choice of equipment used (e.g., cards, book, microfilm, computer), but these are primarily technical details. They are important in practice but not at the theoretical level of this general framework. Retrieval in

[8]   R. H. Lytle compared the effectiveness of retrieval by provenance with retrieval by subject index in "Intellectual Access to Archives: I. Provenance and Content Indexing Methods by Subject Retrieval," *American Archivist* 43, no. 1 (Winter 1980): 64-75; "Intellectual Access to Archives: II. Report of an Experiment Comparing Provenance and Content Indexing Methods of Subject Retrieval," *American Archivist* 43, no. 2 (Spring 1980): 191-207. The two techniques gave comparable results but "The most salient finding of the study was the poor retrieval performance of both methods" (p. 193).

[9]   R. G. Chenhall, *Nomenclature for Museum Cataloging: A System for Classifying Man-made Objects* (Nashville, Tenn.: American Association for State and Local History, 1978).

library services also has these variations and so does not appear to differ significantly from the other sorts of information retrieval.

Becoming informed

There appears to be no reason to suppose that the processes by which people become informed differ in any significant way from one retrieval-based system to another. Therefore the discussion in chapter 9 above would appear to be as valid (or invalid) for archives, etc., as for library services.

Demand

In chapter 10 we analyzed the demand for library services as an economic process. In brief, we concluded that individual's goals derive from personal values: the satisfaction of curiosity, the quest for stimulation or reassurance, the pursuit of personal interests. A real price is involved in using retrieval services because there is "toil and trouble" in using it, though not usually a commercial charge. The real price can be viewed as including time, effort (physical and mental, including the effort involved in changing habits), discomfort, and, where applicable, monetary charges. There is also a price mechanism in the sense that demand is elastic and varies with price. The individual constantly decides what to do, where to go, and what action (if any) to take to become informed. In cybernetic terms the individual is a "system" seeking not only to survive but to maintain an acceptable level of stability Whether or not a particular information service is used will depend on the relative price and each individual's perception of the probable real price (time, effort, discomfort, money) in relation not only to the perceived probable benefit of becoming informed but also to the probable real prices and benefits of alternative courses of action. In seeking to consider other retrieval-based information service in lieu of libraries, no change on the demand component of our theory appears to be necessary.

Allocation

The allocation process as formulated with respect to libraries was seen as being essentially a political process based on sponsorship: Resources ordinarily come from public or other funding rather than from fees. The nature of this process was examined in chapter 11. However, in chapter 12, we broadened the discussion to include situations in which users pay fees. The same general characteristics appear to apply to retrieval-based information services as a class. They are commonly public services (archives, museums), and where they are not (MIS), they are often regarded as support services in large organizations. In both cases direct charges to the user are not the norm. There are also commercial retrieval-based information services that are strictly for profit as well as some that are subsidized. The first impression is that the extension of the discussion of allocation in chapters 11 and 12 remains appropriate.

In recent years there has been discussion of "Information Resources Management," which is generally described as including the planning, budgeting, organizing, directing, training, and control associated with an organization's information, and encompassing both the information itself and related resources such as personnel, equipment, funds, and technology. Information Resources Management has quite specific origins in the paperwork problems of the U.S. government and an emphasis on information as a resource to be managed.[10] Its relationship to existing information-handling activities is not yet clear.

For a comprehensive approach to providing information service in an organization it would seem logical to include in one coherent framework both internally derived information sources (as in archives, records management, and Management Information Systems) and externally derived sources (as in libraries). To be effective one would have to recognize not only the distinguishing characteristics of each of these retrieval-based information systems, but also the underlying similarities, the subordination of each to the mission of the organization, the unifying effects of trends in information technology, and, generally, the indifference of the individual user as to whence and how the information came. Even if a comprehensive approach were not implemented administratively, a detailed comparative analysis of different examples of retrieval-based information services can be expected to yield insights useful about each.[11]

While this discussion cannot be regarded as more than touching upon the issues, the preliminary conclusion is that the conceptual framework developed for considering library services also shows promise for the consideration of the rest of the family of retrieval-based information services.[12]

---

[10] K. B. Levitan, "Information Resource(s) Management—IRM," *Annual Review of Information Science and Technology* 17 (1982): 227-66; R. H. Lytle, "Information Resource Management: 1981-1986," *Annual Review of Information Science and Technology* 21 (1986): 309-36.

[11] See J. Rogalla von Bieberstein, *Archiv, Bibliothek und Museum als Dokumentationsbereiche: Einheit und gegenseitige Abgrenzung* (Bibliothekspraxis, Bd 16) (Pullach bei München, F.R.G: Verlag Dokumentation, 1975).

[12] *Intellectual Foundations for Information Professionals*, edited by H. K. Achleitner (Boulder, Colo.: Social Science Monographs, distributed by Columbia University Press, New York, 1987); A. M. Schrader, "In Search of a Name: Information Science and Its Conceptual Antecedents," *Library and Information Science Research* 6, no. 3 (July-September 1984): 227-71.

The flow of information in society

In this section we consider very briefly other sorts of information services that are not retrieval-based. These relate to the framework developed for library services in two ways:

1. The process of becoming informed was depicted in chapter 9 as being affected by prior knowledge of any origin. Whatever has been learned in whatever way affects what else will be understood. The relationship between the effects of all other information sources on the use of library services is shown in the top right corner of figure 13.2. Libraries' support for literacy education and librarians' concern for intellectual freedom are two examples of concern for the broader environment.

2. Library services are in competition with other sources of information in the sense that other sources of information will in some circumstances be preferable. It may often be more advantageous to buy a personal copy of a book, to consult a commercial data base, or to ask somebody else rather than use a library.

In chapter 10 we examined the determinants of demand for library services. The assumption was made that inquiries would be directed to a particular library service if two conditions obtained: The perceived probable benefits exceeded the perceived probable price; *and* use of the library service was perceived as preferable to alternative sources of information. This is represented in figure 13.3. In previous chapters we were concerned only with the decision whether or not to use a given library service. This was a two-valued option: to use or not to use. To extend the framework to include other sources of information that are or could be used we need to expand this two-valued option into as many options as we care to include. This is indicated in the note "1. Other sources of information" in the representation of the environment in figure 13.3. To the extent to which we could model the choice between all available options, we should have a general model of decision making with respect to information-gathering behavior.

Part IV

Some Problems Reconsidered

20

Some Problems Reconsidered

In chapter 2 some quite diverse problems associated with library services were briefly described. It was suggested that progress in dealing with these problems was hindered by inadequate understanding—by inadequate theory. In this final chapter, these problems will be reconsidered in the light of the conceptual framework developed since chapter 2.

Why do libraries differ?

The traditional types of library services (academic, public, school, and special) are generally recognizably different from each other, although each type of library may vary from one country to another. How might this be explained?

The nature of the inquiries that are brought to the library service varies from one sort of context to another. Different sorts of inquiries call for different sorts of services. An author catalog is obviously less useful than a subject catalog for an inquiry framed in terms of subject matter; the ability to browse in open stacks would seem more useful for inquirers whose wants are vaguely defined than for those who know precisely which document they want.

In chapter 6 variation among inquiries was considered and a typology more sophisticated than the traditional known-item/subject inquiry dichotomy was proposed. In chapter 7 we noted the need for each library's collections to reflect the needs and expertise of the population to be served. In chapter 14 the manner in which different sorts of inquiries indicate different patterns of provisions was explored. The conclusion reached was that known differences in the patterns of inquiries provide a plausible explanation of the characteristic differences between types of libraries.

In chapter 11 it was argued that the detailed pattern of provision of library service was largely determined by the allocation of resources to and within the library. Further, since such allocation is fundamentally a political process, it will follow that the values (altruistic or otherwise) of those who do the allocation and such compromises as may be necessitated by the political processes involved will determine the outcome. This, it is suggested, goes a long way to explain differences in the scale and orientation of library services of the same type in different countries. A country with relatively limited resources and other pressing needs for public funds, such as, for example, Zambia, can hardly afford to provide the same level of library service as, for example, Canada, even if the social values were the same. However, even where resources are equally present, differences may be reflected in the proportional allocation of public funds between, say, public libraries, on the one hand, and the restoration of ancient buildings or subsidies for railroads. Such differences in values should not be seen simply as calculated public policy decisions taken by national governments but as reflecting cultures and their traditions. For example, school libraries are unlikely to flourish if the educational philosophy of the school system stresses teaching, standardized curricula, and the authority of the teacher rather than learning and discovery by the child. Even where resources are provided and library use is encouraged, the flavor is likely to differ in detail. North Americans accustomed to viewing the public library as a bulwark of Western, liberal democracy are liable to be surprised to learn that Lenin was an admirer of the public library services of the United States and that he fostered libraries in the Soviet Union. This is surprising only if one fails to distinguish the ideological purpose from the library service as an instrument[1] and also fails to see library services in relation to their cultural context.[2] Differences in motivating values are especially likely to be reflected in the allocation when it comes to selection and censorship.

Differences in fashion and tradition within groups of professional librarians presumably also contribute to variations between libraries. However, the two aspects that derive most directly from the conceptual framework developed in the previous chapters—inquiries and allocation processes—would seem to go a long way to explain the differences between library services.

Why aren't library services used more?

That people do not necessarily want to use library services in all cases when they have a need to do so is understandably a source of regret to librarians. Chapter 10 examined the background to Mooers' dictum that

---

[1] For an account of the role of libraries in a country that is not a Western liberal democracy see Committee for the Compilation of the History of the Library Service, "The Library Service of Our Country During the Last Ten Years," *Union Research Service* (Kowloon) 19, no. 8 (April 26, 1980): 105-15; 19, no. 10 (May 3, 1960): 130-49. (Translated from *Peiping, Pei-ching Tahsueh Hsueh-pao* (Peking University Journal), No. 4, 1959.)

[2] In using the word "cultural," we are following Sir Edward Tyler's classic definition of culture as "that complex whole which includes knowledge, belief, art, morals, custom, and any other capabilities and habits acquired by man as a member of society." *Primitive Culture*, 1871, quoted in R. C. Benge, *Libraries and Cultural Change* (London: Bingley, 1970), p. 11.

"An information retrieval system will tend *not* to be used whenever it is more painful and troublesome for a customer to have information than for him not to have it."[3] The explanation was seen in terms of the balance between the perceived probable cost (the "real price") to the user relative to the perceived probable benefit and also relative to the perceived probable cost of alternatives to the library service and to not bothering at all.

How should catalogs be evalulated?

The problem of the evaluation of catalogs and other retrieval systems was addressed in chapter 8. Critically important is the separation of three different processes: formulation of the inquiry in the terms of the system; the retrieval process itself; and utilization of the data retrieved.

The retrieval system itself can only retrieve stored data in terms of the attributes used as the basis for retrieval. To the extent to which data consistent with the specifications of the inquiry as formulated are yielded, the retrieval system can be said to be responsive. Whether or not the retrieved data are found by a user to have utility depends not on the retrieval system but on the human being who examines the data.[4]

There are, then, two different bases for evaluation. Evaluation in the narrow sense of an evaluation of the retrieval system itself is a matter of responsiveness, of ability to yield consistently the data that fit the descriptions expressed in the formulated inquiry. Evaluation in a wider sense has to do with the utility of the data that have been retrieved and examined. This differs from the narrow definition in two ways: (1) it is not an evaluation of the retrieval system but of the combination of a retrieval system and its users; and (2) it is concerned with human values from which alone utility and beneficial effects derive. It is, therefore, different in scope and different in kind.

Evaluation in the narrower sense—of the capability of the retrieval system—need not be rejected on the grounds that capability is less important than utility since attributes other than utility can be used as predictors of utility. For example, a system that can retrieve documents pertinent to Austrian history reliably and consistently can, in practice, be expected to yield documents useful to a student of Austrian history.

---

[3] C. N. Mooers, "Mooers' Law or, Why Some Retrieval Systems Are Used and Others Are Not," *American Documentation* 11 (1960): 204.

[4] "Value is not inherent in, nor is it carried by, an information message. Consequently a message has value only in context. It is given value by its users." R. S. Taylor, *Value-Added Processes in Information Systems* (Norwood, N.J.: Ablex, 1986), p. 203.

How large should libraries be?

In many areas of manufacturing, commerce, and engineering, matters of size and scale are of central interest. One might reasonably have expected the same to be true in librarianship. After all, every increment in size costs money. Yet, beyond a general belief that bigger is better, the literature of librarianship is almost silent on the topic—and what little there is does not get one very far and, one suspects, is little read.[5] In brief, the literature is very limited on what one might have expected to have been a central concern.

There may be circumstances in which library books ought to be relegated to less accessible storage (or even discarded) and there may be circumstances in which staffing ought to be increased relative to (and even at the expense of) acquisitions. A change in size is a change in kind and some restructuring of the pattern or provision, such as decentralization or automation, may become desirable. However, after all appropriate restructuring, the acquisition of one more book would seem to continue to be advantageous, even though, with diminishing returns, the advantage might become very small. In other words, the marginal benefit of increased size appears to remain positive, however slight. Bigger, from this perspective, remains better. The restraint lies *outside* of the library. At some point, the marginal increase in the benefit to be derived from the next dollar to be spent on books is less than the benefit to the city of the next dollar to be spent on road repairs or the benefit to the university in increasing the number of teaching assistants, or whatever. We should, therefore, expect the literature of librarianship to be (or to become) rich in dealing with the problems of handling increases in size or in the development of a budget of any given size. However, we cannot expect it to be other than impotent in relation to optimal library size because the problem is, in large measure, external to librarianship and can only be resolved in relation to the *context* of library service and by the political processes of allocation that deal with the allocation of resources both to the library and to rival uses of the same resources.

[5] A noteworthy contribution is D. Gore, ed., *Farewell to Alexandria: Solutions to Space, Growth, and Performance Problems of Libraries* (Westport, Conn.: Greenwood Press, 1976). Other writings include B. C. Brookes, "Optimum $p\%$ Library of Scientific Periodicals," *Nature* 232, No. 5311 (August 1971): 458-61; M. K. Buckland, *Book Availability and the Library User* (New York: Pergamon Press, 1975), chap. 2 and Appendix A. See also references in footnote 15 of chapter 2. For an informal discussion of responses to growth of university library collections, see. R. C. Swank, "Too Much and Too Little: Observations on the Current Status of University Library Resources," *Library Resources and Technical Services* 3, no. 1 (Winter 1959): 20-31. (Reprinted in R. C. Swank, *A Unifying Influence* (Metuchen, N.J.: Scarecrow Press, 1981), pp. 65-80.) See also M. D. Cooper, "Economies of Scale in Academic Libraries," *Library and Information Science Research* 5, no. 2 (Summer 1983): 207-19; M. D. Cooper, "Economies of Scale in Large Academic Libraries," *Library and Information Science Research* 6, no. 3 (July-September 1984): 321-33.

Adaptability and the survival of library services

Another of the problems posed in chapter 2 was the paradox of the survival of library services in the apparent absence of the effective, reliable feedback that is needed for adaptation. This topic was examined in chapter 10, where the existence of a second and largely independent mechanism of feedback and adjustment was noted: the adaptiveness of the user.

Although library staff may often be unaware of failures in the use of library services, the user knows when the wanted document or the desired data have not been found. To the extent that service is perceived by the users as less than satisfactory, demand can be expected to be reduced. As demand diminishes, pressures on the library are eased. In other words, survival can be as much the result of feedback and adaptation on the part of the user as on the part of the librarian.

It is not suggested that the presence of *two* feedback mechanisms is a complete explanation or the only one. For example, as noted in chapters 11 and 12, users can and do share in the political processes that determine the detailed allocation and reallocation of resources and, thereby, the pattern of library provision. Nevertheless, viewing the situation as involving two feedback loops appears to go a long way to resolve the paradox.

Library goodness

How does one know whether one library is better than another, or that a given library is currently improving or degenerating? Can there be a single usable measure of library goodness? If so, what is it? If not, why not.[6]

One *can* concoct measures of library goodness[7] but their credibility is undermined by the number of arbitrary assumptions that have to be made to piece the parts together. Nor should this be surprising. If one wants to choose an automobile, one considers a variety of different factors: safety, appearance, economy, speed, comfort, and so on. The problem is to relate this battery of factors to one's resources, intentions, and personal set of values.

Although the quest for the Grail of Library Goodness has not (yet) been successful, there has been no lack of measures of performance proposed, nor of people proposing them.[8] There have been plenty of suggestions. What is lacking is a sense of coherence—a sense of fitting

---

[6] This section is based on M. K. Buckland, "Concepts of Library Goodness," *Canadian Library Journal* 39, no. 2 (April 1982): 63-6.

[7] For example, "document exposure," see M. Hamburg et al., *Library Planning and Decision-Making Systems* (Cambridge, Mass.: MIT Press, 1974).

[8] The principal guide to this area is F. W. Lancaster, *Measurement and Evaluation of Library Services* (Washington, D.C.: Information Resources Press, 1977).

together to form a whole. It is not that there has been no progress. Yet there is a long way to go, and it is noticeable that the numerous empirical efforts need to be counterbalanced by a greater attention to theory, to context, and to how the bits and pieces fit together.

Orr's schema

A discussion that can be very helpful in trying to grapple with concepts of library goodness was published by Orr,[9] who points out that there is a fundamental ambiguity in discussions of library goodness because there are two quite different sorts of goodness:

1. How good is it?—a measure of *quality*.
2. What good does it do?—a measure of *value*.

Suppose, for example, that one were to amass a collection of Persian prayer books and that, through assiduous purchasing and photocopying, this collection came to be the largest collection of its kind in the world. Unquestionably, this would be a good collection. If one were to add good cataloging and knowledgeable staff, then one would have a good library. It would be good in the sense of quality. We can, in fact, say more than this. Quality in this sense implies *capability*. Such a library collection is of good quality because it is highly *capable* of meeting the needs of persons seeking to learn about Persian prayer books.

On the other hand, it does not necessarily follow that even the highest quality library will have beneficial effects. Let us imagine that this collection of Persian prayer books were to be located in Bella Bella, British Columbia, or some other relatively inaccessible and sparsely populated area. What good would it do? In the absence of utilization, it is difficult to imagine beneficial effects.

Unfortunately, both quality (capability) and value (beneficial effects) are difficult to measure, especially the latter. In practice, we tend to fall back on surrogate measures (see figure 20.1). In particular, income or resources are assumed to indicate capability: "With a book budget that low they can't do much!" or "That should be a good library, just look at the resources they have!" There is an implied causal connection. So there should be in the sense that a skilled librarian ought to be able to improve the quality of a library service if given improved resources. However, the improvement is not automatic any more than buying expensive ingredients guarantees a good meal since the chef may make mistakes. Similarly, it is assumed that if utilization is increasing, then the beneficial effects

---

[9] R. M. Orr, "Measuring the Goodness of Library Services: A General Framework for Considering Quantitative Measures," *Journal of Documentation* 29, no. 3 (September 1973): 315-32, esp. p. 319.

F_{IG.} 20.1   Concepts of library goodness

Source: R. M. Orr, "Measuring the Goodness of Library Services:
A General Framework for Considering Quantitative Measures,"
Journal of Documentation 29, no. 3 (September 1973): 315-32.

are increasing. "The children's library is very busy, it must be doing a good job."

These assumed connections, which are depicted by dashed lines in figure 20.1, are not unreasonable so long as it is remembered that the tightness of the connection can vary. Several things can go wrong. In particular, the type of capability being provided needs to be related to the sort of demand to be served. The capability being offered may be more or less *inappropriate* for the pattern of demand in the context where the library service is provided. One can imagine library collections more appropriate to the probable demand in Bella Bella than Persian prayer books. Similarly, relocating the latter to Vancouver—or, better yet, Teheran— would increase utilization and hence, presumably, beneficial effects.

The distinction between capability and beneficial effects helps illuminate the questions addressed earlier in this chapter. Libraries differ both because different capabilities are appropriate for different needs and because views and preferences regarding beneficial effects vary from one cultural context to another. Lenin recognized the capability of the public libraries of the United States. He chose to adapt them to a different definition of beneficial effects—the development of a Marxist society rather than a capitalist democracy. The evaluation of catalogs and other retrieval systems in the narrow sense of their responsiveness is concerned with capability: the study of the utility derived from their use is a matter of beneficial effects. The larger the library's collection, the greater its capability, although increasing a library's capability by adding more books needs to be balanced against other ways of improving libraries, such as longer hours of service and better assistance. Converting resources into capability is primarily a matter of technique and technology. Deciding what sort of capability to provide—and how much of it—is a political decision, as is the evaluation of the probable increase in beneficial effects to be expected from increasing the capability of the library compared with the beneficial effects that might be derived from expenditure on other things outside of the library.

The concept of library goodness is ambiguous: "How good is it?" and "What good does it do?" are valid but quite different questions. Orr suggests another goodness—the goodness of library management—that would be reflected in tighter connections between the elements in his schema: more capability for any given increase in resources, more utilization for every increase in capability, and so on.[10]

Such improvement in the effectiveness of library management and in our ability to grapple with concepts of library goodness calls for greater attention to library services in theory and in context.

[10] Ibid.

Bibliographical Note

Some of the material in this book has appeared in different form in other publications.

Parts of chapters 2 and 20 appeared in "Concepts of Library Goodness," *Canadian Library Journal* 39, no. 2 (April. 1982): 63-6. Chapter 3 draws on "Looking Ahead—and Around," *Information Reports and Bibliographies* 7, nos. 4-5 (1978): 15-18; and "Library Education—meeting the Needs of the Future," *Catholic Library World* 50, no. 10 (May 1979): 424-6. Parts of chapters 6 and 14 are based on "Types of Search and the Allocation of Library Resources," *Journal of the American Society for Information Science* 30, no. 3 (May 1979): 143-7. Chapter 7 is similar to "Library Materials: Paper, Microfilm, Database," *College and Research Libraries* (forthcoming, 1988). A section of chapter 8 is discussed in a similar manner in "Relatedness, Relevance, and Responsiveness in Retrieval Systems," *Information Processing and Management* 19, no. 3 (1983): 237-41. An earlier version of part of chapter 10 appeared in *Progress in Cybernetics and Systems Research*, vol. XI, edited by R. Trappl et al. (Washington, D.C.: Hemisphere, 1982), pp. 147-51. Discussions of the logistics of books' availability in chapter 10 and elsewhere are based on *Book Availability and the Library User* (New York: Pergamon Press, 1975). Chapter 14 develops ideas in M. K. Buckland and A. Hindle, "Acquisitions, Growth and Performance Control Through Systems Analysis," in *Farewell to Alexandria: Solutions to Space, Growth, and Performance Problems of Libraries*, edited by D. Gore (Westport, Conn.: Greenwood Press, 1976), pp. 44-61. An earlier version of chapter 16 appeared as "Ten Years Progress in Quantitative Research on Libraries," *Socio-Economic Planning Sciences* 12, no. 6 (1978): 333-9. The impact of new technology on library catalogs, discussed in chapter 17, is more fully developed in "Bibliography, Library Records, and the Redefinition of the Library Catalog," *Library Resources and Technical Services* (forthcoming, 1988). Chapter 18 is based on "Education for Librarianship in the Next Century," *Library Trends* 34, no. 4 (Spring 1986): 777-87.

Index

About the Author

Michael Buckland is Professor, and formerly Dean, at the School of Library and Information Studies at the University of California, Berkeley. His principal professional interests are library management and the analysis of information services. He entered library work as a trainee at the Bodleian Library of Oxford University after studying History at that University. After taking his professional qualification in librarianship from Sheffield University, he joined the library staff at the University of Lancaster with primarily bibliographical duties. From 1967 to 1972 he was responsible on a day-to-day basis for the University of Lancaster Library Research Unit where a series of studies were undertaken concerning book usage, book availability, and library management games. Meanwhile he received a Ph.D. from Sheffield University. His doctoral dissertation was published as *Book Availability and the Library User* (Pergamon Press, 1975). In 1972 he moved to the United States to Purdue University Libraries where he was Assistant Director of Libraries for Technical Services before going to Berkeley where he served as Dean from 1976 to 1984. From 1983 to 1987 he was Assistant Vice President in the system-wide administration of the University of California with responsibilities for library planning and library automation. He has also served as Vice President of the Indiana Cooperative Library Services Authority and as Visiting Professor at the University of Klagenfurt, Austria, where most of the first edition of this book was written. His publications include numerous papers and technical reports on the analysis of library problems, on library management, and education for information service.